Advance Praise for *Aligning Strategy and Sales*

"In his practical and no-nonsense style, Frank Cespedes breaks down the essence of why most strategies fail in the field and what senior executives must do to change that. Cespedes acknowledges the complexity of the strategy-to-sales process and refutes the naïve belief that our strategies fail simply 'because the salespeople were outsold' or 'we don't have the right sales incentive plan.' While those things are often true, the reality is a lot more complex. Cespedes forces us to face the complexity and shows us a model for how to manage it and increase our strategy's odds of success."

—Lisa S. Thompson, Principal, Deloitte Consulting LLP

"By reading and applying the lessons from *Aligning Strategy and Sales*, you will gain strategic advice, practical techniques, and great insights into how to accelerate strategy and sales results. These will be useful to executives who want to help their companies deliver superior value and real solutions to a world of increasingly demanding customers."

—Michael Eckhardt, Managing Director, Chasm Institute

"*Aligning Strategy and Sales* presents a multifaceted look at the drivers of effective sales and sales management. As a human resources practitioner, I was pleased to see a comprehensive discussion of performance management. And the discussion on team effectiveness through cross-functional interactions provides insights on working 'laterally,' which requires considerable effort and attention in many organizations."

—Toby S. Mannheimer, Senior Vice President,
Human Resources, Finmeccanica
North America and DRS Technologies

ALIGNING STRATEGY

AND SALES

ALIGNING

STRATEGY

AND SALES

THE CHOICES, SYSTEMS, AND BEHAVIORS
THAT DRIVE EFFECTIVE SELLING

Frank V. Cespedes

HARVARD BUSINESS REVIEW PRESS

Boston, Massachusetts

Copyright 2014 Frank V. Cespedes
All rights reserved
Printed in the United States of America

10 9 8 7 6 5 4 3 2 1

No part of this publication may be reproduced, stored in or introduced into
a retrieval system, or transmitted, in any form, or by any means (electronic,
mechanical, photocopying, recording, or otherwise), without the prior permission
of the publisher. Requests for permission should be directed to permissions@
hbsp.harvard.edu, or mailed to Permissions, Harvard Business School Publishing,
60 Harvard Way, Boston, Massachusetts 02163.

The web addresses referenced in this book were live and correct at the time of the
book's publication but may be subject to change.

Library of Congress Cataloging-in-Publication Data

Cespedes, Frank V., 1950-
  Aligning strategy and sales : the choices, systems, and behaviors that drive
  effective selling / Frank V. Cespedes.
    pages cm
Includes bibliographical references.
ISBN 978-1-4221-9605-2 (alk. paper)

1. Sales management. 2. Selling. 3. Strategic planning. I. Title.
HF5438.4.C426 2014
658.8'101—dc23

2013050975

The paper used in this publication meets the requirements of the American National
Standard for Permanence of Paper for Publications and Documents in Libraries and
Archives Z39.48-1992.

Contents

Preface

Here is one big thing I have learned from running a business, consulting with companies around the world, and teaching executives and MBAs at a good business school for nearly twenty years: for most firms, the largest, most difficult, and most expensive part of strategy implementation is aligning sales and go-to-market efforts with the company's espoused strategies and goals.

This alignment challenge is the largest in multiple dimensions. Doing this well is essential for marketplace success and company valuations. A key to meeting growth potential is eliminating the gulf between big-picture strategy and field execution. Yet, in a recent survey of more than eighteen hundred executives, more than half (56 percent) say their biggest challenges are ensuring that day-to-day decisions are in line with strategy and allocating resources in a way that supports the strategy.[1] Poor alignment of sales and strategy means direct and opportunity costs. Selling is, by far, the most expensive part of implementation for most firms. Look at the income statements of US companies. The amount invested in sales forces (including salaries, benefits, and other components of SG&A—selling, general and administrative expenses) is about $900 billion annually. This is more than five times the $170 billion spent on all media advertising in 2012 and more than twenty times the $40 billion spent on all online advertising and marketing in 2013.[2]

Aligning strategy and sales is the most difficult part of implementation because it involves a combination of factors: a coherent strategy, the right incentives, hiring, developing a performance culture, and sustaining field behaviors in the face of market changes largely outside the control of the seller. This is hard stuff, and despite the aspirations (some would say, pretensions) of management professors like me, business is not and never will be like physics. Unlike the math and concepts in the Higgs boson or string theories, most important things in business are easy to say—advice from a fortune cookie: be customer focused, strategy should drive structure, work as a team, and so forth—but hard to do. A sales force consists of people—"a messy variable," as a research colleague once said—with different capabilities and motivators. Unlike thermostats, you can't "regulate" people via an algorithm. Good salespeople bring flexibility, street smarts, and the ability to customize a value proposition, build relationships, and work within their own company to marshal resources into a winning team. They also "bring egos and the need for security and meaning. Unlike advertising, salespeople cannot be turned on and off. Unlike a website, they cannot be expanded and upgraded overnight."[3]

These activities are also increasing as a portion of costs. Continuous improvement in production and back-office functions has been driving managerial attention for decades. Companies have pursued goals such as six-sigma quality and tenfold reductions in cycle times. Ideas have consequences and sometimes good consequences. This attention to production activities has yielded results and, as consumers, we benefit. But as in any competitive interaction where winning is ultimately measured by *relative* advantage, the very success of these activities means that the focus of productivity improvement is shifting. In the first decade of the twenty-first century, production efficiencies enabled an average S&P 500 company to reduce its cost of goods sold by about 250 basis points, but SG&A as a percentage of revenue has not declined.[4] Where would you look next for a source of competitive advantage?

Mind the Gap

Because aligning strategy with sales is vital to business success, this topic must be a priority for business schools and practitioners, right? Wrong.

On the academic side, there is little written about how to link strategy with the nitty-gritty of field execution. Certainly, there are now *many* books and articles about strategy formulation and strategic planning. Some are based on industry analysis, and some on finding points of differentiation independent of industry conditions (e.g., "blue ocean" strategies). But few have much to say about the role(s) of a company's sales channels in executing strategy. In fact, a combination of "reorganizing" and "incentives" is usually the prescription if sales is even discussed. But there is no one best way to organize (see chapter 8), and reorganizations in sales are always costly and risky because they disrupt established call patterns and client relationships. Experienced sales executives also know that appropriate incentives are a necessary but not sufficient cause of getting field behavior to align with espoused goals. So the strategy literature essentially leaves sales with the kindly parson's suggestion about how to get to heaven: "Always do good and avoid evil." Undoubtedly great advice, but, like most sermons, it may work when you're preaching to the already converted, but it's too abstract if you're not.

If we descend from the Parnassus of strategy to the olive groves of marketing, the picture is not that different. Sales is a notoriously underrepresented stepchild in the curricula and research of business schools.[5] The exigencies of academic publication rites mean that an extreme focus is the norm. A business is strategy *and* operations *and* marketing *and* sales *and* HR . . . and other activities that comprise a business model. But cross-functional research is difficult to do in the "right" journals, and faculty aspiring for promotion tend to avoid it. What does exist, of course, is a vast trade literature (much of it anecdotal but some grounded in good research), mainly from consultants and trainers who believe in the efficacy of a particular selling approach. But they also treat selling in isolation from strategy, and the focus of much sales training can have a perverse effect: it often leads a company's sales force to work harder but not necessarily smarter.

The current reality, then, is that nearly all of the advice to managers focuses on *either* selling skills *or* business strategy. It's a bit like the satiric poster I once saw in a manager's office: "Theory is when you know everything but nothing works. Practice is when everything works but no one knows why. In this place, theory and practice come together: nothing works and no one knows why!"

None of this would matter much if, outside posters and power points and in the realm of practice, de facto alignment were the norm. But it's not. Addressing that gap, actionably and with attention to the available scholarship, is the focus of this book.

Part One

WE HAVE A PROBLEM

Time is a great teacher.
Unfortunately, it kills all its pupils.

—Hector Berlioz

Chapter 1
The Dialogue That Rarely Happens

This book looks at how to get sales results that link with strategy. Chapter 1 discusses the relevant players, what needs to be linked, why in many organizations this linkage is broken, the financial and human consequences of this disconnect, and therefore why it's worth your time and effort to fix it.

Chapter 2
Diagnosing the Problem

If you don't understand the cause-and-effect relationships in a business situation, then you are likely to pull the wrong levers, trying to improve the execution of a flawed strategy or changing strategic direction when you should focus on better execution. This chapter examines three situations and asks, what's the problem—the firm's strategy and/or the sales channel tasked with executing that strategy?

Chapter 3
Fixing the Problem

Chapter 3 provides a framework for addressing the various interactive processes—market characteristics, selling behaviors, sales force environment, and so forth—that shape effective selling efforts. These interactions are relevant to aligning strategy and sales in any organization. The chapter explains why this framework can help your company where it counts—in daily encounters with diverse customers—and outlines the logic and plan for the rest of this book.

1

The Dialogue That Rarely Happens

Jim Koch, the founder and CEO of Boston Beer Company (BBC, maker of Sam Adams and other leading craft beers), is one of the smartest and most analytical business leaders I have ever met. Jim has three degrees from Harvard, but to his credit, he overcame the handicaps.

After graduating from business school and law school, he worked for seven years as a strategy consultant with the Boston Consulting Group (BCG) before starting BBC in 1984. For some time, Jim was the sales force at BBC, and he makes regular sales calls to this day. In a "street sales" business, this involves many cold calls on bartenders, wholesalers, and other impatient customers. Like Willy Loman reminiscing about the New England territory or Odysseus recalling his encounter with the Cyclops, he has stories: "I routinely have bartenders tell me that the manager isn't in today when the manager is standing ten feet away. I was once thrown out of a New York City grocery store because the owner saw me removing competitors' stickers that were blocking Sam Adams. I've had a customer pull a gun on me. Selling isn't for sissies." But after thirty years, he also emphasizes something crucial about sales and strategy: "I've come to see making a sales call as one of the most challenging intellectual activities there is—certainly more immediately challenging than anything I did at BCG . . . When I walk into a bar, I have about thirty seconds to understand the economics of the place: What is its strategy, and who are the clientele? How does it make money? What's the weakest draft line, and how would sales increase if we replaced it with one of ours? Who's the decision maker? Then you need to connect personally."[1]

In pharmaceutical sales, the window of opportunity is estimated to be about five minutes; in enterprise software, the selling cycle can take months; in certain key-account situations, it can take years. But Jim Koch is describing the moment of truth in *any* strategy for *every* company *across* industries: what happens to all the analysis, vision, planning, and (if it truly exists) strategic direction when your people are in front of a potential customer? As Churchill reportedly said to the Admiralty after Gallipoli, "However beautiful the strategy, you should occasionally look at the results."

This book looks at how to get sales results that link with strategy. In doing this, I hope to help address a glaring gap in both management theory and practice. It's a gap, moreover, that new technologies and changing buyer behavior increasingly expose. But to deal usefully with that gap, we must first understand the relevant players, what needs to be linked, and why it's worth your time and effort.

Strategy Priests

Late in life, the painter Georges Braque was asked for his opinion about his old friend Picasso: "Pablo? He used to be a good painter, but now he's just a genius." Whether or not you agree with Braque's opinion about the later Picasso, you have in most organizations undoubtedly met the kind of person he describes: long on vision, short on craft and tactics, eloquent about ideas, but basically speechless when it comes to the implementation realities and requirements. I once attended a presentation at GE by a corporate executive about a proposed cross-selling strategy. At one point, one of the veteran line-of-business heads sitting next to me whispered in my ear: "This guy is one of our strategy priests: he operates where the rubber meets the sky." It was not a compliment about "thinking outside the box," and the proposal went nowhere.

In my career as a business manager, a consultant, and an academic, I have probably been part of as many strategy meetings as anyone. My experience is that very few actually articulate the implications of espoused strategies for customer-contact behaviors in the field. In fact, few strategic plans even mention sales activities in relation to financial goals, brand aspirations, and alleged competitive advantages. Moreover, the process for introducing and reviewing these plans often exacerbates the separation of the "strategists" from the "doers" in the field. The typical process is a kick-off sales meeting followed by a string of emails from headquarters with periodic reports back to headquarters on sales results. Each communication is mainly one-way, and there is too little of it. One result is that the root causes of underperformance are often effectively hidden from both groups.

Research indicates that my experience is representative. In the twenty-first century, corporations spend an estimated $100 billion annually on management consulting and allied training, most of it aimed at creating or changing strategy.[2] In response, business schools graduate annually tens of thousands of aspiring strategists and big-picture thinkers. Yet, according to surveys by strategy consulting firms themselves, less than half of frontline employees say they are clear about their firm's strategy, and customers are even more mystified: 80 percent of managers said they believed their companies had strongly differentiated strategies and products, but fewer than 10 percent of these firms' customers agreed.[3]

One result is that, like clockwork every few years, someone publishes a study that finds that relatively few—some research indicates less than 10 percent—of even effectively formulated strategies carry through to successful execution.[4] Moreover, on average, companies deliver only 50 to 60 percent of the financial performance that their strategies and forecasts promise.[5] At the risk of being pedantic, let me point out that this means something like 90 percent of companies fail to execute strategies and that, if management were to realize the espoused potential of its strategy, the increase in value—to employees, shareholders, and, ultimately, society—could be as much as 60 to 100 percent.

What's the problem? One big problem (as one often hears whispered about organizations) indeed starts at the top . . . in the hushed halls and assumptions of the people nominally in charge. My colleague Cynthia Montgomery conducts a revealing exercise in senior-executive programs at Harvard. She is a strategy professor in these programs, and the participants are typically CEOs or other C-level executives. Toward the outset of each program, she asks executives to list three words that come to mind when they hear the word *strategy*.

The result of doing this with groups from across industries and with a global sample of senior leadership thinking about this core aspect of business? "Collectively, they have produced 109 words, frequently giving top billing to *plan, direction,* and *competitive advantage.* In more than 2,000 responses, only 2 had anything to do with people: one said *leadership,* another *visionary.* No one has ever mentioned *strategist.*"[6] And no one ever mentions *sales.* Also, I think you will agree that even *leadership* and *vision,* while essential, are still a long way from implementation where it counts: in your organization's encounters with current and prospective customers.

Given this lack of attention to field realities, you can see why a simple statement—"I'm from Corporate, and I'm here to help you"—is one of the oldest jokes in most firms. Many field managers relate to corporate strategy pronouncements as just a nice chart, another presentation, a vision that has little to say about how sales should allocate money, time, and people. Someone once defined a critic as a person who knows the way but can't drive the car. The fact is, in many firms the top managers, removed from the realities of customer contact, are often blithely unaware of the embedded strategic commitments and competitive tests that field activities daily represent. Yet, as Jim Koch emphasizes, understanding those activities demands and deserves at least as much effort as strategy formulation.

Sales Sinners

If the strategic shepherds often issue pronouncements severed from realities in the field, then admittedly many in sales are a wayward flock focused on the ground immediately in front of them.

For over twenty-five years, Andris Zoltners has been teaching an executive course to sales leaders at Northwestern University and other venues. Each time, he asks the sales leaders in attendance, "How do you know when you have a successful sales force?" and "What issues are you currently faced with?" Over the years, he has built a database of more than 2,400 responses from more than 850 sales leaders. According to his categorization of the results, their responses overwhelmingly focus on metrics and operational improvements *within* the sales function, independent of strategic objectives.[7] Some 84 percent of the responses cite current selling efficiency issues such as:

- "Salespeople lack closing skills . . . don't spend enough time prospecting."

- "We are not achieving quota consistently . . . Goal setting processes result in unfair sales targets."

- "Territory alignment needs to change: large differences in territory potential are creating unfairness in the sales force."

- And, of course (as with nearly all executives), complaints about IT and lack of "enough" information: "Sales information is lacking: accuracy and timeliness of sales dashboards are inadequate due to IT problems."

Only 13 percent cite issues external to the sales force, divided between market issues such as "We must adapt to changing customer needs and new technologies" and internal company issues such as "The company product line is shifting." Finally, just 3 percent focus on sales effectiveness issues, and even these responses are typically defined by internal rather than external market criteria: "We just launched a new Sales Effectiveness and Growth Initiative aimed at improving sales force performance" and "Management has taken a keen interest in improving global sales effectiveness" (imagine that!).

This tendency to focus almost exclusively on tactics and current operations, while failing to think or act strategically, is not unique to sales. But it is exacerbated in sales for a few reasons. One is the nature of life in this area of business. Sales management involves hundreds of decisions in market time, not company time. Life inside any sales organization is filled with deadlines, calls, periodic crises, pressures to perform, and (in contrast to many other areas of business) common management assumptions that there are seemingly straightforward and transparent metrics to judge performance: sales per quarter, sales per employee, did she or didn't she meet quota? As a sales manager once said to me, "In this job, if you don't survive the short term, you don't need to worry about the long term."

Another reason is the disconnect between planning processes and the requirements of sales decision making. According to surveys, about two-thirds of companies treat strategic planning as a periodic event, typically once per year and as a precursor to the annual budgeting and capital-approval process. Companies tend to do plans by business unit, irrespective of the firm's go-to-market approach (which, for good reasons, often spans business units). Forget, for a moment, that strategy is *not* the same thing as a financial plan or capital budget. "The numbers" in financial models should express plans and their resource-allocation implications in quantitative terms. If not, they're basically important-sounding garnish on a pitch—something venture capitalists recognize when they evaluate entrepreneurs' business plans.

We will return to this issue in chapter 4. Instead, consider the following description of the typical planning process, based on research with over 150 companies worldwide:

> Companies that follow the traditional strategic planning model develop a strategy plan for each business unit at some point during the year. A cross-functional team dedicates less than nine weeks to developing the unit's plan. The executive committee reviews each plan—typically in daylong, on-site meetings . . . The plans are consolidated to produce a companywide strategic plan for review by the board of directors.
>
> Once the strategic-planning cycle is complete, the units dedicate another eight to nine weeks to budgeting and capital planning (in most companies, these processes are not explicitly linked to strategic planning). The executive committee then holds another round of meetings with each of the business units to negotiate performance targets, resource commitments, and (in many cases) compensation for managers.[8]

Nine weeks plus nine weeks plus "another round of meetings" equals somewhere between four and five months of "planning." While this is going on, the market is doing what the market will do. No wonder only 11 percent of executives in this survey said they were highly satisfied that strategic planning is worth the effort. No wonder more than half (53 percent) in another survey of more than eighteen hundred executives say their strategy is not understood by employees and customers.[9] Buying processes at customers have no responsibility or interest in accommodating your planning process, and sales must respond issue by issue and account by account. In other words, even if the output of planning is a great strategy (a big if), the process itself often makes it irrelevant to sales executives, who must make important decisions throughout the year in accord with external buying rhythms and selling cycles at multiple accounts.

Strategy priests and *sales sinners*: my terminology may be fanciful, but the gap is real. It is also costly. Virtually every discussion of effective strategy implementation you have read, and will read, stresses the importance of alignment. This is especially true when it comes to the links between strategic intent and sales action, which should be a two-way street: strategic direction is essential for sales effectiveness, and sales knowledge of actual customer behavior is essential for ongoing strategic relevance. But the current situation between strategy and sales at most companies brings to mind Gandhi's quip when asked his opinion about Western civilization: "I think it would be a good idea."

Competency Traps

And it can get worse because, as happens in organizational life, "no good deed goes unpunished." The focus on improving selling efficiencies often has negative unintended consequences. Much sales training is based on gimmicks, unsupported assumptions, and glib generalizations about "selling" that simply don't apply. But much is based on sound fundamentals about listening, problem identification, and understanding value from the customer's point of view. The problem is that, disconnected from strategy, even good training can have a perverse effect: the sales force gets better and better at things that customers care less and less about . . . and the cycle can be self-reinforcing.

A popular sales training course preaches—and I mean *preaches*—a common message to sales sinners: "There is only one reason salespeople lose orders: They are OUTSOLD . . . You have a personal responsibility to be competitive . . . It's like a street fight."[10] No, there are lots of reasons that a salesperson can lose an order, and it's important to disentangle the correct cause-and-effect relationships. If you don't, all the investment and effort and passion can unfortunately lead to what I and others have described as "competency traps." Each function in the firm, including sales, gets better at routines within its domain, but these same routines keep the firm, and its top team as well as salespeople, from gaining experience with procedures more relevant to changing market conditions.[11]

To understand competency traps in practice, an analogy can be helpful and scary. In 1961, Nikita Khrushchev pledged to outproduce the United States in steel, coal, cement, and fertilizer within twenty years. You may have seen old news reports of Khrushchev pounding his shoe on a table at the United Nations and pledging that "we will bury you!"—somewhat like the typical football-and-war rhetoric of many motivational speakers at sales meetings. What we tend to forget is that the Soviet Union actually made quota, producing more of these goods by 1981 than did the United States. The difference, of course, is that over that time, the United States was adapting to a changing world and pioneering a different economy, one based on plastics, silicon, transistors, the web, life sciences, and many other innovations, while the Soviet Union (like some companies) "lumbered on building its mighty edifice of obsolescence."[12] As a leader in your firm, you can worry prudently and diligently all you want about "disruptive innovations," but you ultimately need a sales effort aligned with strategy to do something about it.

Over time, the strategy-sales gap can affect the entire culture of the firm, just as it affected daily life and organizational interactions in Communist states. Unrealistic plans generate a growing expectation that plans and forecasts will not be met. Then, as the "I told you so" becomes the repeated experience of business heads and other people in the field, it can become the normal expectation that performance commitments won't be kept—which, in fact, is what the data about strategic forecasts versus actual implementation results indicates. Performance reviews (discussed in chapter 10) then become like Lake Wobegon, where everyone is above average because a culture of underperformance has managed expectations downward. And managers, expecting not to meet forecasts, spend more time rationalizing results and protecting themselves—the finger-pointing or CYA syndrome, as some have called it, that characterizes a culture of underperformance.[13] The sales organization becomes less intellectually honest about its capabilities in relation to the market today and tomorrow (not yesterday), and strategy discussions are therefore based on less reliable information. And so on, in a downward spiral reminiscent of the slogan that the Solidarity union used when it organized worker slowdowns in the Gdansk shipyard under Communist rule: "They pretend to pay us, so we'll pretend to work!"

Avoiding the Traps

Linking sales efforts with strategy is vital for implementation and profitable growth. Conversely, daily sales practices affect strategy and ongoing strategic options: those selling efforts—successful or unsuccessful, focused or diffused, smart or stupid—constrain and redirect strategies in various, often unintended ways. In any situation where you have interacting variables like this, you must confront the interactions and diagnose the problem. That's what's needed to improve selling *and* strategy.

2

Diagnosing the Problem

Lewis Thomas was dean of Yale University and New York University Medical Schools, president of Memorial Sloan-Kettering Institute, and generally acknowledged as "the father of modern immunology." Thomas once estimated that before the twentieth century, going to a hospital *lowered* your odds of survival. The state of the art meant that diagnoses were uncertain, sanitary conditions spread infections, and therefore the prescribed medical strategy more often than not had multiple unintended consequences. Indeed, some estimate that this was true for decades into the twentieth century, until disinfectants and penicillin for civilian use became common. Hence, Count Nicolas de Chamfort's aphorism about medicine and philosophy in his day: "lots of drugs, few remedies, and hardly any complete cures." Judging by the results reported in the previous chapter, one can't help but wonder: in many companies today, is strategy deployment and implementation in sales essentially at the level of hospital care a century or more ago?

Begin with diagnosis. If you don't understand the cause-and-effect relationships in a business situation, then you are more likely to pull the wrong levers in attempts to fix it and, like pre-twentieth-century hospitals, lower the odds of survival. Consider the following three situations and ask, what's the problem—the firm's strategy or the sales channel tasked with executing that strategy, or both?

MANY VARIABLES

There is a firm—let's call it "Document Security Management, Inc." (DSM)—that throughout the 1980s and 1990s built a great business by picking up boxes at corporations, law firms, and other organizations and then either shredding or storing those documents in secured warehouses. DSM was a growth-stock pick for years, and justifiably proud of it. One source of its competitive advantage was its early-mover advantage and one-stop-shop value proposition: because DSM provided a complete managed-document service, firms could outsource to DSM the entire activity and so dedicate their high-paid lawyers, executives, and other professionals to better uses. Another source of advantage was its sales force, which had greater scope and numbers than its competitors and which had (over the years) developed great relationships with, and knowledge of, relevant buyers and users at target customers.

By the early twenty-first century, however, it became apparent that online digital technology was affecting the core of the business, and the CEO was determined not to be fatally disrupted by an emerging technology. DSM hired one of the world's leading consulting firms to look into this and recommend a strategy. The consultants did three things. First, they restated the obvious with empirical data: more customers were using online storage services, and these services were priced a lot less than DSM's service. Second, DSM should not hide its head in the sand and, instead, should introduce its own online storage service and leverage its installed customer-base advantage. Third, DSM should then train its sales force to sell these digital services in a bundle with the traditional managed-document service.

DSM accepted the recommendations, but the results were awful. Digital document management meant that DSM's sales force had to develop relationships with, and knowledge of, different buyers and influencers at accounts. IT departments became more important in the buying process, and they talked a different language, with different priorities, than the front-office executives and administrative assistants to whom the sales force had traditionally sold. Pricing the bundle was a problem: inherently, the high-touch and high-tech document services had very different cost implications for DSM and therefore different prices. Despite the training, salespeople took the path of least resistance and often unbundled the package or just sold the lower-priced digital service. Contract renewals on the managed-document service declined, and so did DSM's profitability and earnings per share. So DSM altered its sales compensation policies. Contract renewals on the managed-document service then increased, but digital service sales declined and emerging competitors established strong footholds with multiyear contracts, effectively locking DSM out of accounts as storage increasingly migrated to the cloud.

In a few years, both salespeople and customers raised "branding" issues: "Who in fact *is* DSM in this marketplace: a full-service document management company, or another cloud server company?" The result: DSM finally divested its digital unit. DSM is now a profitable but smaller company and no longer a high-flying growth stock in the capital markets.

What was the problem in this situation? Surely it is hard to disagree with the basic strategic intent. Anyone who has read and absorbed the lessons of Clay Christensen's work on disruptive innovation would, I believe, find it hard to argue that DSM should *not* have responded to emerging market reality.[1] That's a recipe for becoming yet another case study about market myopia.

Should we blame the strategy consultants, because this is another instance of consultants' "taking your watch and telling you what time it is"? Well, all organizations have a lot of accumulated inertia. If, for whatever reasons, no one else is willing to say, "The big hand on the watch is here and the little hand is there," then outside consultants add value. This is especially true when, as with DSM, the consultants bring data to disparate executives' functional windows on the market and salespeople's tendencies to conflate "the market" with whatever they heard on their last sales call.

Was pricing the culprit, because the attempt to sell two very differently priced products to the same customer was doomed to fail? Well, pricing here did reflect DSM's cost to serve (see chapter 10) when it sold these different services. Despite what you hear from some "new-economy" gurus, it really is hard to make money by selling below cost. (And recall Peter Drucker's comment in an interview: business-people call them "gurus" because it's easier to spell than "charlatan.")

Perhaps the issue was sales force structure and deployment—as many advocate when you're trying to introduce a new technology, DSM should have sold its digital service through a separate sales force. Well, if you do, what happens to DSM's installed-base advantage and selling costs, and wouldn't two sales forces only have exacerbated the pricing and branding issues?

Or was the basic issue really about sales compensation and incentives? Anyone who tells you that compensation structure is not an important behavioral driver is living in Disneyland. (Consider my next example for an illustration.) But then DSM cannot be faulted for trying many different compensation plans. Also, as discussed in chapter 9, you can pay people any way you want, but if, at the end of the day, they don't know what to do when they're in front of potential customers or can't get access to the right buyers, the comp plan won't solve your problem.

So perhaps the issue was that DSM's sales training was inadequate and (as we've heard the sales trainer exhort sales sinners) there was really only one reason DSM lost orders: it was OUTSOLD? For sure, whether or not top management realized it, this strategy meant a very different set of sales tasks, and therefore executing the strategy required different selling behaviors. It also required different incentives; a different approach to pricing and account management; and a change in sales control systems, including how people are measured and coached in performance reviews. The company also needed a cultural change in how field information gets back to management. Furthermore, DSM had to change how top management reviews and reacts to that input from sales about the strategy. Can a sales training program fix all that? If you find one, buy it and let me know.

The point is that there are many variables—including people, that impeccably messy variable—relevant to diagnosing implementation problems and then aligning strategy and sales. And as in any recovery process, the beginning of wisdom is to acknowledge this and not to pretend—as so many management books do—that you can manage it solely through training *or* compensation *or* the sheer brilliance of the strategy itself. In fact, what we can say with certainty is that in the DSM situation, embarking on a strategy without considering the realities facing the people key to executing that strategy at customers is the biggest problem of all.

UNINTENDED CONSEQUENCES

Some years ago, I worked with a private-equity firm that had recently bought a consumer goods company, "Packaged Products Company" (PPCo). Nuts and potato chips were its largest product lines, and nationally, PPCo had leading market-share positions in those categories. The partners at the private-equity (PE) firm asked me to help them address the following situation, which they described as a "sales channel not selling as profitably as it can and as profitably as we need to grow this business and deliver on our investment thesis."

PPCo sold its products through three main channels. Supermarkets, mass merchandisers, and convenience stores accounted for over 80 percent of its dollar volume. The latter two classes of trade were growing faster than supermarkets and, because of their self-service business models, required more service from their suppliers. In its main product categories, PPCo also faced increased competition for shelf space from many new light-calorie and microwave product forms. One result was that nuts and chips were declining as a percentage of overall salty-snack volume and, because of price competition, also declining in profitability for PPCo. The good news: PPCo had other, higher-margin products to sell to the growing channels, and its market research indicated these products were well received by consumers. The bad news: the sales force continued to focus on nuts and chips and was not allocating enough time and effort to the other categories. Why?

One reason was the sales compensation plan, which rewarded salespeople in terms of case volume. Since nuts and chips were, by far, the highest-volume items, that's where they focused their efforts. And to spur volume, they negotiated many forward-buying deals with trade buyers—that is, they offered price promotions that motivated the trade buyer to stock up on the products being promoted in a given quarter and then buyers' purchases dropped precipitously the following quarter. In effect, the sales force was simply reshuffling demand, and this also played havoc with manufacturing and logistics, damaging PPCo's cash flow and profits. But as one sales rep candidly explained to me, "We sold the deals, and if that caused problems in other areas of the business, so be it."

What to do? We redesigned the sales comp plan so that bonus was no longer primarily driven by volume irrespective of products sold. Instead, "points" were allocated to different items, and there was now a bigger incentive to sell PPCo's higher-margin products and not only nuts and chips. We also redeployed the sales force to reflect changes across and within the classes of trade in the customer base. PPCo had been over-allocating salespeople to supermarkets and under-allocating to mass merchandisers and convenience stores. We also redesigned sales responsibilities. Salespeople had been responsible for both selling and service activities at their accounts, and the growing channels were significantly more service intensive. My activity analysis indicated that sales reps were spending as much as 40 percent of their time on service, not selling, and that PPCo could add three part-time merchandisers to do the service for the fully burdened cost of one full-time sales rep. So we did that.

The good news? PPCo salespeople indeed sold lots more of the higher-margin items and with fewer forward-buying promotions, and with merchandisers in place, PPCo's costs of serving trade customers decreased while the time available for selling increased. The bad news? PPCo also sold a lot less nuts and chips, and this had a domino effect on the business. It impacted purchasing because now PPCo had less bargaining power with suppliers and less ability to get volume discounts on materials that were used across its product lines, not only in peanuts and potato chips. It affected transportation and logistics: their big trucks were not full, and these costs also increased. It impacted what was and was not profitable: because these purchasing and transport costs were allocated across product lines, the lower overall volume meant that the seemingly higher-margin items, which now had to absorb more of the shared cost burden, were not so high margin after all.

At the point of sale in stores, moreover, the addition of merchandisers had a consequence unforeseen by my crisp activity analysis. Those service activities were, in fact, part of selling: they provided PPCo's salespeople with opportunities to get more face time with store and regional managers at trade accounts, get more information about plan-o-grams and other crucial in-store tools, and then help with sell-in for PPCo's product programs. But now salespeople were not doing service and the merchandisers were not able to do (or even aware of) these direct and indirect selling tasks.

The result? Two years after implementing these sales management changes, PPCo's EBITDA (earnings before interest, taxes, depreciation, and amortization) had declined and we were back to the drawing board.

Like most people, I hate using a bad-practice example when I am part of the bad practice. It's more fun to do after-the-fact corrections of others. But what goes around comes around. Management writers who don't acknowledge their own mistakes either are perfect (very unlikely), have never managed (common), or are incapable of learning because business and selling are for big stretches about learning (as efficiently and effectively as possible) from inevitable mistakes.[2] The PPCo example illustrates important connections between strategy and sales—connections that affect every enterprise.

Each change to PPCo's sales system had a sound rationale. But the changes inevitably affected other elements throughout the value chain of the company. The sales compensation plan was indeed dysfunctional, and the sales force was clearly not optimizing PPCo's product capabilities in a changing market. But despite what many of my economist colleagues say, a sales comp plan is never only an exercise in incentives. The emphasis in the plan will inevitably affect the quantity and kinds of orders the firm receives in operations, the cash-flow profile managed by finance, the recruitment and training needs faced by HR, and organizational interactions between sales and other functional areas. Similarly, there was nothing wrong or "greedy" in the PE partners' desire to sell more profitably and deliver on their investment thesis. That's what a strategic objective (in this case, preparing for a future liquidity event) is for, and current sales behavior should not be a reason to abandon relevant strategic goals.

But aligning sales with those goals is an intertwined strategy *and* leadership *and* sales issue. It's not possible in this situation, as in others, to separate strategy and sales implementation, because there is seldom only one cause of suboptimal sales or most other business problems. Even within the realm of sales management, it's important to recognize the interacting dimensions that must be managed to link selling effectiveness with strategy. PPCo's salespeople are selling, but are they selling across product lines the way the strategy and market realities require? Salespeople are selling, but are they allocating their time and efforts to the right activities in the right proportions? Salespeople are selling, but do they have the skills, capabilities, and motivation to sell on criteria other than price?

Finally, note the crucial embedded knowledge that my own analysis overlooked: the connection between seemingly mundane in-store service activities like stocking and arranging the shelves with the core selling tasks in the business. You wouldn't know this from your desk at headquarters, and if you are a C-level executive and don't regularly leave the building to meet with customers, I guarantee that you don't know other important things about your business. It's why Jim Koch, CEO of Boston Beer, still makes sales calls. And it's what John Maynard Keynes was getting at when he expressed the wish (never granted, as far as I can tell) that "if economists could manage to get themselves thought of as humble, competent people on a level with dentists, that would be splendid": the knowledge of what really happens "out there" and the ability to use that knowledge without messing up other important things.[3]

OUTSOLD?

One of the best books about selling, ever, is David Dorsey's *The Force*. Written in the mid-1990s, Dorsey's book turns a year in a Xerox sales district in Cleveland into a riveting drama about people, accounts, the operatic highs and lows of the sales cycle, and the triumph of making quota. Dorsey focuses on Fred Thomas and his major-account sales team and the sometimes strange but effective motivational techniques of his district manager, Frank Pacetta. It is a great ethnographic study of B2B selling for capital goods.

But when it is viewed through the lens I am outlining in this chapter, there is a pathos throughout this wonderful book. Even as Thomas and Pacetta make their sales, Xerox itself is missing the strategic point, although the facts are staring right at them in every office where Thomas and his team make their sales calls: more and more copies are being handled by printers linked to personal computers, not by copying machines. Thomas and Pacetta are doing their best to maintain Xerox's share in copiers. But the disconnect between sales efforts and strategy (in this case, a lack of strategy to deal with a technology that is redefining the market and customer behavior) is the dramatic subtext of the book.

Even Dorsey, as great a writer and observer as he is, doesn't get it. In his author's note, he explains that "I wanted to write an American success story. I wanted to tell in vivid terms the story of how a top salesman—along with his team—attains certain goals over the course of a typical sales year, and what impact this effort has on the personal lives of the people involved."[4] Here, he succeeds admirably. But he also notes that Xerox by the 1990s competed in a "document" market, and he lists the competition: Kodak, Canon, Ricoh, 3M, Minolta, Savin, and others . . . yet makes no mention at all of HP, Brother, and the other makers of low-cost computer printers that were eating Xerox's lunch in the document market. It makes Dorsey's summation of his story a non sequitur: "A once-thriving American business loses share to the Pacific Rim, gets scared, adopts Total Quality Management practices, raises productivity, and begins to win back business. The way the Cleveland district sells copiers illustrates . . . this comeback."[5] Not quite. How could it be when selling, however interesting and effective, is divorced from the main strategic reality facing the firm?

Managing the Variables

You see the common thread running through all of these examples. Many "sales" problems are really strategic alignment issues. They cannot be resolved without linking your firm's go-to-market initiatives with espoused strategic goals. When leaders don't recognize and diagnose these situations appropriately, then—like DSM, PPCo, and Xerox at the time—they can press for and actually achieve better execution when what they need is a better strategy, or they change strategic direction with great cost and turmoil when they should be focusing on the basics of sales execution. Organizationally, it's a dialogue that never happens: you may formulate and preach strategy, but sales wanders off and overall company performance declines.

To forge and keep relevant the appropriate links, strategists and salespeople need a framework that helps them diagnose and distinguish the interacting factors, provides a common language of performance, and breaks a complex issue into parts that can be measured and managed. Based on experience (including good and bad practice) and work with lots of companies, I have a framework you should consider. It can improve dialogue between these groups and, in turn, improve selling *and* strategy formulation.

3

Fixing the Problem

A framework refers to physical structures but also mental models, "a set of assumptions, concepts, values, and practices that constitute a way of viewing reality."[1] Especially when dealing with the conjunction of complex and moving parts like strategy (which concerns your organization today in relation to an uncertain future) and sales (which is about customers and their motivations in relation to evolving choices), you need a model, a way of isolating key features of that complexity and making "the business" manageable.

Good models, as Emanuel Derman (an accomplished modeler in physics and finance) points out, "are vulgar in a sophisticated way."[2] They are vulgar because, like a caricature, they emphasize some features at the expense of others. You can have anything you want in a model, but not everything that actually exists in the thing itself. And that's a model's purpose. The map is not the terrain, and we the people must decide what matters in a model for a given purpose.

As Derman emphasizes, doing business with people is more complicated than doing physics about matter: "It's not that physics is 'better,' but rather that . . . in physics you're playing against God, and He doesn't change his laws very often . . . In [business] you're playing against God's creatures, agents who value assets based on their ephemeral opinions. They don't know when they've lost, so they keep trying."[3] If you think Derman—a quantum physics researcher at Oxford, Rockefeller University, and Bell Labs and then head of Quantitative Research at Goldman Sachs and Salomon Brothers, where he made original contributions to financial options theory—is just being modest, then consider this: Isaac Newton was a lot smarter than you or I, but in 1720 he also invested heavily in the South Sea Company and lost almost $5 million in today's money. Business *is* tougher than physics, as Newton himself implicitly acknowledged: "I could calculate the motions of the heavenly bodies, but not the madness of people."

But good models are also sophisticated. They embody "worldly knowledge or refinement," as the dictionary defines sophistication. A good framework isolates features that explain most of the variance and that enable you to track cause-and-effect linkages, make things managerial, and focus time and effort. A vulgarly sophisticated framework is one that can be used because, in any organization, a way of viewing reality "is not just a battle for finding the truth, but also a battle for the hearts and minds of the people who use it."[4] Sales managers will ignore analytics or prescriptions that lack worldly knowledge or can't be applied where they live: in daily encounters with diverse customers.

Linking Strategy and Sales: A Framework

Figure 3-1 depicts graphically the framework that I want you to consider and that organizes the rest of this book. In words, here is the basic logic of the framework.

To align strategy and sales usefully, you must first understand the externals in your business and then make choices about how your strategy proposes to deal with the opportunities and threats inherent in those market realities. In any business, value is created or destroyed in the marketplace with customers, not in conference rooms or planning meetings. Key externals include the industry you compete in, the market and product segments where you choose to play, and the nature of the decision-making and buying processes at the customers that you sell and service. These factors, displayed along the top of figure 3-1, determine the required

FIGURE 3-1

The seller's compass: linking strategy and sales

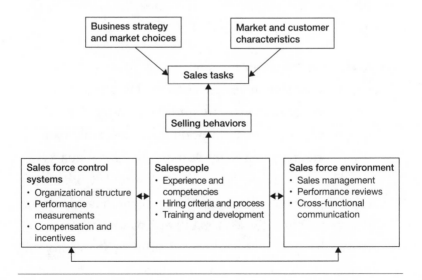

sales tasks—what your go-to-market initiatives must accomplish to deliver and extract value, and therefore what your salespeople (and other customer-facing personnel—e.g., service) must be especially good at to implement your strategy effectively.

Then, the issue is aligning *selling behaviors* with the required *sales tasks* and using the appropriate levers for doing so. The key levers are displayed along the bottom of figure 3-1:

- *Salespeople:* who they are, what they know, how you hire and then develop their skills and attitudes over time, so that they are good at executing *your* strategy's required sales tasks, not those of a generic selling methodology or what they learned at another company that made a different set of strategic choices.

- *Sales Force Control Systems:* the systems that shape ongoing performance management practices, including how the sales effort is organized and deployed, key performance indicators used to measure effectiveness, and sales compensation and incentive systems.

- *Sales Force Environment:* the environment in which go-to-market initiatives are developed and executed, and how well sales staff are informed, engaged, and supported: how communication does or doesn't work across organizational boundaries; how sales managers are selected and developed; how salespeople work as a team if and when that kind of coordination is important; the conduct and consequences of performance reviews—one of the more powerful but underutilized levers for influencing behavior in organizations.

No framework is all-encompassing. But this one defines the actionable core for alignment in any organization that deals with customers: the connections between the enterprise, its strategy, and the required implementation tasks; and then the connections between people, control systems, and management practices that largely determine whether actual behaviors align with those tasks. The framework also reflects the worldly reality that alignment of strategy and sales involves both the *what* (the integration of strategic choices and activities in response to the marketplace) and the ongoing *how* (the actions, allocation of resources, and skill sets that enable managers to connect people's behaviors to those choices and tasks).

Shining Light on the Links

At one level, a framework is a checklist. Just as checklists, complemented by experience, reduce mistakes by surgeons, pilots, structural engineers, and others, they can help business strategists and sales managers.[5] This framework takes an inherently multidimensional issue—forging relevant links between big-picture strategy and specific selling efforts— and breaks it into parts that can be managed. It focuses on sales accountabilities while reminding you that effective selling is the *outcome* of strategic choices and organizational systems, not only sales efforts.

Enabling effective selling in an organization requires the ability to diagnose these interactions and translate that understanding into action plans that *can* be measured, managed, and used by people in the field. It's worth the effort, because it can change what you do in sales *and* how you do strategy.

For example, you often hear about "coin-operated" sales forces where, allegedly, the key driver for salespeople is the structure of a compensation plan and where ongoing management is a very secondary activity. Money matters. But as I show in chapter 6, effective (and ineffective) salespeople come in all shapes and sizes; sweeping generalizations about selling and salespeople are just not supported by decades of empirical research; and the particular selling tasks inherent in a business strategy determine what it takes to be good at selling in a given situation. In turn, recognizing this affects how you should manage to get the most from your sales investment. And as chapter 8 explains, any sales force is a diverse group of people; the job is to manage this portfolio of talent. As chapter 9 explains, it's difficult if not impossible to craft one incentive plan that satisfies all of the diverse motivations in this portfolio. Like it or not, as a sales leader, you must learn to operate along all three dimensions outlined at the base of figure 3-1: people, the compensation dimension of control systems, and the ongoing sales management portion of the sales force environment.

Similarly, firms spend significant time, effort, and resources on determining sales quotas. But is that in fact the best place to start? As chapter 10 shows, appropriate goals depend on strategic objectives and the market environment in which you are competing today and tomorrow, not yesterday. And for goals to motivate, feedback is necessary: that's why performance reviews (sales force environment) link with performance measurements (sales force control systems) and why both affect who and how you hire and develop (salespeople).

Cause and effect also moves the other way: from sales to strategy. As chapter 6 shows, sales decisions directly affect a company's top line and hence the cash-flow profile of the business brought to finance, the orders received by operations, and the recruiting and training needs facing sales, HR, and other functions. This framework can therefore serve two purposes in strategy discussions. First, as chapters 4 and 5 discuss, it helps to clarify and articulate strategic choices in ways that translate into field behaviors, and so provide a necessary complement to broad and often content-free statements of mission or purpose. Second, it can also help strategists keep their eye on determinants of effective implementation in most organizations: the external customer factors and choices that determine sales tasks and the management levers that affect whether selling behaviors align with those tasks.

The basic idea is that aligning strategy and sales requires an ongoing systemic approach and not, unfortunately, a quick-fix motivational speech, a grand off-site, or an allegedly all-purpose selling methodology. You must integrate three factors internal to the sales organization—the people involved, the control systems that influence their behaviors, and how those controls are applied in the sales force and company environment—with factors external to the sales organization: your business strategy and the target market/customer characteristics that (if you in fact have a strategy) flow from those strategic choices. The latter largely determine what sales tasks are required, while the former influence selling behaviors so those tasks are done in ways consistent with strategy. When there is coherent integration among these factors, sales results *and* strategy formulation improve.

The Rest of This Book

The subsequent chapters look at each component of the
framework and how it affects the alignment of strategy and
sales. Here is the logic and plan.

Part II, "Linking Strategy and Sales," concerns core elements of each side of this duo.

- Chapter 4 looks at a foundational prerequisite: the
  presence of a coherent strategy. I will not discuss
  strategy-formulation methods in any detail. These
  days, by the time people reach senior positions in their
  companies, most have been exposed to many strategy
  techniques (Five Forces, SWOT, Value Chain Analysis,
  Game Theory, and so on) in an MBA or executive
  education program. Rather, I look at issues that often
  get muddled in firms amid techniques: the goal of *any*
  business strategy, the need for and impediments to
  making strategic choices, and—last but not least—
  the difference between strategy and other important
  things like mission or purpose.

- Clarity about the elements discussed in chapter 4
  is the prerequisite for doing what chapter 5 discusses:
  articulate a strategy in ways that busy people in the
  field can understand and embrace.

- Chapter 6 focuses on how effective executives translate
  strategic choices into practical, day-to-day sales tasks.
  If you're a sales manager, this chapter may change how
  you select and use available selling resources. If you're
  a strategist, it should motivate you to leave the office
  and talk to salespeople and customers. And if you're

a CEO or board member evaluating sales numbers, it will encourage you to always start with getting your people to dissect the sales tasks and never be a sucker for glib generalizations about selling or "sales" personalities.

Part III, "Performance Management," then focuses on the nitty-gritty of sales management.

- Chapter 7 looks at what's involved in embodying the required sales tasks in actual selling behaviors, and so being able to scale a sales process, via customer selection and account management practices. Chapters 8 to 10 then discuss research and guidelines for managing each of the levers along the bottom part of figure 3-1.

- Chapter 8 is all about people: hiring and development, the options for organizing salespeople, and the impact of new technologies and online shopping methods on both the sales organization and the required capabilities of salespeople.

- Chapter 9 examines a core sales force control system: sales compensation and incentives. Both elements are very important, but their role and impact are often misunderstood. If you're a CEO, a CFO, or other C-level strategist, this chapter may save you money and/or redirect how you spend that money. And if you're a sales manager, it can remind you what you're being paid for and that you can't substitute money for management.

- Chapter 10 then looks at a key dimension of sales force environment—performance reviews—and how it interacts with an element of control systems: the performance metrics used by sales managers and strategists to measure sales effectiveness.

Part IV, "Closing," examines broader management and company requirements for effective selling and strategy implementation.

- Chapter 11 discusses a key fulcrum and perennial sore point in most firms: developing sales managers that can manage. If you're a current or an aspiring sales leader, this chapter should motivate you to reexamine your promotion criteria and your own career, and if you're in HR, it should motivate you to forge closer links with the management teams in sales.

- Chapter 12 is about making connections: it looks at the coordination—between sales and other functions—required for sales success and suggests a practical way of improving that coordination. I also conclude with summary advice to sales leaders and strategists about aligning strategy and sales.

That's the plot of the rest of this book. Like all authors, I share the secret wish of that character who, in Terrence McNally's comedy about actors, *Golden Age*, always whispers before he goes on stage, "May the subtlety and the humility I have tried to bring to my performance be appreciated by someone other than myself." But, like all customers, that's for you to judge.

Part Two

LINKING STRATEGY AND SALES

The main thing is to keep the main thing the main thing.

**—Attributed to Jim Barksdale, Stephen Covey, Steve Jobs,
the band Last Call, and others**

Chapter 4
The Goal of Strategy

In most companies, people use the word *strategy* in different ways. This chapter looks at why so many executives misunderstand the goal of strategy and confuse strategy with other important but distinct processes in a company. See if you, and your colleagues, can pass the test discussed in this chapter.

Chapter 5
Making and Articulating Strategic Choices

Strategy is choice, and important choices inevitably cascade throughout a firm. This chapter examines that cascade and provides a practical way of articulating and communicating strategic choices in a manner that busy people in the field can understand and use.

Chapter 6
Sales Tasks and Strategy

Selling is probably the most contextually determined set of skills in a company: what works there does not necessarily work here. This chapter discusses what research tells us about sales effectiveness, how to translate a strategy into customer-selection criteria, and what it takes to be good in sales. If you're a sales manager, this chapter may change how you select and use available selling resources, and if you're a CEO, strategist, or board member evaluating sales numbers, it can help you to dissect sales tasks in your company and avoid being a sucker for glib generalizations about selling.

4

The Goal of Strategy

Let's take a test that I have given to hundreds of managers. Because I've spent years in a B-school, it probably won't surprise you that the test involves a two-by-two matrix (figure 4-1).

On the vertical axis is economic profit (EP) or what some have branded as economic value added (EVA). Essentially, EP is what's left after subtracting the cost of capital from net operating profit. When a firm makes an investment—a choice to commit time and capital to build a new plant, hire a new salesperson, or invest in training, for example—that investment should, at a minimum, recover the firm's cost of capital, including its opportunity cost (that is, whatever else the firm could have done with that money, those people, or the time expended). Hence, on the top of the vertical axis in figure 4-1, EP is positive (that's good), and on the bottom, it's negative (that's bad). On the horizontal axis is top-line revenue growth, or sales. At the right side, revenue growth is high and increasing. By contrast, at the left side of the horizontal axis, revenue growth is low, maybe flat, and perhaps

FIGURE 4-1

The goal of strategy is profitable growth

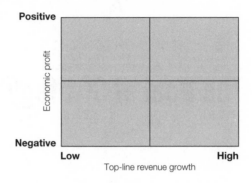

even declining. Now, let's take the test, which has three questions:

Question 1: In which of the four cells of this matrix is the best place for a company to be?

The answer is the upper-right quadrant, where EP is positive and revenue growth is high. In that situation, you want to grow that initiative as much as possible, because each increment of growth adds enterprise value. As Mae West put it, "Too much of a good thing can be wonderful." In my dealings with managers, nearly everybody answers question 1 correctly.

Question 2: Where is the second-best *place for a company to be on this matrix?*

The answer is the upper-left quadrant, where EP stays positive even if top-line growth slows. About 80 to 90 percent of managers correctly answer this question. In many ways, the situation in the upper-left quadrant is what finance, accounting, and investment review committees get paid for, and it's *not* a popular job in most firms. Essentially, the job is to look at the requests for time, money, and people in the plans from R&D, marketing, operations, sales, HR, and other colleagues, and say, "This is ingenious, but may I test the assumptions, run the numbers, and see if we recoup our cost of capital with that initiative you're planning—or in which you have already invested capital and, by the way, *your* reputation in this company?" You'll have a hard time, Doctor No, winning employee-of-the-month awards if you're really doing your job in that role, as evidenced by the language and jokes: "bean counters," "green eye-shade type," "the introvert accountant looks at his shoes when he talks to you, the extrovert accountant looks at your shoes." It's not popular. But it's necessary for the health of the business.

This brings us to the final question on the exam. Notice that you have a fifty-fifty chance of getting the answer right. So, please pay attention to how I word the question:

Question 3: Where is the worst *place for a company to be on this matrix? Is the worst place to be (a) in the lower-right quadrant, where EP is negative but where we are adding customers and growing our top line? Or, is it (b) the lower-left quadrant, where EP is also negative and top-line revenue is low, flat, and maybe even declining as in 10, 9, 8, 7, 6 . . . ?*

The answer is (a) or the lower-right quadrant, and it's *a lot* worse than the alternative (b). When economic profit is negative, additional investments in that initiative only *accelerate* the destruction of value in the enterprise. It's the Charge of the Light Brigade, and while you may salute their gallantry and persistence, you should sell short as soon as the troops start down that awful valley. Or, think of it this way: if you're on the *Titanic* or another sinking ship, you hope the ship sinks slowly, not faster, because that buys time for you to use available resources for other potentially lifesaving or business-improvement activities. In my experience, fewer than a third of managers answer question 3 correctly and, in many firms (especially tech firms), much less than a third. And if you think this is just an arbitrary test without worldly consequences, think again. This confusion about the dynamics of sales and economic profit is reflected, and in fact magnified, in companies' actual financial and market performance.

Going back to 1990, the consulting firm Bain and Company has done a study of companies' performance. Bain looked at companies worldwide with sales of at least $500 million and asked three questions: over the course of a decade, how many of these firms achieved a relatively modest rate of growth (5.5 percent in real terms) in (1) sales and (2) operating income, while also (3) earning their cost of capital? Why 5.5 percent, you ask? Because over 90 percent of firms say in their annual reports and strategic plans that they aspire to at least this level of performance. In a sense, Bain is conducting a put-up-or-shut-up type of inquiry. The result? Many companies meet the top-line revenue criterion. Many fewer do that while growing operating income commensurately. Include cost of capital (and you should), and the results are disheartening. For the decade of 1990–2000, only 13 percent of companies achieved all three criteria, and for 2001–2010, it was only 9 percent—fewer than one in ten companies.[1] A McKinsey study reached similar results: an analysis of EP for nearly three thousand large nonfinancial companies from 2007 to 2011 indicates that the top quintile of firms accounted for 90 percent of *all* the EP measured, while the bottom two quintiles *destroyed* more than $450 billion in EP during this period.[2] The goal of strategy is profitable growth, and EP should be part of that goal. But sustained profitable growth is rare.

The Avoidance of Strategy

Going back to my test: why do so many experienced and well-educated executives answer question 3 incorrectly? The reasons vary. In testy moods with critics, the novelist Saul Bellow liked to explain the difference between ignorance and indifference this way: "I don't know and I don't care."[3] Place the following reasons in the "I don't know" category.

Lack of Information. In many firms, managers (including C-suite executives) don't know their firm's cost of capital.[4] Calculations like this are "what finance does" (if finance does them) or are the focus of a pseudo-scholarly debate about *the* correct way to compute the equation. One good thing about PE firms is that their debt covenants force managers in their portfolio companies to get up to speed about this aspect of the business, resolve the debate, and make sure that it's reflected in resource-allocation decisions, not just delegated to people who keep score after the fact. When this is not done, managers are attracted to the allure of sales for their own sake, ignoring the fact that accounting profit can grow even when EP is declining. Sales by itself is a trailing and often misleading indicator of enterprise performance and value.

The Nature of the Concept. The notion of opportunity cost, central to economic profit (and, for that matter, to economics for over a century), is apparently not an easy concept for busy executives. I don't mean that it's an intellectually difficult notion. We all know the basic idea. Opportunity cost is the sacrifice you make related to the next-best alternative available; it's what you forgo when you make a choice for X rather than Y or Z. The issue is not IQ. Rather, as usual in business, it's living the idea in practice, because opportunity costs are not just financial; they also include the lost time, effort, and other activities associated with resource allocation.

When asked to explain why, when EP is negative, they said selling more (the lower-right quadrant in figure 4-1) is better than selling less or not selling at all (the lower-left quadrant), executives invariably say that those sales can "keep things going" or maintain "morale" and "customer relationships." But consider the arithmetic: if that sale does not recoup your cost of capital, you're digging a deeper hole, however good you, your colleagues, and sales reps feel about that sale. It's what accountants call the *sunk-cost fallacy*: throwing good money after bad. Fundamentally, these responses ignore opportunity costs: what *else* you could do with that time, money, and people to keep things going, maintain morale, and (very important) preserve and build valuable customer relationships.

Performance Metrics. By contrast, place the following reason for exam failure in Bellow's "I don't care" category: performance metrics. You can understand that something will not help enterprise value but if you are paid to do it—and punished if you don't, either financially or in terms of prestige and status—you will probably do it. Performance metrics tied to volume or market share irrespective of economic profit predominate in sales organizations. Many executives in explaining their answer to question 3 will frankly acknowledge that "increasing share is what I get paid for, it's what drives the allocation of resources in the annual budgeting process, and it determines my bonus." To paraphrase the old Groucho routine, "Who are you going to believe: your eyes or your paycheck?"

Consider the global subprime mortgage debacle. As Michael Lewis and others have documented, many people, including frontline people at the banks and mortgage companies, knew then that these loans were a colossal example of doing business in the lower-right quadrant of figure 4-1.[5] We also know, in retrospect, that this destroyed huge amounts of economic value as well as many companies. But mortgage brokers made their bonuses through 2007 and into part of 2008 before the music stopped. On a global scale and with bigger consequences than peanuts, this was a version of what the PPCo sales rep told me: "We sold the deals and if that caused problems in other areas of the business, so be it." And it's not uncommon. Years ago, Steve Kerr wrote a classic analysis of performance metrics that pay off for one behavior while the rewarder somehow hopes for another. His title beautifully summarized the situation: "On the Folly of Rewarding A, While Hoping for B."[6]

The Need for Strategy

But another factor in executive behavior is neither ignorance nor indifference. It is a rational belief that the lower-right quadrant in figure 4-1 is often about an investment and that there is a dynamic investment cycle inherent in answering question 3.

You must often spend money before you make money. So yes, say executives, we are in the negative EP quadrant today, but that's necessary to make real profit tomorrow. In other words, we have a plan for migrating the firm or that initiative, over time, from the lower-right to the sweet spot in the upper-right quadrant. In various forms, this is what you are asked to believe in most annual reports, investor presentations, new-product plans, and sales programs. It's the argument behind claims for "first-mover advantages" or "freemium" pricing or "razor-and-blade" sales approaches: build the base (or the "eyeballs" or "hits" on a website) and then monetize the base.

I have yet to see an entrepreneur, an executive, or a hedge fund manager say that someone should back them because their plan won't ever make money. Doesn't happen, except in *The Producers*. The issue is not whether there is an investment cycle. Rather, what criteria should we use to distinguish between a plausible pitch, with reasonable investment of money, time, and people, and a hockey-stick projection where we hemorrhage money for years but then—"picnic/lightning"—we will suddenly make money (usually, by the way, in year 3 of the plan)? It can't just be that we like the person making the claim, or that the power points are awesome (don't laugh; I've sat on boards and worked with venture-capital firms, and it can happen). One basic criterion must be the plan (not just the assertion or the passion) for getting to the upper-right quadrant. Does it make sense, is it in touch with market and customer realities—in other words, is it a coherent *strategy*?

Consider consumer internet companies. The common business model here is called a two-sided platform with a chicken-and-egg dynamic: you must attract users in order to attract people or firms willing to use your site and pay you to advertise on your site. Hence, a key initial sales strategy is to sign up users, most often by not charging for the service. You see what this means for the venture's cash-flow curve: it's a deep trough. But the strategy is to build the customer base to attract suppliers who in turn attract more users and suppliers, and so on. With a plan like this, many firms raised billions of dollars during the initial internet boom until that bubble burst. We know, with hindsight, that most of those plans were literally not worth the paper or computer they were written on. They ignored fundamentals and lacked a strategy for dealing with the market conditions in which those firms proposed to sell and compete: low entry barriers, many choices and high buyer power, burgeoning substitutes, and so on.[7] Yet, at the same time, there is Amazon, eBay, and other successful two-sided platform firms from this era that have survived and grown in the same industry conditions.

Pricing is a moment of truth in strategy and sales. So fast-forward from the initial internet boom, and consider current approaches in this space. In 2012, almost 80 percent of the one hundred top-grossing mobile apps in Apple's App Store used freemium pricing (versus 4 percent just two years earlier), and it sounds both plausible and fun as a selling approach.[8] It's plausible because there's almost no marginal cost to digital goods, so you can acquire users with free services until inertia or switching costs kick in and then you charge for additional capacity, extras, or premium features. It's fun because lots of people know how to sell things for nothing, and on the internet, your sales force (if you have one) is negligible. It seems to work splendidly for companies like Dropbox, LinkedIn, and Skype. But so many others are truly enacting the old joke about selling each pencil below cost yet somehow hoping to make it up in volume. Why?

Typically only 1 or 2 percent of users will upgrade to a paid product. So the size of the target market counts in crafting a strategy here: you need a product or service with a large-enough market that 1 to 2 percent is economically meaningful and can support fixed costs and scaling costs. Choice of features for free is important: offer too many, and there's no customer incentive to upgrade, but offer too few, and you can't generate enough initial demand. A varied product line is often necessary: paid users expect to get better or different versions of the free service. The customer context (which is where sales lives) is, as always, crucial. Note the dynamics of services like Dropbox, LinkedIn, and Skype: in part you use them because other important people in your life use them. The presence or absence of peer pressure and social switching costs are also pertinent in crafting a selling approach in this market. By contrast, when Apple proudly announced that it had more than 100,000 iPhone apps in its App Store, a little-known fact was that over 98 percent of customers had shown *no* interest in the 99,000 least popular apps.

Success and failure in business are not only due to luck, timing, and effort. These things matter. But so does a strategy that makes coherent choices, effectively allocates available resources, and communicates to people in the field. So, what is and is not strategy, and what must you recognize before you can craft a coherent and communicable strategy for sales?

What Strategy Is Not

Strategy is now one of the most fungible words in the business lexicon. Different people use the word in different ways, in the same company and sometimes in the same sentence. One result is that for many firms and even for prominent strategy consultants, the concept has shrunk to nothing more than setting "Big, Hairy, Audacious Goals" (BHAG) or "adaptability" or "just-in-time decision making" or "a few critical initiatives . . . built around deep capabilities."[9]

The economist Fritz Machlup once wrote an essay about "weaselwords," by which he meant "words concealing voids of thought . . . used to avoid commitment . . . which destroy the force of a statement, as a weasel ruins an egg by sucking out its content."[10] Machlup was talking about how economists often use words like "structure" in lieu of empirical cause-and-effect linkages. Ironically, after decades of books, articles, and MBA programs so dedicated to strategic thinking, that's the current danger with how the word *strategy* is used in many business meetings. It's too often a way of sounding smart or leader-like, and it's used and confused with other important but distinct things.

Machlup explained how this can happen. As he pointed out, when an economist uses the word *labor*, no one "will ever think of the painful muscle contractions preceding childbirth, and if we say 'capital' he may not know precisely what we mean, but he will rarely confuse it with the seat of government in a state or country." But when multiple words used to refer to different aspects of complex phenomena have overlapping meanings, then "the context [cannot] be relied upon to indicate which meaning is intended [and] the writer or speaker has a moral duty, I would say, to state what he means."[11] So say I. So let's first clarify what strategy is *not*.

Strategy is not the same thing as a goal, an aspiration, or a vision of what we want to be—big or small, hairy or bald, audacious or timid. I'm of course referring here to Jim Collins's influential notion of BHAG as the strategic essence and starting point of "great" companies. In his books, Collins has as many smart things to say about organization as anyone since Peter Drucker (and, in my book, that is sincere high praise).[12] But he's just reflecting and not improving current practice with this notion.

So many companies confuse strategy with aspirational statements like "We will be number one or number two in our markets" or "Our strategy is to be the world leader in . . ." or "Our strategy is to provide superior shareholder returns." When you cut through the rhetoric, too many strategic planning meetings are already optimistic forecasting exercises (call it a BHAG rather than saying the glass is half-empty) followed by the knights at that round table taking a vow: "Let's pick a big number and go for it!" That may be motivational. It may, as Collins suggests, help to stimulate ideas. Objectives are undeniably important (see the next chapter). But it's not strategy, and it does not help people in the field to build the skills, processes, and relationships required to execute a strategy.

Strategy is not the same as mission or purpose. These terms refer to the way a firm describes why it exists, the value it adds to customers and society, and why it matters. Over forty years ago, Kenneth Andrews emphasized that a CEO is, for good or ill, an "architect of purpose" about the organization's mission in society, with and beyond its customers.[13] Clarity of purpose can provide a foundation for strategy. But confusing the two—as so many firms do: check out their websites and investor presentations on those sites—can hurt, not help. Here are statements of core purpose by firms lauded repeatedly in discussions of "great" companies:[14]

3M: To solve unsolved problems innovatively

Cargill: To improve the standard of living around the world

Mary Kay: To give unlimited opportunities to women

Merck: To preserve and improve human life

Nike: To experience the emotion of competition, winning, and crushing competitors

Walt Disney: To make people happy

These statements are ennobling and make a difference in how employees feel about their jobs. But these statements are also so nebulous that they are analytically useless for doing what any coherent strategy must do: specify where we do and don't play in this world, and how we propose to win in those places where we do choose to play. 3M doesn't go after any unsolved problem. There are many ways to improve living standards in addition to the productivity-enhancing animal feeds that Cargill sells. You can make people happy with money, drugs, or many other things besides the great animated characters devised by the wizards at Disney's Pixar subsidiary. Strategy requires choice, but purpose is about the other part of the yin-yang: expanding the role and possibilities of the enterprise. And no organization's purpose is independent of how much the world changes. As Keynes said, when asked in the 1930s why he had changed his mind about government intervention in the economy, "When the facts change, I change my mind. Tell me, sir, what do you do?" If you simply cling to purpose, you're just stubborn, not principled, or you may believe your purpose is just too big to fail; it's not.

Confusing purpose with strategy is bad news: for your firm and your career. For years as P&G's CEO, Bob McDonald spoke about the "purpose" of the company, wanting P&G to "touch and improve the lives of more consumers, in more parts of the world, more completely." But in the absence of results, he finally abandoned that rhetoric when he cut almost six thousand jobs and made core strategic decisions about where and how to allocate resources: a focus on forty country/product combinations. McDonald recognized the difference too late: he was fired in 2013.[15] Purpose is not strategy.

Strategy is not the same as values. Values refer to the principles that people in an organization believe and that help to guide how they behave. Values are important. As I'll discuss in a later chapter, they help to establish the ground for the "rules of engagement" required between sales and other functions. They also typically provide an important ethical reminder about the principles, beyond legal compliance, under which firms should operate, and that's especially important in sales.

Here are some of the published core values of Apple, which, by early 2014, was one of the most valuable companies in the world and is a remarkable example of how leadership (including values) can revive a company that, only a decade ago, was given up for dead by many observers: "We believe that we are on the face of the earth to make great products . . . We constantly focus on innovation . . . We don't settle for anything less than excellence . . ."

Nordstrom: "Service to the customer above all else . . . Excellence in reputation . . ."

Disney: "No cynicism . . . Creativity, dreams, and imagination . . ."

Merck: "Unequivocal excellence in all aspects of the company . . . Science-based innovation . . . Honesty and integrity . . ."

Nike: "It is our nature to innovate . . . Simplify and go . . . Do the right thing . . ."[16]

These are not just empty words to people in successful companies. But they often are just empty words in unsuccessful companies. It's not always possible, despite Disney, for people to avoid cynicism. We cite the values of successful firms but not others. Check out the espoused values of Enron, Lehman Brothers, Bear Stearns, or other defunct and disgraced companies, and you'll see many of these same statements. What's cause and what's effect? Also, note the overlapping themes of innovation, excellence, honesty, and integrity in the values of companies in wildly disparate businesses. In a competitive market, who could be (at least publicly) in favor of mediocre products or poor customer service or lack of innovation or behaving dishonestly?

Values are real in action, not on websites or in speeches. Like the advice to "buy low and sell high," it's an important principle. But it is a strategy that provides direction about where to buy, how to sell, and when not to. Yet, many executives somehow expect a sales response when they say, "Our strategy is to provide superior products and services . . ." or "constant innovation" or "great service." This may play well at Davos or on *Charlie Rose*, but not in the trenches. And speaking of the trenches . . .

Business strategy is not the same as war or a battle plan. The word *strategy* comes from the ancient Greek for a "general" in a military campaign. Strategy gurus constantly use analogies with battle plans for "competitive advantage" versus the enemy. But the metaphor is not suitable because business, unlike a war or battle, is not primarily about defeating an enemy. Business is primarily about customer value: targeting customer groups and tailoring sales and other activities to serve those groups better or differently than others. You don't learn much about that from studying Caesar, Napoleon, Sun Tzu, Lee, or whoever your favorite general is. The analogies are also used selectively and inconsistently. A repeated example is Hannibal's defeat of the larger Roman army at Cannae by his pioneering use of flanking tactics and cavalry. But we don't often hear about Fabius Maximus, a Roman general nicknamed "The Delayer," who simply wore down Hannibal's invading army by avoiding pitched battles. Hannibal *lost* that war. Or Clausewitz tells us that detailed planning is everything but drop the plan once the shooting starts: which is it? We already know that the business world, like other mortal activities, is uncertain. As Damon Runyan said, "All life is six-to-four against." So what gain really comes from the military analogy?

And there should be a significant gain to justify the common loss. The military metaphors lead executives to conflate strategy with the aggregation of tactical plans à la Napoleon at Waterloo or Lee at Gettysburg (those geniuses of "military intelligence" also lost, didn't they?). "Wait for the element of surprise" becomes double the R&D budget; "take the right flank" becomes increase production capacity; "provide air cover" becomes globalize; and "charge!" is a motivational sales meeting. But studies show that a big problem with corporate planning processes is that the resulting "strategy" turns out to be the bland compilation of business-unit plans that, in turn, are a compilation (not integration) of functional initiatives.[17] I support our troops as much as the next person, but let's demobilize and drop the battle metaphors. As Peter Drucker put it over a half-century ago, "The purpose of a business is to create a customer." That's also the purpose of purpose and any business strategy. Make customers, not war.

In fact, effective strategy aligned with sales is more like the Appalachian Trail than any battle plan. The 2,000-mile footpath was initially sketched out by Benton MacKaye in 1921 and, with the help of thousands of volunteers, opened in 1937. Unlike a concrete highway or a military invasion, the exact route of the Appalachian Trail is in constant negotiation with the forest, changing somewhat with each winter storm and spring flood—the external environment. It's estimated that only about 1 percent of the original footpath remains.[18] But about 3 million people hike some portion of the trail each year, and it's the model for other long-distance trails around the world. The soil changes, but the strategic direction and therefore the choices of where to place a given portion of the path hold up nicely.

What Is Strategy?

The confusion of business strategy with complementary but distinct concepts can lead executives into a debilitating form of "Fed-speak" when they try to articulate strategic direction. Years after resigning his position, former Fed chairman Alan Greenspan explained why and how he did it:

> As Fed chairman, every time I expressed a view, I added or subtracted 10 basis points from the credit market. That was not helpful. But I nonetheless had to testify before Congress . . . and so you construct what we used to call Fed-speak. I would hypothetically think of a little plate in front of my eyes, which was the *Washington Post*, the following morning's headline, and I would catch myself in the middle of a sentence. Then, instead of just stopping, I would continue on resolving the sentence in some obscure way which made it incomprehensible. But nobody was quite sure I wasn't saying something profound when I wasn't.[19]

Arguably, Greenspan had good motives for his obscure and incomprehensible statements. But if you need to articulate a strategy that people in sales and other functions can understand and embrace behaviorally (and you do, you most certainly do), this is not helpful.

So, what *is* strategy? It's fundamentally the movement of an organization from its present position to a desirable but inherently uncertain future position. The path from here to there is both analytical (a series of linked hypotheses about objectives; where we play; how we play; and what this means for the customer value proposition, sales tasks, and other activities) and behavioral (the coordinated efforts of people who work in different functions but must align for effective selling to happen). And the trail begins with making and communicating some core choices inherent in any coherent strategy.

5

Making and Articulating Strategic Choices

In his wonderfully titled book, *Build a Better Life by Stealing Office Supplies*, Scott Adams, the creator of *Dilbert*, has a cartoon called "The Importance of Strategies" (figure 5-1). In the first panel, Dogbert notes that "All companies need a strategy . . ." What too often follows that sentence, as chapter 4 argued, is a catchy aphorism (you need a strategy because without one, no road will take you there, etc.). But Dogbert says that all companies need a strategy "so the employees will know what they don't do." The remaining panels of the cartoon are a before-and-after parable about strategy.

In the second panel, at the company with no strategy, the phone is ringing. Who's on the phone? It's a customer, supplier, channel partner, or sales manager with a potential deal. But the executive, Dilbert, is paralyzed and uncertain: "Uh-oh . . . what should I do? I don't know what our strategy is, so how do I know if my answer will allocate resources

FIGURE 5-1

"The Importance of Strategies"

Source: Scott Adams, *Build a Better Life by Stealing Office Supplies*, 1991.

appropriately?" The third panel is the "after" situation at the company with a strategy. Again, the phone rings and now Dilbert does not hesitate. He listens politely, responds, "No, we don't do that" and—click!—he hangs up on the caller.

Adams is having fun with this notion. But Dilbert, in the final panel, is basically correct. Strategy involves "no" as well as "yes." Without "no," you get what most companies get as a result of planning meetings: a list of possibilities, a vision at 30,000 feet that many managers simply don't understand ("What does this mean for money, time, and my people . . . uh-oh, what should I do?"), or a series of incremental initiatives for the next year. In fact, if you attend a "strategy" meeting, and after the meeting it's not clear which customers you would *not* serve, what services you would *not* provide, or what activities in sales and other areas you will *not* invest in, the odds are that it was not a strategy meeting. It may have been a useful motivational meeting, and people may leave feeling good about the company. But without clarity about "no" as well as "yes," there is no strategy.

Strategy and Choice

Business strategy is about the choices that a company makes in its attempts to achieve competitive advantage in a market. Some choices are explicit. They are documented in a plan or discussed at meetings. But many important choices are implicit in the myriad decisions we make, often without thinking of them as strategic, in the flow of running the business or on a project-by-project basis. This includes the hurdle rates used to evaluate capital requests, or the assumptions about risk and reward implicit in how finance calculates the firm's cost of capital or the questions that you are expected to ask and answer when you develop an R&D, marketing, operations, or sales initiative.

Any budget involves choices about who and what gets more or less of finite resources. Firms are always making choices about which products or sales efforts to support, and which not to support with as much time, people, and money. There is no "ignorance is bliss" dimension to this aspect of business. You are better off being explicit. The focus of most people in a firm most of the time is on near-term operating issues. Nothing wrong with that. But without clarity about key choices, people can only pick up random, disconnected cues about strategy as they work, and alignment is then hit-or-miss.

Equally important, the raison d'être of strategy is to maximize the value of what your firm brings to the table—the capabilities that *distinguish* you from competitors in ways that customers value. Strategy means being smart about being different. In mass-merchant retailing, Target sells for higher prices than Wal-Mart. As Target's chairman notes, "If we're in the business of selling the same stuff that the guy down the street has, we're not going to be able to sell it for more."[1] A strategy must answer the question "Where and how are we going to win?" Without that clarity, the firm and its sales efforts run the risk of global mediocrity: you become OK at many things, but not very good at any specific things.

Cascading Choices

Important strategic choices cascade throughout a firm. One way to think about this is figure 5-2. First, what are our goals and objectives with respect to the value we do or can bring to customers (customer value) and the value we expect to get from customers (financial value)? A customer value proposition is always at the core of any successful strategy. Yet research indicates that as many as 75 percent of executive teams lack consensus about this basic element.[2] You can see why. In most firms, up-to-date information about what customers value is held by frontline people in sales, service,

FIGURE 5-2

Cascading choices

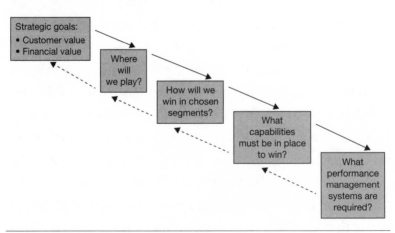

and marketing. Meanwhile, information about costs is best known to a combination of people in procurement, operations, finance, accounting, and product/service groups. And consensus about the value proposition is not enough. You must serve customers in ways that produce good economic returns for your firm: a strategy also requires choices about how you *extract* financial value.

That leads to the next set of choices: Where will we play in the opportunity spaces available in our market(s)? Which customers and segments can we serve distinctively and profitably? That is the *scope* dimension in a coherent strategy. In areas where we choose to play, how will we win? I'll define winning the way customer and capital markets do: winning in business is achieving above-average value-delivery to customers and returns to investors. All else in a competitive market is survival or getting the chance to play again. Winning is being above average in both customer and financial terms.

That, in turn, leads to choices about the capabilities needed in sales and other areas in order to win. At what tasks must we excel and be world-class in relation to the best at those tasks? Conversely, what are the tasks that we must do but should not overengineer? In other words, where do we need to be just good enough and not necessarily the very best? These are the *advantage* dimensions in a strategy, and they involve "no" as well as "yes." A strategy means continually asking, "Where are we spending too little *and* too much time, people, or capital?" Companies with coherent strategies do not treat all functions equally. Some are more important, and get more resources, than others.

Choices about goals, where to compete, sources of advantage, and capabilities are incomplete without performance management—the practices that develop and keep relevant the information and capabilities needed to execute a strategy. In the field, core performance management choices involve shaping selling behaviors, organizing the sales effort, the measures used to evaluate effectiveness, hiring and development criteria, and—last but not least—compensation and incentives.

Finally, you see dotted lines in figure 5-2 leading back to strategic goals, because this should be an iterative process. Goals determine choices about customers and capabilities, and performance management practices should align with those choices. But a competitive market environment is like the wind and rain on the Appalachian Trail. It's not the responsibility of competitors and customers to align with our goals and capabilities; it's our responsibility to keep in touch with market changes. Alignment is a process, not a single decision or action. It's a pattern of choices over time.

Put differently, what makes a company great—and what makes for a coherent strategy versus a slogan—is *not* the fact that the firm may have a great value proposition or has a terrific blue-ocean opportunity or is very good at R&D, engineering, marketing, sales, or social media. What makes a company great and a strategy something more than a wish list is *how* these things fit together.[3] Alignment provides the information needed to keep the links relevant to today and tomorrow, not yesterday.

Articulating Strategy

These cascading choices play out at multiple levels. They determine which customers get real attention and their perceptions of who you are (your *brand*). They determine where people, time, and money get allocated in the daily running of the business. They ultimately determine (more than vision, mission, or purpose statements) what is and is not a priority opportunity, threat, and behavioral value in the firm. So it's important to translate the choices in a strategy into statements that people in sales and other functions can understand and use.

As the Dilbert cartoon suggests, it's tough for people to execute a plan they don't understand. Studies indicate that communication of priorities to the front line is highly correlated with business performance and, conversely, that this "middle ground" is often where strategy execution breaks down in companies.[4] Other studies find that employees need information to understand the strategic and bottom-line impact of their daily choices, that communicating strategic identity is the first step, and that "strategy maps" or other visual devices can play important roles.[5] Yet, many executives actively and passively resist making their strategy explicit. Years ago, Kenneth Andrews cited common reasons voiced by executives for not articulating strategy.[6] You hear these reasons as often now as you did then.

Competitor Concerns. One reason Andrews cited was "the desirability of keeping strategic plans confidential for security reasons." But the strategies of successful firms are usually well publicized. How many books, articles, and case studies get written about Apple, IKEA, Nike, Southwest Airlines, and other examples? For decades, Toyota has allowed outside groups to study its factories on-site. This may increase knowledge of current best practice in production (which is not the same thing as strategy). More often, as a four-year study of Toyota's production system across forty plants concluded, "observers confuse the tools and practices they see on their plant visits with the system itself."[7] In a world with a global infrastructure of consulting firms and others paid to disseminate information about best practices, confidentiality as a reason not to articulate strategy is both myopic (the information is just not that hard for interested competitors to acquire) and often beside the point (you have bigger things to worry about than competitors reading your strategy documents if *your* people don't know your strategy and therefore don't execute it well).

Intuition and Incrementalism. As Andrews explained, "Managers who prefer muddling through . . . never commit themselves to an articulate strategy." Businesspeople never really needed Emerson to remind them that "a foolish consistency" is not a prerequisite for the corner office. But you can and should be alert to market changes while also providing employees with more than enigmatic descriptions of strategic choices and why certain tasks are important. If you don't, then as in a Rorschach ink-blot test, employees— and especially salespeople—will fill in the blanks with their own constructions. The result is diverse behaviors driven by multiple imaginary strategies that subvert the process implied by careful "muddling through." And if the strategy is implicit in the intuition of a gifted leader, then, at best, it's only as strong as that person's reach and, more often, as weak as the weakest link in the organization.

Belief That "We Know It and Don't Need to Articulate It." According to Andrews, some executives claim that "a firm that has internalized its strategy does not feel the need to keep saying what it is, valuable as that information might be to new members." The current way of saying this is to cite culture or principles as the secret sauce of success. These are important, but not the same as a set of known strategic choices that interact with customers. An unstated or vague strategy cannot be tested and contested as market conditions change. As Andrews noted, "To cover in empty phrases an absence of analysis . . . is worse than to remain silent, for it conveys the illusion of a commitment when none has been made . . . A strategy must be explicit to be effective."[8]

Information and Change. I add this other common rationale because the speed of information flows and change in business allegedly makes articulating strategy an ephemeral exercise that's not worth it.[9] But how different are we, really? "Information overload" was the basis of Alvin Toffler's pop-sociology book *Future Shock* in 1970. That's a few business generations ago: think mainframes with spindle cards, Nixon, gas-guzzlers, and your parents were probably younger than you are now. Look at history: "creative destruction" has been the fruitful norm, as Schumpeter emphasized, at least since the steam engine. Indeed, the pace of change was cited by Alfred Sloan and others *for* the importance of communicating plans throughout an organization.[10] The more things change, the more they change. But the fact of change is perennial. As in any arms race, moreover, both sides beef up: there is more information *and* more "big data" ways of analyzing information. Adaptability is important, but consider the status of this point of view in your organization: is this an argument for not articulating strategy, or is it what people say when they're too lazy to get the data or don't want to commit to choices? And *not* articulating strategy never helped any company adapt to disruptive change—from Western Union in the nineteenth century to the latest firm upended by a new technology or business model in the twenty-first.

Strategic choices are required, whether or not you acknowledge and communicate them within and beyond the C-suite. If your firm doesn't choose, then over time in any competitive market, one or both of two other parties will choose for you: either your competitors or (in voting with their feet) customers. Neither group necessarily has your best interests at heart.

Objectives, Scope, Advantage

My colleague David Collis and the late Michael Rukstad have a useful way of articulating strategy.[11] They point out that any coherent strategy statement should specify, at a minimum, three components: objectives, scope, and advantage. Clarifying these elements forces leaders to sharpen their external market positioning and to specify the implementation tasks inherent in that strategy. Their approach is especially useful when you're communicating strategic direction to the field.

Objectives

This component indicates the ends that strategy hopes to achieve: the primary goals that will motivate behavior and resource allocations in the firm. Goals can be quantitative and qualitative and chosen from a range of possible outcomes within a specified time frame: profitability, market share, the well-being of patients in a health-care organization, or other objectives. But as Fred Smith, founder of Federal Express, once put it, "Every successful business has, at its heart, a theory of the business—an underlying set of supporting objectives . . . that gives people a foundation on which to operate. Working inside that framework, they've got an idea of what we want them to do [and] to prioritize."[12]

If there are multiple objectives, the hierarchy should be clear because a choice or redefinition of objective has a big impact. When a firm's primary objective is profits over market share (or vice versa), or scale and throughput over premium service, the results cascade through the organization and especially in sales. Consider key account programs designed to implement a strategy with a market share objective. These sales programs typically involve specialized support in areas like applications engineering, custom design services, and expedited delivery as well as volume discounts. These costs take their toll on profit margins. Often, the rise in volume is simply not enough to offset the loss in operating income and the call goes forth to reorganize sales or change the strategy. But what *is* our objective? Articulating strategy to the field begins with a clear-eyed answer to that question.

Scope

This is the where-to-play element of strategy. Again, there are multiple dimensions from which you can choose: segments, geographical markets, product or service categories, or others. But choose you must: every firm is always making it easier or harder for certain types of customers to do business with it, and customer selection (discussed in chapter 6) is a core strategic and selling decision.

It's a decision that should *not* be delegated to sales. In many ways, salespeople lack the frame of reference needed to make good scope decisions. Their training, daily attempts to connect and build relationships with buyers, and often financial incentives predispose them to say yes to any need a customer expresses. In addition, in most companies it is other functions, not sales, that deal with the terms and conditions struck in a sales deal. Predictably, studies indicate that "loss of focus" is the most common reason that companies stall and strategies fail.[13] A purely sales-driven culture will proliferate customer segments and services, increase the seller's cost to serve, and dissipate scope choices.

Scope decisions require a delineation of the boundaries (e.g., the types of customers, products, or services) that we should not go beyond, given the current strategy. Clarifying scope provides a necessary template for framing and debating the inevitable trade-offs facing any firm as customers, competitors, suppliers, new technologies, and other market factors make competing demands on limited time, talent, or capital. Consider the following example.

I worked with a medical products company that had a division performing poorly. Sales and profits were down, factory utilization was below 60 percent, and price pressures were increasing. However, with surprisingly minimal capital-expenditure investment, the factory could also be used to produce paintball equipment for that growing consumer leisure activity. Should the company do it? Before you decide, note that at the time this proposal was made to the board, paintball equipment was a fragmented and fast-growing market where gross margins were an estimated 30 percent *higher* than margins on the company's medical equipment. Moreover, the people behind the proposal were good operating managers who understood the ramifications for distribution and brand. They proposed to distribute paintball equipment through manufacturers' rep (MR) organizations and with a different label, thus minimizing impact on the current channels and perceptions of the firm and brand by buyers at its hospital accounts. Should they do it?

The board was divided but, for good reasons, finally voted no. Let's assume that all of the operating and economic assumptions in the proposed plan panned out. This redefinition of scope was still ill advised. The paintball market, unlike that for medical products, would be driven by multiple new-product introductions to retail channels, by style and fashion, and (as entrants in this currently fragmented but high-margin market inevitably occur) by increased competition likely to accelerate new products, styles, and required advertising expenditures. The division had no experience in, or capabilities for, dealing with any of these factors, and an MR channel would provide less, not more, information about these market developments over time. Notice, also, that the increased scope would mean that every erg of time, talent, and capital expended on the paintball market would *not* have been available for dealing with the problems in the core market. The issue in this situation was not whether to add paintball production capabilities. The real choice was a tough portfolio decision: should we keep or sell the medical-products division?

Scope decisions like this confront all firms constantly, even in downturns. A survey of four hundred executives in North America, Europe, and Asia was conducted in March 2011—in the midst of the Great Recession and growing fears at the time about the European Union, the continued growth of China's economy, and banks and credit markets everywhere.

Only 15 percent of respondents, even in bad times, said their growth was inhibited by lack of attractive opportunities.[14] There will *always* be opportunities that sales can chase. But marketplace success and the voice of experience indicate that the "no" part of strategy is vital. Many small and medium-sized firms, as well as start-ups, succeed with scope discipline: focusing on specific groups of customers or products. This allows them to know those segments in detail and build selling efforts geared to those customers. Vanguard, the mutual fund company, has as one of its articulated strategy principles a key scope choice: "We will not pay for distribution of our products." Its CEO notes that this choice helps "in the difficult decisions where we decide not to do something as a result. Often the things you say no to turn out to be among the most important choices."[15] Similarly, Steve Jobs, in an interview not long before his untimely death, was asked to cite the biggest lessons he learned in his career: "Focus . . . means saying no to the 100 other good ideas that there are. You have to pick carefully. I'm actually as proud of the things we haven't done as the things we have done."[16]

Advantage

By advantage, I mean what the firm does differently, better, or world-class (as well as the best) to deliver and extract value in areas where it does compete. Advantage is about the means that we rely on to *win* with chosen customer groups, and you can divide it into two components: the value proposition to external customers and the internal activities that support the external value proposition.

Any strategy lives or dies on the basis of its customer value proposition. As the old maxim puts it, "When the customers don't want to come, *nothing* can stop them!" Businesspeople regularly get advice about typologies relevant to crafting a value proposition, because there are many ways to win customers, including price, quality, service, speed, innovation, and so forth. But the question in the advantage component of a strategy statement is, What is the center of gravity in our approach? Do we ultimately compete on the basis of our cost structure (e.g., Ryanair and Wal-Mart) or on some other basis that increases our target customer's willingness to pay (e.g., Singapore Airlines and Nordstrom)? In other words, will we *sell it for more* or *make it for less*, and coordinate and allocate resources accordingly?

Nearly all competitive markets confront companies with this choice. In retailing, there is Wal-Mart, Dollar General, warehouse club stores, and category killers. But there is also Nordstrom, Louis Vuitton, Tiffany's, and many high-end boutiques. In pharmaceuticals, there is Pfizer's Lipitor and other blockbuster drugs targeted at wide-scope, mass-market customer segments. But there is also Alexion, a firm founded by Leonard Bell. Alexion sells one product, Soliris, a drug used to treat certain diseases of the blood and kidneys that afflict no more than twenty thousand patients worldwide. Soliris costs about $400,000 *per patient* annually. But insurers have paid this price, because Soliris is the only safe and effective treatment for these diseases and that price is less than the total cost of alternative treatments. By 2013, Alexion had grown from $25 million in sales in 2007 to almost $1 billion with a market cap of $18 billion.

Sell It for More. In this form of advantage, you believe that your products or services provide better performance on attributes that are important for target customers, and for this they are willing to pay a premium. To truly be an advantage, this approach must continually avoid the following pitfalls:

- *Meaningless or False Differentiation:* the points of superiority are either unimportant to the customer or based on a false presumption of superiority.

- *Uneconomic or Invisible Differentiation:* the customer is unwilling to pay for the additional performance or is unaware of the difference.

- *Unsustainable Differentiation:* the innovative product features or service components are easily imitated.

Make It for Less. In this form of advantage, your cost structure allows you to make money at prices that competitors cannot. Many firms compete successfully in this manner. But realities in most industries typically allow only a few firms to build a sustainable cost advantage. Once this advantage is established, moreover, the very success of these firms makes it difficult for others to duplicate. To truly be an advantage, therefore, this approach must continually avoid these potential pitfalls:

- *Price Wars:* any cost advantage is lost in price competition; no one extracts value.

- *Substitutes:* we may indeed have a sustainable cost advantage over direct competitors, but not over substitutes available to our target customers.

- *Cost Reductions versus Lowest Costs:* lowering cost does not necessarily mean your cost is lower than that of the relevant competition, and in any market, there is ultimately only one lowest-cost competitor. Never confuse these different cost positions.

Where is *your* business along this spectrum? Do others agree with you? Does sales know?

1	2	3	4	5	6	7
Make it for less						Sell it for more

Be clear about this. If not, you will run into problems. Externally, there will always be someone out there who can beat you on cost and price or someone else who knows more about a given segment and can tailor its operations and sales efforts to the performance and buying criteria of that segment better than you can. Internally, important HR issues flow from lack of clarity about advantage. Salespeople cannot be premium service sellers in the morning and cost hawks in the afternoon. It doesn't work that way.

From Strategy Statement to Sales Actions

The value of the objectives, scope, advantage approach is that, when done well, it allows people to understand the key choices, test them in the marketplace, provide feedback, and set in motion actions that facilitate effective selling, as outlined in figure 5-3.

These choices are interlinked in selling. Depending upon the objective and sources of advantage, sales will face different buyers and selling tasks and require different performance management practices to deliver the value proposition. Internally, different assets will be needed for the cross-functional activities required for effective selling in

FIGURE 5-3

From strategy articulation to sales actions

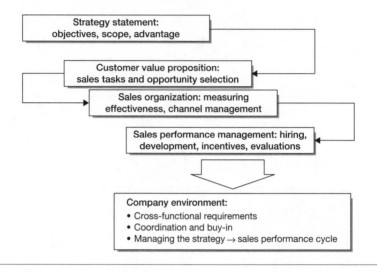

line with that strategic objective. Conversely, clarifying the value proposition embedded in a strategy should help sales focus with more precision, qualify customers, and allow the firm to align resources accordingly—the focus of chapter 7.

In turn, clarity about customer and opportunity selection helps field managers to organize more efficiently, specify the role or roles of the sales force in customer acquisition and retention, choose relevant metrics for measuring sales effectiveness, and understand how best to use selling resources with channel partners and new technologies relevant to sales pipeline management. These decisions are the relevant context for sales performance management practices, including hiring and development, compensation plans, and performance evaluations—the focus of chapters 8 through 10, respectively.

Performance management practices in the field not only help to sharpen productivity in sales. They also help people, across the organization, to understand the kinds of coordination and buy-in needed for effective selling and, in so doing, help the C-suite as well as the front line to manage the cycle of strategy and sales performance—topics discussed in chapters 11 and 12.

I do not want to oversell the power of words. Saying is not the same as doing. I'm sure you can cite, from your own experience, examples of finely articulated strategies that were poorly implemented, and elaborate strategy banners that were ultimately just wall hangings in branch offices. Alignment is a process, not a one-shot deal, and even clear statements are not a substitute for actual behaviors.

But I guarantee that, whatever else your people are good at, they are *not* good mind-readers. It begins with strategy articulation and communication. If you can't say it, clearly and concisely, then they will have more trouble understanding and executing it, efficiently and effectively. Let's look next at a central part of that process: defining sales tasks as a result of strategic choices.

6

Sales Tasks and Strategy

What is a salesperson? What does it take to be good in sales? These are questions posed by generations of researchers and managers, and the search for generalized traits of effective salespeople has been alternately comic and inconclusive. It's important to understand why. It's also important to understand how to translate the choices in a coherent strategy into criteria for customer selection and opportunity management, and how this affects sales tasks and what it takes to be good in sales.

What Research Does and Doesn't Tell Us about Sales Effectiveness

Research on sales long focused on uncovering personalities related to performance. For most of the twentieth century, "mental alertness tests" were accepted tools for identifying these traits. In 1916, the Carnegie Institute of Technology (now Carnegie Mellon University) founded a Bureau of Salesmanship Research to create psychological tests for salesmen.

Conversely, psychologists tried to explain the changes that occurred to nerve cells in the brain when customers heard sales pitches.[1] Research of both sorts continued throughout the century. For example, John Watson, the founder of behaviorism in psychology, left an academic career to join the J. Walter Thompson ad agency, which assigned him to work first as a traveling salesman and then as a retail clerk at Macy's. You encounter descendants of this research in current studies about how much buying behavior is based on—surprise!—reactions in the amygdala rather than reason or logic.

Also influential for decades was phrenology: studying the shape of heads in the belief that head shape revealed traits of character and selling capability. In July 1916, for example, over three thousand people met in Detroit for the World's Salesmanship Congress. President Woodrow Wilson was the keynote speaker. He was followed by the acclaimed phrenologist Grant Nablo, who told his audience to look for a high forehead when hiring (denotes "imagination") and avoid applicants with "a flat back head" (they are "quick starts but slow finishers"). "Look around you," said Nablo, "and you will see heads like that." Look around you now, and you will see currently respectable embodiments of this type of research: generalized assessment tests; selling typologies that allegedly apply across selling situations; and—phrenology was silly, wasn't it?—brain-scan and "neuro-marketing" generalizations about buying and selling. As Walter Friedman documents, "The work of phrenologists and physiognomists in deciphering the elements of salesmanship continued . . . long after these 'sciences' had been discredited . . . More than anything else, [they] revealed the growing desire to find applicable laws of salesmanship."[2]

The search for these laws continued in more careful and less trendy research. Studies explored the effectiveness of "hard sell" emotional appeals versus "soft sell" rational appeals, "canned" versus "extemporaneous" presentations, and product-oriented versus personal-oriented selling approaches (focusing on product features versus "selling yourself" to a prospective customer). Correlational studies investigated the relationships between personality traits (e.g., "forcefulness" or "sociability") and sales performance, between demographics (e.g., age, education, years of sales experience) and performance; and between qualities like "emotional intelligence" and performance. As a recent review of these studies puts it, "The results of this research have simply failed to identify behavioral predispositions or aptitudes that account for a large amount of variance in performance for salespeople. In addition, the results of this research are quite inconsistent and, in some cases, even contradictory."[3]

What can a manager take away from research on the topic? First, the fact (and this is a fact) that even good research is inconclusive does *not* mean that these links are nonexistent. Depending upon the sales situation, many of these traits may be vitally important, and it is difficult to train and motivate poorly selected people to effective performance. Many experienced managers, reflecting on what it takes to sell in their business, can legitimately claim, "I know it when I see it."

Second, the inconsistent results tell us something significant: a search for universal sales rules is misguided. So much depends on the sales situation that what researchers call a contingency approach—one that incorporates contextual circumstances—is necessary. More simply stated, the research suggests that certain common stereotypes of a "good" salesperson (e.g., pleasing personality, deep inventory of stories, "hard-wired" for sociability, and so on) are indeed stereotypes—"conventional, formulaic, and oversimplified conception[s] or image[s]"—that obscure the realities of a situation.[4]

Test this conclusion against your own experience. In business, you are constantly presented with so many factoids and opinions about what makes for a good salesperson. However, most read like a bland summary of the *Boy Scout Handbook* and include descriptors like *modesty, conscientiousness, an achievement orientation, curiosity,* and *a lack of discouragement.* These lists of generalized traits are so broad that, at best, they simply remind us that people tend to do business with people they like (but not always and not as often as many sales trainers assume). At worst, the lists just lead us back to the old cynical description of a salesperson: he or she who practices the art "of arresting the human intelligence long enough to get money from it."[5] Look at successful entrepreneurs—most of whom, in early-stage ventures, *must* sell—and their diverse backgrounds, temperaments, and paths to success. Or consider the diversity on *Inc.* magazine's list, "10 Greatest Salespeople of All Time":[6]

- There is Dale Carnegie, who believed selling required "effective communicators ... healthy team dynamics ... [and] work-life balance." But also on the list is John H. Patterson: "The founder and CEO of the National Cash Register Company was known to be a stern control freak." Patterson's sales control systems were not just temperamental in a family-owned firm dependent on internal financing and where his salespeople, working on highly leveraged commission plans, were also responsible for on-time collections in cash from customers.[7]

- We encounter David Ogilvy, the legendary ad executive whose basic sales advice was, never be boring:
"Foster any attempt to talk about other things; the
longer you stay, the better you get to know the prospect, and the more you will be trusted." But we also
meet Joe Girard, allegedly the greatest car salesman of the post–World War II era. Girard believed
that "sales operated according to a law of averages"
and so preached and practiced a form of disciplined
pipeline management: don't waste time talking to
nonprospects. Think about the differences between
executives reviewing and buying advertising campaigns and people buying cars at a dealer.

- There is Ron Popeil, who pioneered fast-talking,
buy-now infomercials for the Veg-O-Matic,
Mr. Microphone, the Pocket Fisherman, and other
products. Popeil believed selling required people
(like him) who integrated the functions of inventor and
entertaining pitchman. But there is also Erica Feidner,
who sold more than $40 million in Steinway pianos
during her career. "It is not unusual for Feidner's
customers to describe her as a force of nature," the
journalist James B. Stewart (one of her clients) wrote
in a profile of Feidner in *The New Yorker.* "This is not
because they feel pressured by her but because after
they meet her many soon find themselves in the grip
of musical ambitions they never knew they harbored.
These ambitions often include buying a specific piano
that they feel they can no longer live without, even
if it strains both their living rooms and their bank
accounts."[8]

- There is Larry Ellison, "the king of aggressive corporate technology sales" in a business where, if you win, you win a long-term software contract and a string of licensing fees, and if you lose, you're effectively out of that account for years. Be aggressive in that situation. And there is Mary Kay Ash, who focused her cosmetics salespeople on a combination of visible incentives (the signature pink Cadillacs), the intrinsic rewards and constant celebration of female achievement when outlets for such achievements were more limited, and the power of social networks. You probably should not be too aggressive in your friend's living room or when selling to your friend's friends.

- Finally, the list also contains Zig Ziglar, the sales trainer and motivational speaker who encouraged all salespeople to commit to a lifetime of learning and training (see the connection?) *and* "to be extremely shrewd when it comes to setting and thereby exceeding goals and quotas." Here, the interesting question for behavioral economists is, *Why* would a manager invite to a sales meeting someone who advises lowballing sales forecasts?

Sales talent comes in all temperaments. No size fits all. It can vary from the aggressive tones of an Ellison or a Patterson to the subtle harmonies of a Feidner, from the hard sell of a Popeil to the social sell of a Mary Kay Ash, *depending upon the selling situation.* Philip Delves Broughton interviewed people in different cultures and fields of selling, from rug traders in Tangiers to art gallery owners to infomercial specialists. He wanted to understand what they did and how they did it. Reflecting on the array of humanity his research encompassed, he drew this conclusion: "What enables a sales-person to succeed is that they've found a match between who they are and what they are being required to do. Some people are wooers, compelled to win over everyone they meet in an instant. They do well in jobs where they must close a lot of transactions every day . . . Others prefer to build networks of deep relationships over time . . . Some salespeople will be coin-operated, motivated entirely by commission and competition with their peers . . . But the first step for anyone selling, man-aging, or hiring a sales force is to understand these dynamics between personality, self-perception, and role."[9] Amen.

Boundary Role Person

Selling jobs vary greatly in the kind of product or service sold, the customers a salesperson is responsible for, and other requirements such as the relative importance of techni-cal knowledge, number and types of people contacted during sales calls, and the relevance of dinners and other relation-ship-building efforts. The correct answer to the questions "What is a salesperson?" and "What does it take to be good in sales?" is lots of different things, depending upon the industry, the buyers, and other factors. Selling effectiveness is *not* a generalized trait. It's a function of the *sales task*.[10] And the task will vary according to the selling company's strategy and the customer's buying process.

As the words *sales representative* imply, a salesperson *rep-resents* the company and its products, services, and promised capabilities to the customer. Academics call this a *bound-ary role person*—someone who operates at the boundaries of different organizations and must therefore respond to the often conflicting rules, procedures, and requirements of each.[11] As seen in figure 6-1, the sales rep represents the buyer in the selling organization and his or her organization to the customer. Hence, salespeople (more than others in a company) must interact internally with people in marketing, operations, engineering, finance, and others across the firm, and depending upon the buying process, they deal externally with a host of people at clients. Each group has its own operating procedures. Yet the essence of most selling jobs is to manage and, in practice, to negotiate this boundary between the selling organization and potential customers. That's one reason why coordination across the organization—the focus of chapter 12—is so important to effective selling.

This view of the salesperson focuses attention on how hiring, deployment, and other organizational procedures do,

FIGURE 6-1

Boundary role person

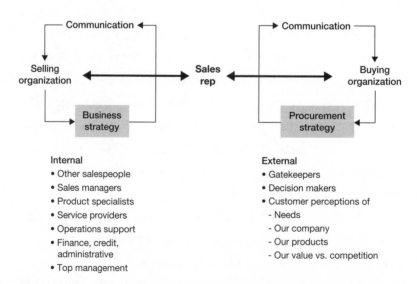

Source: Adapted from Frank V. Cespedes, "Aspects of Sales Management: An Introduction," Harvard Business School Publishing, Case 9-589-061 (Boston: Harvard Business School, 2006).

or do not, support the behaviors required to perform the role effectively in a given sales job. In turn, this means paying attention to important differences in sales tasks and avoiding glib generalizations about selling. For example, consider how, despite so many generalizations about globalization, sales tasks vary significantly by market and country *for the same products*:

- James Farley, Ford's group vice president for sales, points out that "the skills required of salespeople often differ between our global markets. In India, for instance, buying a car is an important rite of passage for families that are ascending to the middle class. Car buyers routinely bring their parents, grandparents, aunts, and uncles with them to dealerships . . . and some will ask the salesperson to perform a blessing on the vehicle before they receive the keys."[12] In China and some other countries, many car buyers don't know how to drive, because their only experience has been on motorbikes. So a sales task is to provide rudimentary driving lessons for customers.

- Susan Silberman ran Pfizer's Latin America region and emphasizes that "selling pharmaceuticals in Latin America is not the same as selling them in the United States or Western Europe." Latin American pharma reps have more access and time with physicians. Hence, "they are able to have in-depth conversations," providing information about treatments and clinical trial data. So, as Silberman notes, sales calls in Latin America "start and end a bit differently, because many of our reps stay in their territories longer and can develop deeper relationships with doctors."[13]

Or consider direct selling, a global activity that, for many, represents a paradigm of selling. The tasks vary by country and by location *within* the same country or market.[14] In rural settings in developing economies, you're going door-to-door, building relationships in the local community, and typically with a broad product mix—like the Yankee peddler of that emerging economy known as the nineteenth-century United States.[15] But in urban locations, the direct seller relies primarily on street traffic, often segments potential customers and price points according to their vehicle (are they on a bus or driving a car?), tends to focus on one product, and uses a sales pitch very different than for rural direct sellers.

Direct selling tasks vary in other ways. Eureka Forbes sells vacuum cleaners and water purifiers via more than eight thousand door-to-door salespeople working in 550 cities and towns across India. Suresh Goklaney, vice chairman of Eureka Forbes, notes that "people in the West—the United States in particular—may not like door-to-door sales, because they value their privacy. Our culture in India is different. We routinely drop by friends' houses without calling first, just to visit . . . When our salespeople visit, they interact with the entire family. They use the vacuum cleaner to blow up balloons for the children, making the demo fun, interactive, and engaging." The tasks also vary by company strategy and thus affect hiring, training, metrics, and pipeline management. Goklaney notes that at Eureka Forbes, in contrast to many other direct selling companies, "we don't give price discounts—ever—so making a sale comes down to the salesperson's correctly identifying the family's needs and working to solve them. On average, our salespeople sell one vacuum cleaner or water purifier for every four demonstrations, and our best people close one sale for every two demos. Our new sales recruits are usually 18 to 20 years old, and they make about eight sales a month."[16]

Finally, sales tasks change as the company, its products, and available technology change. Eureka now has a website, and in 2011, two hundred thousand people visited that site and requested a sales call. Those customers, already aware of basic product information, must be sold differently from its traditional customers. (Eureka noticed and made seventy thousand sales on the basis of those web leads in 2011.) It now has fourteen hundred franchises that sell *and* service Eureka equipment. Tasks and opportunities differ when selling and service activities are combined. And Eureka has begun to sell security systems and other home-related products in addition to vacuum cleaners. This changes the nature of the rep's boundary role in the firm.

As these examples illustrate, the key determinants of sales tasks will be the nature of the customer and, therefore, how a firm translates the objectives, advantage, and scope choices in its strategy into customer selection criteria and then opportunity management practices in its selling efforts.

The Importance of Customer Selection

Every customer is *not* a good customer. Customer selection is a crucial decision. It affects the relevant value proposition and, therefore, required selling tasks and internal capabilities. Depending upon the strategy, many factors can be relevant customer-selection criteria.

Order size is probably the most common criterion firms use to judge which customers merit the most sales attention and resources. One reason is the importance of cash, the revenues represented by bigger accounts, and typical selling economics: larger orders are often not proportionately more expensive to sell and fulfill than smaller orders. But depending upon objectives, order size may not optimize customer selection. For example, a premium-priced producer of a differentiated product will find that buyers generating the largest orders are aware of that fact, have more bargaining power as a result of their volume purchases, and can affect prices in other areas where the firm sells its products or services.

The *product mix* purchased by a customer is another common factor. The potential of selling across the product line is often a key consideration in deploying sales resources and defining sales tasks, as in the evolution of Eureka Forbes's sales initiatives. This can be especially important in situations (e.g., many web-based and service ventures) where the selling company's cost of goods sold is approximately equivalent across its product line, but customer price sensitivity varies considerably for some products or services.

Customer profitability can vary considerably when *customer maintenance costs* over time are taken into account. During the development period of buyer-seller relationships, cash flows are often negative for the seller; when the product or service is delivered, licensing or subscription fees may begin, reorders start to materialize, and cash flows turn positive. But in many businesses (e.g., professional services), the seller's expenses *after* the sale differ significantly from one type of customer to the next, making customer maintenance costs (and additional after-sale revenues, if any) an important scope and selection criterion.

Beyond economics, *qualitative criteria* can affect customer selection. Some accounts help to generate sales at other customers. Venture capitalists understand the role of "name" accounts in establishing credibility for a start-up and aiding sales tasks at other accounts. In health-care markets, teaching hospitals often play this role in the so-called hierarchy of influence: selling to these hospitals has a longer-term advantage, as medical students use and disseminate the product to other institutions. For years Apple pursued an analogous sales approach when it focused on schools.

The key point is that a customer represents a stream of orders for the seller. That order stream, in turn, inevitably generates a domino effect on the seller's business (figure 6-2). Customers always come embedded with transaction costs for the seller. Depending upon your business model, some orders are easier or harder to process (e.g., stocked versus custom items in a manufacturing business; customers that do or don't require multiple proposals in a service business). This has implications upstream in the seller's value chain for capacity utilization: both the mix of what is made (*what kind* of capacity is utilized) and throughput (*how* the

FIGURE 6-2

Impact of customer selection decisions

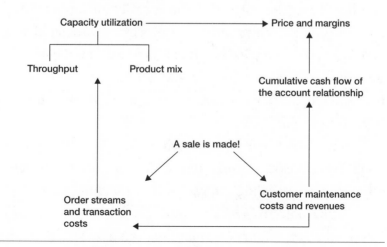

relevant capacity is utilized—e.g., which production lines in manufacturing, or the types of people and skills utilized in a service business). Orders also affect downstream after-sale economics and organizational requirements. Together, these factors help to determine the cumulative net cash flow of that buyer-seller exchange, the price or prices needed to make that customer profitable for the seller, and the margins available for any other business needs.

Partitioning versus Segmenting Customers

Few firms clarify their customer selection criteria. Either directly in sales meetings or implicitly in the compensation plan, most are in effect saying to their salespeople, "Go forth and multiply!" That is indeed what salespeople then do: they sell to anyone willing to pay a certain price (often discounted to make a volume quota target) and so generate an unwieldy array of sales tasks, fragment selling effectiveness, and make profitable growth difficult. As customers buy and use the product, the firm then sets in motion another dimension of the domino effect in figure 6-2: it tends to modify the product and processes associated with making and selling its products, typically in the myriad directions generated by this kind of selling activity, dissipating the company's resources in other areas of the business beyond sales.

This undiscriminating approach inhibits learning and can blind both sales managers and leadership to what is actually going on in selling efforts, as illustrated in figure 6-3.[17] Translating objectives and scope choices into effective customer selection requires *segmenting* a market based on the

FIGURE 6-3

Partitioning versus segmenting customers

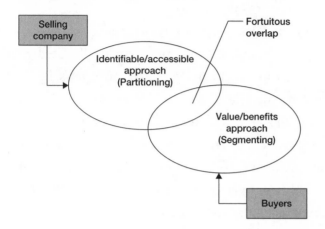

Source: Adapted from discussion in Rowland T. Moriarty, *Industrial Buying Behavior: Concepts, Issues and Applications* (Lexington, MA: Lexington Books, 1983), 123.

benefits the customer receives and perceives in your products and services. Segmentation focuses on the problem or opportunity the buyer confronts. But most firms *partition* their market or markets according to what is accessible via purchased lists, standard industrial classification (SIC) codes, data from a trade association, or the sheer number of cold calls. If and when sales are made, customer value is intermittently uncovered by the "go forth and multiply" approach. But this is a fortuitous overlap—the result of a random-walk process analogous to throwing darts while blindfolded at a diverse array of opportunities. With enough cash and salespeople, and enough throws and investor "patience" (or inertia), the company will indeed stumble over value. But those "hits" can blind management to the limits of its sales process, confuse sales tasks, and prevent scaling of the business. To avoid this trap, you must put into practice some core principles of opportunity management.

Principles of Opportunity Management

The choice to do business with a customer also represents an opportunity cost: money, time, and people allocated to customer A are resources not available to customers B, C, and D. Because a sale has a domino effect on the seller's business system, the fact is that, no matter how large or growing the market, your firm can add and extract more or less value from different opportunities in any portfolio of customer possibilities. In a competitive market, ineffective opportunity management eventually leads to loss of money, time, and positioning with customers who are (or should be) core customers for the firm and, over time, to the nurturing of "commodity competencies": your sales force and firm gets better and better at activities that customers value less and less.

Most markets present firms with an array of customer opportunities. One way to envision that spectrum is depicted in figure 6-4. At one end are *transaction buyers* in what is essentially a "spot market." At the other end are *relationship buyers* in a "solution market." Many customers will be some hybrid along this spectrum, but it's useful to focus on the end points to make the strategy and sales choices clear.

Transaction buyers have short time horizons when purchasing in the category. An example is a trader on a commodities exchange, where, as the saying goes, "long term is after lunch." In those markets, an array of choices and a lack of switching costs make buy/sell adjustments easy. If you sell in a market like that, you make money by "playing the spread" at a point in time, *not* by investing in long-term

FIGURE 6-4

A spectrum of opportunities: who is the "good customer"?

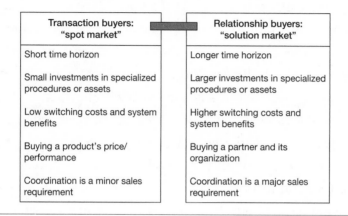

Transaction buyers: "spot market"	Relationship buyers: "solution market"
Short time horizon	Longer time horizon
Small investments in specialized procedures or assets	Larger investments in specialized procedures or assets
Low switching costs and system benefits	Higher switching costs and system benefits
Buying a product's price/ performance	Buying a partner and its organization
Coordination is a minor sales requirement	Coordination is a major sales requirement

relationship-building activities. On the *Inc.* list of great sales-people, think Popeil or Joe Girard, not Mary Kay Ash or David Ogilvy, because at this end of the spectrum, there may not be a long term to extract value from relationships. Trans-action buyers make low investments in specialized proce-dures or assets when purchasing in the category and are less interested in the wider system benefits that your firm may offer. These customers ultimately purchase a specified level of performance at a desired price at a point in time. This does *not* mean that these buyers are uninterested in quality or value. Rather, they define value as meeting specifications and are not willing to pay much (if anything) for what they see as an overengineered product or service whose quality, applications, or features exceed what they want at that point.

By contrast, relationship buyers adopt a longer time horizon when purchasing in a given category. Why? Because there is something about the product, seller, or buyer that motivates these customers to make larger investments in specialized assets or procedures (physical or psychological). Once made, these investments do generate switching costs (physical, psychological, or financial). Historically, enterprise software has been this kind of market. The choice of a vendor was not only about the product features and "user-friendliness." It was also a multiyear choice of support, upgrades, and other processes not easily altered after the fact. Because of these investments and switching costs, these buyers *are* interested in the wider benefits. As well as a product's price/performance at a point in time, they are also "purchasing" a partner and its organization. Hence, they are interested in knowing more about the seller, its R&D plans and commitment to the category, its financial stability for the long term, and the ability and accountability of that account manager to get things done inside the selling firm. Conversely, as a seller, you find ways to sow "fear, uncertainty, and doubt" about competitors, especially new entrants in the category—the famous "FUD" message of established firms for years. With these customer opportunities, think Ellison or Patterson or Ogilvy, not Girard or Popeil.

Who is the "good customer"? In my experience, most executives say "relationship buyers." They argue that prices and, because of switching costs, "customer loyalty" is higher at that end of the spectrum. But the selling cycle is likely to be longer (affecting cash flow), and customization requirements and expenses are also likely to be higher, generating many customer-specific processes and costs along the activity chain outlined in figure 6-2. The answer to the "good customer" question is that it depends upon your objectives, scope, and advantage and how you translate them into a value proposition and sales capabilities with core customers. I'll outline a step-by-step process for developing a core customer profile in the next chapter. But here I want to emphasize the basic choices facing firms in opportunity management and the implications for sales tasks and strategy.

Success and Failure in Opportunity Management

In general, transaction buyers require standardized products and services that are easy to purchase at a point in time. The seller needs to provide appropriate selection and threshold levels of quality at an acceptable price, and it needs salespeople who can close many transactions without much ancillary support. In this situation, you take costs *out* of your go-to-market approach whenever possible, and that will affect hiring, deployment, and other areas of performance management. Relationship buyers put more emphasis on evaluating the applicability of a particular solution and its feasibility over time. The seller must be able to customize the offering and provide continual innovation on a widely used or especially high-performing platform or brand. The firm also needs salespeople—whether they're straight-on aggressive like Ellison or wry and charming like Ogilvy—who can work with these buyers to help imagine and specify a relevant long-term state of affairs. Figure 6-5 illustrates the choices and consequences.

Success is aligning your selling program with the opportunities pursued. When you are focused on solution buyers, then the longer selling cycles, multiple requests for proposals (RFPs), custom requirements, and after-sale support services are key sales tasks, and (if you've done your financial analysis well) the hiring and training for these tasks is worthwhile. A firm can also succeed with transaction opportunities, if it

FIGURE 6-5

Success and failure in opportunity management

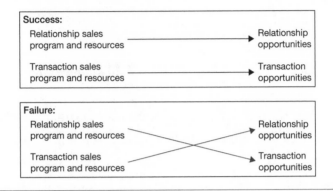

finds ways to take costs *out* of its selling approach, product/ service offering, and support. This has implications for sales management, but also for R&D, finance, and others across the selling organization.

Failure in opportunity management comes in two forms— what statisticians call *type 1* and *type 2* errors. Type 1 error, like a false positive, is approaching transaction buyers with a solutions-selling approach. What do those buyers do? Ultimately, they would be doing your firm a *favor* if they immediately chased your sales reps away. But these buyers tend to seek out more information (typically through multiple RFPs and meetings) about product/service possibilities, and then use that information in setting specifications with transaction sellers from whom they *do* purchase at a given price. This is a direct financial cost to the selling firm. It's common in start-up situations. Because start-ups lack a reputation and buyers worry about the start-up's survival prospects, new ventures with "a great new product" can easily overestimate their ability to acquire relationship buyers. But type 1 errors also plague many established, high-end category leaders when they compete with low-end competitors in a market. Notice how many tales about disruptive innovation—Canon versus Xerox, mini mills versus integrated steel makers, online versus full-service brokerages, and others—are about high-end providers still trying to sell feature-rich, full-service solutions to customers not interested in having it "overengineered" and whose willingness to pay for the solution is therefore decreasing or nonexistent.

Type 2 error is the opposite condition: approaching relationship opportunities with a transaction selling approach. These buyers *do* chase those salespeople away in the sense that the selling firm's offering is not really part of their choice set. This is an opportunity cost to the extent that your firm loses a chance to compete in a market where it wants or needs to compete. Also, notice that while most organizations have financial systems that track revenues minus expenses and thus direct costs, no one has yet developed a good cash register (or an accounting general register) for tabulating opportunity costs. Hence, type 2 errors can linger and repeat with more frequency than type 1 errors, putting an unexpected ceiling on sales and growth and (for entrepreneurs) the ability to scale a venture.

Strategy, Sales Tasks, and Performance

Responding to a customer opportunity, therefore, is a choice but not simply a binary—yes versus no—decision. In some cases, the required response might be a relatively inexpensive additional product feature. Others might require a change in product development or a service activity. Still others might require a different business model to sell successfully to that portion of the spectrum. Translating a strategy into effective selling means making these choices and, in the process, clarifying sales tasks. It's necessary, and as the following example indicates, it can renew a business as well as sales.

For decades, Dow Corning enjoyed profitable double-digit growth by selling innovative silicone products through a high-end sales force that bundled the products with relevant technical services. But growth stopped in the late 1990s.[18] Many silicone buyers faced a margin squeeze on their products as their large customers, especially in the construction materials sector, pressured them to lower their wholesale prices. As a result, Dow's customers increasingly defected to lower-cost rivals, especially smaller local players that, with no R&D investment and with lower overhead, offered commodity silicone products at very low prices. These players also supplied private-label silicone compounds to DIY chains like Home Depot, compounding the price pressures and growing a segment where Dow was not selling.

Dow initially responded with layoffs and other cost-saving measures. But these proved inadequate. So in 2001 a task force (involving sales staff, product managers, and others) reviewed five years of customer data and developed a view of Dow's markets and sales tasks in line with that discussed in this chapter. Customers, they found, could be grouped into two broad categories: those who sought solutions and others whose buying decision was primarily influenced by price. The first group was itself divided into three segments: those seeking "innovative" solutions (early adopters who often did joint R&D with Dow), "proven" solutions (those seeking specific applications and services already available from Dow, such as customized blending, packaging, and recycling), or "cost-effective" solutions (customers willing to pay a premium for high-performance silicone compounds that reduced their finished product's unit cost). These three segments were Dow's traditional customers, who valued its expertise and were willing to pay for solutions to their product- or process-related problems. The problem was the price-seeker buyers, who were experienced purchasers of commonly used silicone materials and who wanted the lowest price and an easy way to buy. One option was to continue ignoring the price-seekers. But this also meant ignoring the market facts and acquiescing to continued decline.

Instead, the team did the following: develop a no-frills offer at a low price and take all traditional sales and service costs out of Dow's participation in this segment. The product could only be ordered on the web with high-volume, minimum-order quantities and with fees for rush orders. No product or technical service was available through this channel, which focused on about 350 silicone compounds out of more than 7,500 offered by Dow Corning. Additionally, a dual-brand marketing approach was adopted: Xiameter was the brand name for the web product, to distinguish it from the silicone product/service bundles sold to solution customers, and organizationally, the no-frills offering constituted a separate P&L unit. Xiameter's sales funnel started with customers registering online, followed by automated and largely self-service steps from order entry to payment. By 2005, Dow Corning's sales had grown by 60 percent to $3.9 billion, and losses had turned to profits of $506 million, with Xiameter an estimated 30 percent of company sales and especially strong in Asia. By 2010, sales and net income were $6 billion and $866 million (a record 14.4 percent of sales), respectively.

The success here illustrates the importance and rewards of effective opportunity management. Dow knew how to sell to solution buyers. But many of those customers can, over time and after repeat purchases, become transaction buyers. It's not their job to understand your strategy. It's *your* job to adapt strategy and sales to market realities. Dow did this by establishing a go-to-market approach compatible with these buyers. In addition to the web and minimum-order quantities, low/no technical service and a light management structure reduced overhead substantially. Notice how the firm managed the domino effect of sales outlined in figure 6-2: the sales system allowed goods to be produced to order and shipped to customers in full truckloads, eliminating inventory and warehousing expenses, optimizing factory utilization and transport savings, and minimizing customer maintenance costs.

Notice, also, that the strategy involved frontline managers in sales, among others. In its boundary role, a key function of sales is to provide timely information about differences along a firm's spectrum of opportunities. But to get and keep relevant that information, sales and C-suite leaders need to establish performance management practices that determine whether actual selling behaviors are aligned with the sales tasks inherent in your strategy. These practices include the field's assumptions about core customers and the implications for hiring and development practices, sales force organization, sales compensation, performance reviews, and measuring sales effectiveness—the focus of part III.

Part Three

PERFORMANCE MANAGEMENT

First salesman: "I made some very valuable contacts today."

Second salesman: "I didn't get any orders, either."

Chapter 7
From Sales Tasks to Selling Behaviors

Aligning selling behaviors with sales tasks is the essence of performance management in this area of business. This chapter provides a process for translating strategy into an ideal-customer profile and improving selling behaviors, and explains why linking tasks and behaviors is necessary if you want selling in your company to go beyond individual heroic efforts and be a scalable platform for profitable growth.

Chapter 8
People: Hiring, Development, and Sales Organization

This chapter looks at recruiting high-potential salespeople by understanding the behaviors necessary for success, and then training those selected. Because much development in sales is experiential learning by doing, the chapter also looks at common forms of sales organization and the impact of new technologies and online shopping methods on organization and the required capabilities of salespeople.

Chapter 9
Control Systems: Compensation and Incentives

Chapter 9 is about money. It examines links between compensation, evaluation, and motivation and discusses why you should reexamine much conventional wisdom about sales incentives. The chapter also provides a step-by-step process for designing a sales compensation plan aligned with strategy. If you're a CEO or chief financial officer, this chapter may save you money and redirect how you spend that money. If you're a sales manager, the discussion can remind you what you're paid for and that you can't substitute money for management.

Chapter 10
Sales Force Environment:
Performance Reviews and Measuring Effectiveness

Performance reviews are among the most underutilized levers for affecting behavior in most organizations. Yet reviews, and the metrics used to evaluate sales results, powerfully influence the environment in which strategy is or is not executed. This chapter concerns the how and why of giving performance feedback and measuring sales effectiveness. Among other things, effective performance measurement and review are essential to making "big data" useful in your firm rather than an unintended garbage-in-garbage-out investment cycle.

7

From Sales Tasks to Selling Behaviors

Aligning selling behaviors with sales tasks is the essence of performance management in this area of business. As chapter 3 indicated, there are multiple levers to do this. This chapter focuses on a factor that should condition how a firm uses those levers: the translation of strategic choices into an ideal-customer profile and how that affects selling behaviors. For much of this chapter, I'll use a start-up example, because early-stage ventures confront these issues in an especially stark manner. But linking selling behaviors with buying processes is necessary in a start-up or big global corporation.

Beat the Devil: Scaling a Sales Process

It's tough to start a business that gets traction with paying customers. In the first decade of the twenty-first century, less than half of all US start-ups were able to survive beyond three years.[1] But it's even harder to grow beyond certain levels of sales. Of the nearly forty-four thousand companies founded in 2000 and listed in the Capital IQ database, fewer than 6 percent achieved more than $10 million in revenues by 2010, and fewer than 2 percent more than $50 million.[2] The increase in angel groups, the advent of crowd funding, and continuing venture-capital investments have made it more possible to start a business. But venture capitalist David Lee has it right: "It has never been easier to start a company, and never harder to build one."[3]

Some in the venture community call this the Bermuda Triangle stage of a firm's life cycle—a reference to a region (also known as the Devil's Triangle) in the Atlantic Ocean where aircraft and ships have disappeared mysteriously. Urban legend attributes the disappearances to paranormal or extraterrestrial activity. Many in business do something similar when faced with the exigencies of scaling sales activities.

Consider Business Processing Inc. (BPI, a disguised name), founded in 2000 by a visionary entrepreneur to provide web-based outsourced payroll services to small and medium-sized businesses. By 2004 it had about $40 million in sales, and seventy-five sales reps with annual quotas of $600,000 each and target compensation at quota of about $60,000 per rep. In 2004, the founder raised $30 million to develop new products, sell more, and scale the business. But two years later, BPI's top line had stagnated and investors were restless. Management tried various tactics, including offering bundled products at a steep discount, six months "free" if customers made annual commitments, and other incentives to close deals. Over the next two years, prices declined faster than revenues increased. By the time the recession hit in 2008, BPI's directors were asking fundamental questions about the business.

What happened at BPI is common. The firm had a product performance advantage but a costly ad hoc process for translating strategy into business development initiatives. Probably the biggest problem was the leadership team's inability to define the firm's core customers. Without that clarity, selling is ultimately a function of individual heroic efforts in the field, *not* a scalable platform for growth. As chapter 6 indicated, there are lots of ways to sell. But specifying the way most appropriate for *your* firm always starts with understanding target customers and their buying behavior.

Research finds no clear cause-and-effect linkages between personality characteristics and sales success. Beware the sales guru with the allegedly all-purpose tool. But research does indicate that salespeople accumulate a base of experiences and learn by doing. Then, successful salespeople organize these experiences into categories of selling situations and apply the relevant "script" to a situation. This is called *adaptive selling*: altering behaviors according to perceptions about the nature of that customer.[4]

This process of sorting through and modifying accrued experiential knowledge to particular situations is not peculiar to sales. It applies to many areas of human behavior where people must adapt to changing circumstances. The chemist Michael Polanyi called it "tacit knowledge," and his example was learning to ride a bicycle: "No amount of printed instruction on how to ride will enable most people to hop on a bicycle for the first time and confidently pedal off."[5] Donald Schön called it the ability to apply a "theory-in-use" in contrast to a theory allegedly relevant across all categories.[6] The ancient Greeks called it *metis*, and their poster child was Odysseus' ability to meet the varied challenges presented by storms, the Cyclops, and other cold calls on the way home.[7] Less grandiosely, it's what people do when, like salespeople, they must work with diverse other people. Mort Lachman wrote for stand-up comics. He said that you can write for someone else only if you can "turn him on in your head . . . You have to hear their voice and their inflections as you type; and hear the difference between how Benny [or] Hope would say it." (We younger folk might think of the difference between Seinfeld and Colbert.) Lachman advised that "if they sound all alike to you, be a plumber. You'll make more money."[8] The same goes for selling: if all customers sound alike to you, do something else; you'll make more money.

Understanding Customers and Required Selling Behaviors

The relevance of experiential scripts depends upon the customers that the strategy requires salespeople to deal with. The following are useful distinctions in analyzing customers and, therefore, the types of selling behaviors relevant in a situation. For sales managers, understanding these distinctions is key to aligning behaviors with tasks along the pipeline from prospecting to closing:[9]

- The difference between products and problems, *from the customer's perspective*

- The common status-quo bias in buying behavior

- The differences between lead users and mainstream customers during the selling cycle

Products versus Problems

Consider a recent McKinsey survey of more than twelve hundred company purchasing decision makers responsible for buying high-tech products and services.[10] First, the survey found big differences between what these buyers *said* was important (price and product features) and what actually drove their decisions about vendors. This should not surprise anyone familiar with studies of buying behavior. Research repeatedly demonstrates that you cannot use attitude scales and responses to predict buying behavior accurately.[11] A recurring example is consumers' espoused attitudes about green or eco-friendly products versus their actual purchasing behavior.

Second, and more interesting, the survey found that of the many things that can undermine selling, the "most destructive" were a salesperson's failure to have adequate product knowledge (20 percent) and a salesperson's contacting customers "*too* frequently" (35 percent). Only 3 percent said they weren't contacted enough. What is going on here? The McKinsey researchers draw one valid conclusion: the data suggest that customers are open to fewer but more meaningful interactions—at least in these high-tech sales situations, which center on technologically dynamic products. But what *is* a "meaningful" interaction in this context?

People pay for satisfactory responses to perceived problems or opportunities. But firms can't make satisfaction itself; they sell the means to attaining satisfaction. One of my revered mentors, Theodore Levitt, taught generations of students that "people don't buy two-inch drill bits; they buy two-inch holes." He coined the term "marketing myopia" for the process of defining a business in terms of product features rather than customer benefits (e.g., a firm that assumes it is in the railroad rather than transportation business and so misses key aspects of market scope, substitutes, and customer motivations to buy or not; or to update Levitt's example, firms that saw themselves in the newspaper rather than news business).[12] Others have revived this distinction in emphasizing that customers "hire" products to get jobs done.[13] The customer's *job*, not the product, is the core unit of sales analysis. A meaningful interaction is about how the product or service addresses that job, problem, or opportunity.

This distinction underlines the difference between what a firm *sells* (features of a product or experience) and what many customers *buy* (the problem solved or satisfaction desired). In many situations (e.g., the high-tech context in the McKinsey research), ignoring this distinction can be fatal. Linking required tasks with appropriate behaviors means that salespeople must also understand the benefits for that customer. This requires the ability to engage customers in a discussion about their business problems and the desired outcomes, to flesh out assumptions about how product features do or don't translate into customer-desired benefits and, often, direct observation of customers' usage experiences in the category.[14] In these contexts, the sales task is to answer questions such as:

- What is the problem or unrealized opportunity the customer faces in this aspect of his or her personal or professional life?

- What result(s) does the customer need to get that job done more satisfactorily than the current means of dealing with the problem or opportunity?

- What combination of product or service functions, applications, or support are relevant?

These questions should not be confused with R&D or research intended to design new products, although good companies do link sales insights with those activities: see the example later in this chapter. The goal here is not to determine how to build the product. Rather, the goal is to determine whether you have a product or service with relevant benefits for that customer. If not, move on.

At one level, the difference between products and problems is akin to the "features" versus "benefits" distinction in many sales-training programs. Features are facts, data, or information about the product or service ("this system has X amount of storage" or "our people have experience with Y," and so on). Benefits show how a feature provides a relevant outcome. To link sales tasks and behaviors effectively, clarify how your strategy affects the relative importance of features versus benefits. Going back to the opportunity management discussion in chapter 6: a strategy focusing on transaction customers is more reliant on product knowledge in its sales tasks; a strategy focusing on solution customers relies more on proactive problem identification and customized benefits. As Neil Rackham has shown, there tends to be a positive relationship between the use of features and sales success in small or routine transactions, but *not* when technical or organizational complexity, and a longer selling cycle, characterize the sales context. Also, the users of a product or service respond more positively to features than do decision makers who are not part of the usage situation.[15] It depends on the type of sale.

Benefits versus Status Quo

Daniel Kahneman won a Nobel Prize for research (conducted over decades with Amos Tversky) about how people assess choices. Responses to alternatives (e.g., new products or services) tend to have four characteristics. First, we evaluate on the basis of perceived value, not just "objective" value. Second, we evaluate new products relative to a reference point, usually the products we already own or consume. Third, people view improvements (or value added) relative to the reference point as gains and treat any shortcomings as losses. Fourth, and most important for sales management, perceived losses have a much *greater* impact on buying behavior than similarly sized gains, a phenomenon that Kahneman and Tversky called "loss aversion" and that others label the "endowment effect."[16] For example, studies across cultures show that most people will not accept a bet with a 50 percent chance of winning or losing $100. Gains must outweigh potential losses by two or three times before most people find the bet attractive. Other research demonstrates this status-quo bias in choices relating to investments, job choices, negotiations (e.g., "give-backs" in labor negotiations), and other areas.

Because potential customers tend to overvalue the benefits of an entrenched usage system, it's not enough that a new product simply deliver better or more benefits. Unless the gains significantly outweigh the perceived losses, customers will not buy it. How much better must a new product or service be? This is a situation-specific issue. But consider the following. On average, according to research, consumers overvalue losses by a factor of roughly three, and my colleague John Gourville points out a common bias: both developers of new products and salespeople are naturally biased in favor of their products and thus overvalue the benefits by a comparable amount.[17] The result is often a mismatch of nine-to-one between what sellers think customers want and what customers will (or will not) do.

When a strategy relies on introducing new products or defending an installed base against new entrants, managing status-quo behavior is a key sales task. New products typically require customers to change behavior, and the changes may bring benefits. But the changes also entail perceived costs. The costs may be economic (e.g., activation fees), learning costs (using a new software program), or obsolescence costs (the perception of my CD collection as a stranded asset if I switch to streaming media). These costs equate to "losses" in relation to status-quo behavior and weigh heavily in customer decisions.

In turn, depending upon where you sit, different selling behaviors are relevant. Think of selling dynamics in the enterprise software market. Firms can spend years installing a new version of Oracle or SAP software—a painful process that requires purchasing a long-term license and, often, more hardware. Yet, chief information officers (CIOs) have bought from Oracle and SAP. There is, from a career point of view, much that can be lost from trying a new technology from a new entrant. The potential costs of failure or disruption often outweigh the future benefits in decision making. If you're trying to enter this market, relevant selling behaviors are the minimization of customer change. A company called Workday does this by selling a web-based service rather than a product that customers must install in their computing centers. But it's also in markets like this that, traditionally, "no one ever got fired for buying X." So if you're defending your installed base, you emphasize any "fear, uncertainty, and doubt" about change, while increasing the status-quo bias by offering up-front volume discounts on long-term licenses.[18]

Buyers can be high-inertia creatures, and as Gourville emphasizes, this typically leads to a face-off: sellers often create value through new product or service innovations, but they capture value best by minimizing the required change at customers. Hence, salespeople must get answers to questions such as:

- What change am I requiring of potential customers? Is that customer's problem or opportunity big enough to justify the change? Some products offer great benefits with minimal change at customers, while others offer some benefits but at the cost of significant changes. Effective selling requires understanding which customers fall into which category—which is why having an ideal-customer profile is so useful in linking strategy and sales.

- Can we establish with the customer a credible and shared language for documenting value and benefits? Salespeople at Rockwell Automation, for example, are trained to gather data and show customers a "value calculator" to demonstrate the gain, at that customer, from using a Rockwell motor package: Power reduction cost savings = current cost [kilowatts spent × operating hours per year × cost per kilowatt-hour × years system is in operation] − Rockwell's cost [kilowatts spent × operating hours per year × cost per kilowatt-hour × years system is in operation].

- Can we demonstrate value in advance of usage and get customers to self-select? Through seventy-plus

years of profitability—a period extending from the
Great Depression through the Great Society to the
Great Recession—Paccar (maker of Kenworth and
Peterbilt trucks) has maintained a price premium of
10 to 20 percent over its rivals. Salespeople qualify
customers with an online interactive detailing of
expenses incurred during the life of a truck. You can
input gasoline costs, tire rolling coefficients, and vehicle weight to quantify the benefits of a Paccar truck
versus lower-priced competitors. You can do the same
for resale value, maintenance, driver retention (useful data if you run a fleet), and financing costs. The
firm's website also provides a fuel-economy primer
aptly titled "Push Less Air, Pull More Profit."

Lead Users versus Mainstream Customers

There is another option for dealing with buying inertia: identify customers who highly value the benefits in your value
proposition or, conversely, only lightly value the changes they
must make. Identifying these lead users is often a key to linking strategy with selling behaviors because these customers
place a higher value on the benefits and lower value on the
status-quo than the average customer does. Geoffrey Moore
notes that these early adopters are often category "visionaries" with different buying criteria from the "pragmatists" or
mainstream customers. Firms that fail to identify these differences are unable to "cross the chasm" in their markets.[19]
What characterizes lead users? Despite what you often read
on blogs, there is no simple answer. Research has generated
multiple and conflicting criteria.[20] And, simply labeling early

adopters as "visionaries" or "evangelists" is tautological and does not help in establishing target criteria and planning sales calls.

To start identifying lead users, understand what is and is not behaviorally compatible with the established usage system in the relevant category. A seller has a higher probability of success if he or she can identify customers who are already dealing with the issue (e.g., Intuit selling check-writing and bookkeeping software to early PC adopters and accountants) or can adapt the product in a way that minimizes the customer's need to change (e.g., Dropbox allows you to keep your current means of saving and sharing files while using Dropbox). This means answering questions such as:

- Can the required change be reduced? This may be a product design issue. But it's often an account management task that determines effective selling: educating a prospect about an unrecognized problem or opportunity, or calling on different people at customers. This means recruiting or developing salespeople comfortable with these call requirements and establishing criteria about the answers to outcome questions that merit additional calls.

- Are we calling on the right prospects? To help identify lead users, you can focus selling on the "unendowed" in a market: prospects who are not using incumbent products. As seen shortly, BPI was able to do that kind of selling once it clarified its ideal-customer profile.

- Do cultural factors characterize early adopters in a category? Lead users take risks that mainstream customers do not. Cultural factors are often relevant in identifying community or organizational norms that support (or at least don't discourage) this risk taking. Some argue that one reason the United States has a relatively productive record of entrepreneurship is that, for historical reasons, the United States has more lead users willing to try new products.[21] US farmers are the world's fastest adopters of genetically modified crops; Silicon Valley benefits from the fact that US companies adopt new technologies faster than other countries, even when one looks at technology adoption in non-US locations by US multinationals. Scandinavian customers have adopted green products faster than other customers have. Other cultural factors—national, ethnic, or community norms—often have implications for lead-user identification, and social media are a tool for helping to isolate relevant characteristics.

None of these distinctions relevant to understanding buying behavior—products versus problems, benefits versus status quo, lead users versus mainstream customers—imply normative judgments. The point is not, for example, that lead users are somehow better than mainstream customers. That depends on choices in your strategy. Notice also that *all* of these distinctions are characteristics of the customer, *not* the seller. So you need a way of disaggregating the big issue of "predicting" or "divining" customer behavior into smaller, more manageable issues that can be investigated empirically and used to align required tasks (and performance management practices) with selling behaviors. In other words, you need a way of identifying who is your ideal customer.

Developing an Ideal-Customer Profile

Let's return to Business Processing Inc. During the firm's darkest hours, a BPI board member asked, "What is the profile of our 'ideal client'?" Answering that question illustrates a practical process for aligning sales tasks and behaviors and reveals the implications in areas ranging from hiring and pipeline management to pricing, sales organization, and channel management.[22] Initially, the CEO cited "small independently owned restaurants and food stores": by 2008, they were 40 percent of BPI's customer base at any given time and a focus of selling efforts. But the ideal-customer profile (ICP) uncovered other facts.

1. Assemble and Analyze Customer Data

BPI first assembled a small team of senior leaders (CEO, chief financial officer [CFO], vice president of sales, and an outside director) to analyze its customer data. The team listed *all* potentially relevant attributes. Customers' revenues, profits, number of employees, industry, location: any attributes could be relevant criteria but, at this stage, the issue is generating the information, not screening the list. At BPI, a customer relationship management (CRM) system had been well maintained, and the CFO developed a software tool that allowed the team to analyze the data.

Win-loss analyses then identified three primary differences among BPI's customers—location, vertical market, and number of employees—which correlated with the following sales metrics: selling cycle length, average sale price, churn rate, and up-sell rate. Every firm will have some customer differences unique to its business, but all should know how those attributes link to core selling metrics. A one-day team meeting discussed the findings and reached the following interim conclusions:

- *Profitability:* Profitability was generally proportional to the number of customer employees at the customer company. BPI had relatively high fixed but low marginal costs required to support more employees at a client. This underscored the importance of pricing and customer selection.

- *Cost of Sales:* This metric directly correlated with the length of the selling cycle: longer cycles typically meant multiple requests for proposals and demos and more calls. This affected sales productivity *and* the involvement of other functions at BPI—costs hidden in the basic gross margin data that management had been using to organize and deploy selling resources.

- *Customer Lifetime Value:* BPI was not increasing sales, but overall satisfaction with its services was high. As a result, the value of relationships with growing companies tended to be higher. These customers also churned less than others, including small restaurants and food stores, where financial difficulties and seasonality were a recurring source of cancellations.

2. Develop Preliminary Hypotheses

After analyzing its customer data, the team then identified the following characteristics of "good customers":

- *Size:* Professional services firms with fifteen to fifty employees were large enough to require repeatable payroll processes, but could not afford significant internal IT staff. Their make-versus-buy decisions tilted toward outsourced payroll services. The team also believed these firms chose BPI out of dissatisfaction with the non-priority treatment they received from BPI's larger competitors.

- *Urban Location:* Firms in cities allowed BPI to achieve selling economies, were generally earlier adopters of technology solutions in BPI's category, and (at the time of the analysis) were more likely to have high-speed internet connectivity.

- *Operating History:* Customer churn correlated with how long a firm had been in business. Firms in business for at least five years had lower churn rates and higher lifetime value for BPI.

These hypotheses were based on criteria and data that BPI could document and then use to test with its people and in the marketplace. Among other things, an ICP analysis contributes to fact-driven dialogue and therefore *faster* decision making in any firm where leaders and individual salespeople have strong embedded opinions about why things have or have not worked.

3. Refine and Modify the Hypotheses with Broader Input

With preliminary hypotheses, the team solicited feedback from others at BPI. At a two-day offsite of the team and functional leaders, the participants received a briefing package with the data, and each customer attribute was examined: What are the trends? How long does it take to close with customers in different verticals? How does service mix affect order fulfillment? If we could only invest our sales, marketing, or R&D money and time in pursuing one segment, which would we choose? What are the attributes of customers in that segment? With these discussions, changes were made to the hypotheses. Equally important, the participants left with buy-in about the importance of customer selection for growth.

But you can't stop here. The best understanding of customer behavior and its cost implications for the seller is held by a combination of people in frontline positions. So attendees agreed to get input "two levels down." Among other things, this feedback provided clarity about the cross-functional impact of BPI's selling efforts when it was discussed at a follow-up team session. This time, the starting point was the ICP hypotheses: What did we miss in our initial hypotheses about the domino effect of sales orders on our business? Are there other explanations for the impact? What have we heard that raises questions about the logic of our ICP? What are the implications for selling behaviors?

4. From Ideas to Action: Communicate the Ideal-Customer Profile and the Implications

As a result of this process, BPI shifted its selling focus and defined its core customer as a professional services firm with more than fifteen employees. The new focus had implications externally and internally. Externally, small accounting firms became a priority on sales call lists. Previously viewed as competitors, they now became a source of referrals to target customers. With the ICP, sales reps identified ways to reach and work with these channel partners. For example, BPI found that most small CPA firms lacked the resources or desire to handle payroll processing at their clients, and most were indifferent about who did. A combination of focus, incentives, and a tailored sales pitch made BPI the preferred partner for CPA firms and, in turn, allowed them to be seen as adding value to *their* customers.

Internally, performance metrics changed. BPI had measured sales only on bookings, with no consideration given to order quality or customer renewal rates. Now, metrics for selling through CPAs were set and monitored weekly. BPI found a clear relationship in its sales funnel between the number of meetings a sales rep had with local CPA firms and referrals received. In turn, referrals led to demos at target customers and closed sales. A rep was now expected to contact a certain number of CPAs in his or her territory, and this was measured through a report application. And to reinforce the strategic importance of this behavior, commissions were paid *only* for deals matching the ICP. This was a bold move, but it paid off. The number of sales reps dropped from seventy-five to thirty-five. By focusing on professional services firms (and CPAs as a way to access them), call patterns improved, and with the activity metrics, it soon became clear which reps could execute the new approach. Recruiting efforts also improved as BPI sought people with contacts or experience at CPA firms. An ICP also means a better understanding of relevant skills and experience for HR managers. Similarly, marketing was redirected to include events at venues and conferences where these customers and channel partners gathered.

In R&D, a payroll-HR bundle was developed to allow customers to track employees' date of hire, benefits package, salary history, and performance reviews. This new product increased customer renewal rates because, once BPI became the conduit for this data, the stickiness of the customer relationship increased. In the past, some at BPI had suggested adding HR functionality to the product, but others had rejected this because "we're a payroll company." Now, because BPI could tie this R&D expenditure to customer lifetime value, that debate was resolved and the ICP also helped to pinpoint the relevant product features. It also prompted changes in BPI's strategy with nonideal customers. When a CPA firm provided referrals to these companies, they were treated as transaction customers. BPI contacted these leads via email, directed them to an online demo and self-service set-up. Close rates were lower than for prospects that received in-person sales calls and demos, but each sale was now less expensive and more profitable.

The breadth of these changes meant that communication was critical. BPI's leaders devoted time and effort to discussing the rationale for the ICP and the implications across the business. The results were worth the effort. It took three months from the initial ideal-client question to the roll-out of BPI's sales changes. Within six months of roll-out, nearly a third of the sales force departed: they were not meeting quota or activity goals, and many found the new selling behaviors alien to their skill set and personal preferences. But over the next year, bookings increased 25 percent with fewer reps, and new clients churned at half the average rate of the installed customer base, driving increases in profitability and revenue. BPI's recruitment, on-boarding, and training processes (e.g., sales hires were educated about how CPA and other professional services firms were organized) also improved, and reps became productive in one-third the time it had taken previously. BPI also now had a scalable sales model *and* a process for adapting that model in the face of inevitable market changes: to monitor if and when the current ICP becomes obsolete, leadership reviews it regularly and embeds an ICP discussion in its strategic planning activities.

From Selling Behaviors to Performance Management

Opportunity management is a strategic choice. But translating that scope choice into customer selection and field behaviors is a sales performance issue. Understanding your ideal customer affects sales productivity and pipeline management, cost management, and how leaders across functions think about profitable growth and monitoring achievement of strategic goals.

Consider sales productivity and pipeline value—a recurring topic for entrepreneurs and investors as well as sales managers in corporations. To improve productivity, you can get people to work harder: make more calls and/or do a better job at lead generation. At BPI, fewer reps sold more because the ICP improved lead generation and allowed more fruitful sales calls. You also juice productivity by working smarter: focus on high-impact sales tasks and offload the lower-impact tasks so the sales force has more time to sell, as BPI did when its ICP was translated into new activity metrics and sales responsibilities.

Consider cost management and especially SG&A costs. You can lower selling costs *without* harming selling because an ICP aids knowing where and where not to cut. BPI now understood cause-and-effect relationships between internal activities and customer acquisition and retention, and thus the ability to devote more resources to the important activities. Better customer selection also meant shorter selling cycles, better close rates and cash flows, and the ability to improve sales training and call lists.

Consider the issues of identifying customer value, the cross-functional culture required to create and deliver that value, and how to align an organization for growth. Another ICP analysis, at a large company, can illustrate these linked issues. Information Services Inc. (ISI) is a technology research firm where, by the later 1990s, most revenue came from research subscriptions. Buyers included CIOs and IT leaders in corporations, and ISI grew rapidly through the 1990s as the pace of technology accelerated and clients sought more information. But when the dot-com bubble burst, ISI had fourteen consecutive quarters of declining bookings, which resulted in layoffs of nearly 20 percent of its employees; repeated downward revisions of sales forecasts; and, finally, a mandate from the board to the CEO: reverse the "death spiral."

ISI initiated an ideal-customer process, and as at BPI, the starting point was to analyze extant data. Because ISI's biggest sales were with public companies, their financials were available. In 90 percent of the cases examined, if a firm had lost money in the previous fiscal year, it would *not* buy ISI services. Worse, 30 percent of ISI's pipeline was with this kind of company. ISI then conducted other analyses and interviews and established the following profile of those customers most likely to have the shortest sales cycles commensurate with the highest prices and up-sell/cross-sell potential: multilocation (often but not always multinational companies) with at least $500 million in revenues, profitable for the past four quarters, and where IT spending was at least 5 percent of revenue. This data could be quickly assembled and kept current. In turn, the ICP initiated changes in the selling approach. Instead of calling on more than fifty prospects, each ISI rep was assigned five or six named accounts that fit the criteria. Coverage for all other companies was shifted to telesales. The focus was supported by a revised account planning process and performance metrics, and a commitment to regular coaching and review with management. A year after starting this process, ISI had its first bookings increase in over three years, doubling the firm's stock price.

The ISI example illustrates important links between sales tasks and performance management, and typical differences in managing these links at big corporations versus smaller companies:

- *A Common Language of Value:* In smaller firms, the availability of data is often a challenge. But at ISI—as at many big companies—the issue was too much data: there were five incompatible CRM systems in use, in addition to volumes of reports and spreadsheets, each driven by different assumptions and criteria in product and sales divisions. This patchwork of data allowed managers to justify almost any strategy, further contributing to the firm's malaise for fourteen quarters, because there was no agreed-upon version of customer reality. In addition to clarifying sales tasks, the ICP process itself typically has value at a big company: it helps to reestablish a common language and shared vision across functions and divisions about what the firm is good at. Conversely, without that common language, the current enthusiasm for "big data" and associated analytics is likely to be another iteration of garbage-in-garbage-out investments.

- *Profitable Growth:* Both ISI and BPI improved sales and profitability substantially by refocusing their selling resources, *not* by entering new markets, making acquisitions, or seeking previously unexplored market spaces. This is a message that many corporate executives need to remember. Currently popular strategy advice has many big companies sailing off, like Ahab or Sinbad, in search of "blue oceans" where no one else is allegedly fishing. Avoiding competition is always nice work if you can get it. But most firms are better off emulating wily Odysseus, the sailor who sought prosperity closer to home—in the opportunities inherent in translating strategic choices into an ideal-customer profile and the implications for required selling behaviors and performance management practices.

8

People

Hiring, Development, and Sales Organization

A core performance competency is selecting high-potential salespeople by understanding the behaviors necessary for success, recruiting in accord with those attributes, and training those selected. Because much development in sales is experiential learning by doing, moreover, how the sales force is organized will affect the people you need and the skills they develop. So it's also important to understand the strengths and limits of common forms of sales organization and, in the twenty-first century, how new technologies are affecting the go-to-market tasks involved in aligning strategy and sales.

The People Parts

Most managers never say it this way, but many may resonate with a comment attributed to Terry Gou, chairman of Foxconn, a contract manufacturing company for Apple and other firms. In 2012, Foxconn had more than 1.4 million employees and plans to install more than a million robots in its factories over the next few years. Gou was blunt in explaining his investment rationale to the official Xinhua news agency: "Human beings are also animals [and] to manage one million animals gives me a headache."[1] Perhaps Gou should have made his point the way Caspar David Friedrich, the reclusive German painter of barren landscapes, did: "To love people, I must avoid their company." In speeches and articles, most executives espouse a different view: "People are our most important asset. (In fact, some of my best friends are people!)" and "We hire the best—only the 'A' players, only the stars."

In sales, both approaches to talent management are misguided. Any business process is only as good as the people involved. Terry Gou may be right or wrong in substituting capital for labor in his factories. But differences in individual performance are especially stark in sales activities and cannot be explained by differences in tenure or product mix or account assignments. Some salespeople work harder and/or smarter than others. HR studies indicate that the 85th percentile of a firm's sales staff frequently generates five to ten times the revenue of those in the 50th percentile.[2] Studies in B2B sales contexts find that rep performance in similar territories often varies by 300 percent between top and bottom quintiles, while in retail stores selling productivity typically varies by a factor of three to four.[3]

In other words, there *are* sales stars in most organizations. Here's a specific example: in 2010, Groupon put itself on the map and generated buzz about its IPO prospects with the help of a few high-profile deals. It sold over 440,000 coupons to Gap in August 2010, then 625,000 to Nordstrom three months later, and then a Groupon deal was featured in Oprah Winfrey's 2010 list of "Favorite Things." At the time, Groupon had over forty-five hundred salespeople. But both the Gap and the Nordstrom deals were closed by one salesperson, Jayna Cooke, who also persuaded Winfrey's producers to feature Groupon. Cooke was the firm's top salesperson in terms of gross billings in 2010 and 2011. When she left in 2012 to join a start-up, that loss was not easily recouped by reshuffling account assignments.

Performance in operations, perhaps because internal processes can be more tightly controlled and standardized than external selling processes, typically varies much less.[4] In this respect, sales is more like other creative, nonroutine, knowledge-worker occupations where the phenomenon of stardom is well documented. Studies have found that in complex jobs, the top 1 percent of employees often outperform average performers by 125 percent or more; that there is an eight-to-one productivity difference between star and average computer programmers; that the top 1 percent of inventors across industries are five to ten times as productive as average inventors; and that, historically, data from different eras and disciplines show that a small number of scientists and artists account for a very large number of publications and acknowledged classics.[5] Don't react to this data like the rock guitarists Pete Townshend and Eric Clapton who, when they first saw Jimi Hendrix perform, were so impressed and intimidated that (according to Townshend) they found themselves holding hands in joint submission. Talent indeed matters, and salesperson selection and development has lots of room for improvement in most firms. But you don't need to move everyone to the 90th percentile; moving up a quartile would be a big deal.

At the same time, focusing only on "the best," as many firms say they do, is *not* the best approach to recruiting salespeople, for multiple reasons. Done well, recruiting is not easy. Given the money and management resources required, most firms just can't afford to have stars in all sales positions. And stars are the targets of other companies. When firms are polled about their recruiting criteria, over half say they look for "selling experience within the industry." This means that you and your competitors shop first among each other's stars, not the laggards.[6] Also, stardom is not easily portable. Boris Groysberg has documented how the performance of star stock analysts typically plummeted, permanently, when they left the place where they first performed so well.[7] Why? According to his research, less than half of performance in these jobs stems from individual capabilities, and more than half from firm-specific qualities and resources—brand, technologies, leadership, training, team chemistry, and other factors. As this book indicates, sales tasks are determined by a firm's business strategy and its choices about where to play and which customers to focus on: those are firm-specific factors. In turn, selling behaviors will be affected by your sales control systems and culture, as well as whom you hire and how you develop people: those are also firm-specific factors. When you hire a star, or when a competitor hires one from you, that salesperson leaves all of that behind.

The lesson is that, ultimately, a company must primarily grow its own, especially in sales, through disciplined hiring approaches, focused training initiatives, and market-right organizing principles. It then must strive to retain the best and keep them the best by helping them broaden their skills even as markets and sales tasks change. Sorry, but almost all serious research about people in business underscores the abiding necessity of these fundamentals and debunks glib prescriptions about talent acquisition. Competitive advantage and selling effectiveness reside in *how* you do these fundamentals.

A People Process

HubSpot is a firm founded in Cambridge, Massachusetts, in 2006 to provide web-based inbound marketing services to small and medium-sized businesses. When Mark Roberge joined in 2007, he had never run a sales organization: "I didn't know the conventional techniques that sales managers use. Instead, I relied on my background as an MIT-trained engineer to create a system of hiring and development that relies on metrics and quantitative analysis."[8] Roberge defined his goal as "scalable, predictable revenue growth," and he focused on recruitment, training, and organizational processes that affect how salespeople work externally with customers and internally with other functions at HubSpot.

As Roberge notes, "Most companies screen sales candidates on 'gut feel,' which does not scale. I aimed to inject quantitative analysis into this normally unscientific process." Roberge began by listing criteria that he thought would correlate with sales success at HubSpot. The criteria were weighted by relative importance, and the scores—on a scale of one to ten—were defined as to what each meant for a potential hire. Then after twelve months, five hundred interviews, and twenty hires, Roberge hired an MIT student to run a regression analysis correlating the ex-ante interview scores with ex-post sales success. "By repeating this analysis every 6 to 12 months," says Roberge, "we continually fine-tuned the index to our business. Today, as we hire 5 to 10 sales reps per month, I sleep better knowing this process is established."

In training, Roberge found that "when I asked candidates how they were trained in their last job, many responded that they simply shadowed one of that company's top salespeople for a few weeks. That approach concerned me." Roberge soon recognized what the research outlined previously and in chapter 6 indicates: focusing only on the particular behaviors of stars and attempting to find a universal set of selling traits are bad ideas. "Our best salespeople are great, but they each tend to be great for very different reasons. Most of them are great at one aspect of sales (say, asking great questions) and mediocre at others. So no one sales rep can teach the whole package." He established a process where new sales hires spend their first month in classroom-style training, and then must pass a 150-question exam and six certification tests about HubSpot's product, its sales methodology, and the concept of inbound marketing. For product knowledge, every new rep must create a blog and website from scratch during training. "These exams and certifications," Roberge emphasizes, "ensure that new hires will leave training with the same foundation of skills . . . [And] they experience the actual pains and successes of our primary customers: professional marketers who need to generate leads online. As a result, our salespeople are able to connect on a far deeper level with our prospects and leads."

In organization, Roberge notes that HubSpot's sales tasks "require an unprecedented level of sales and marketing alignment." He put in place some of the linking mechanisms I will discuss in chapter 12. But he also recognized that any sales structure involved trade-offs: "Should I provide each salesperson with one lead and have them call the lead 1,000 times in the month? Or should I provide each salesperson with 1,000 leads and have them call each lead once? Obviously, the answer is somewhere in between—but where?" In a fast-growing start-up, he knew sales organization should be continually reexamined, but felt that "this is another set of questions that many companies answer using nothing more than 'gut feel.' When you have just a handful of salespeople, it can seem like this is an adequate approach—it's hard to see the variability. But with hundreds of salespeople working thousands of leads . . . we've worked hard at HubSpot to create a culture of rigorous self-analysis and review. We are forever poking at the numbers, prodding the data to tell us more."

By 2012, HubSpot had over two hundred salespeople, with 7,000-plus customers, and was the thirty-third fastest-growing company in America on the *Inc. 500* List. "The key takeaway," according to Roberge, "is the process, not the actual results or the criteria. Each sales context is different. Each salesperson has a unique style. Some fit your context and some do not. The process helps to understand these differences." Roberge touches on many of the core activities relevant to the people parts of aligning strategy and sales. I'll describe that process as follows:

- *Build Your Team, Not Another Firm's Team:* Hire and select by identifying the selling behaviors required by *your* firm's strategy; understand what that means for building and managing a portfolio of sales talent; and then put your best talent where it counts most.

- *Develop the Fundamentals:* Train and develop your salespeople in a consistent, customized, measurable way with attention to behaviors and follow-up activities.

- *Choose Your Strengths and Limitations:* There is no one best way to organize a sales force. Understand the strengths and limits of common forms of sales organization, and then choose—and manage—your problems and opportunities.

- *Focus on Buying Behavior:* Sales tasks across industries are being altered by new buying options. Multichannel management is now the norm. That has important implications for people and organization in linking strategy with sales.

Build *Your* Team: Recruitment and Selection

Putting the right team on the field is crucial. As the saying goes, "You hire your problems." Recruitment and selection are now more important for various reasons. Due to the data and analytical tasks facing many sales forces, productivity ramp-up times have increased. Each hire then represents a bigger sunk cost for a longer time. As baby boomers retire, they must be replaced. In addition, there were layoffs in sales (and other functions) throughout the recession starting in 2008. As firms seek to grow, putting more "feet on the street" (or in inside sales positions) increases hiring. And the math, as Jim Dickie and Barry Trailer document, is daunting. In surveys, their data has been consistent for years: involuntary turnover in sales organizations has remained at 13 percent, since peaking at 14.6 percent in 2009, and total turnover (involuntary and voluntary—i.e., retirements, moves, etc.) in both good and bad times runs between 25 and 30 percent.[9] This means that the equivalent of the entire sales force must be replaced at many firms every four years or so. And the time frame shrinks if and when companies increase revenue targets.

So while strategy should drive search and selection, the exigencies of time and labor markets make this, as Roberge discovered, an ad hoc process at many firms. Most adopt a simple decision rule: look at the best reps, and try to hire more like them. But you'll never have enough stars for all sales positions and, in fact, don't want stars in all jobs. In any organization, some activities exhibit high performance variability but have little strategic impact.[10] Think, in many selling situations, about the design of PowerPoint presentations: some folks are much better than others in doing this, but how much impact do the slides have versus other sales tasks? Other activities may be important strategically but exhibit relatively little performance variability—because the tasks are standard, because the firm or industry has reduced variability, or because the business model limits the bandwidth of performance variance. Think about the difference between sales personnel at Nordstrom, where personalized service and advice are integral to strategy execution, and Costco, where low price and product availability make selling activities less complex and variable. Or, more generally, think again about transaction versus solution customers in your pipeline, discussed in chapter 6, and how those sales activities vary.

You want your stars in activities that exhibit both high impact and high variability. That may be prospecting *or* account management; it may be transaction selling *or* solution selling; it may be call frequency *or* managing key channel partners. In activities with low impact or little variability, you don't need stars and should not overpay, either in money or in time. In other words, effective hiring and selection in sales is about building the right portfolio of talent. This has actionable implications.

Focus on how the salesperson makes a difference. Continually ask, "Where are we spending too much—and too little—time, money, and talent across our sales tasks?" The strategic choices discussed in chapter 5 cascade to selection criteria. Also, the key activities will be affected by sales structure (see following) and the necessity—or not—of team selling (see chapter 10) and will change as your markets change. In subscription-based businesses like software and many consumer web services, sales activities with high variance and impact early on are about customer acquisition. But as the market matures, key activities tend to shift toward account management, reducing churn, working with engineering on custom applications, and up-selling or cross-selling additional services. Allocation of sales talent should change.

Focus on behaviors in selection. In many firms, this means upgrading assessment skills. Managers are excessively confident about their ability to evaluate candidates via one or two interviews. But studies across job categories indicate there is only about a 14 percent correlation between interview predictions and job success.[11] This is especially true in sales. A job where individual performance can make a big difference inevitably leads to a cloning bias—many sales managers hire in their own image because how each manager achieved that performance is what got him or her promoted and in a position to hire. But the best results, by far, occur when recruiters can observe the relevant job behaviors.

There are many ways to observe potential hires' behaviors, including simulations, the kinds of tests used at HubSpot, or interviewing techniques. Many sales organizations could emulate the practice used by investment banks and consulting firms when hiring MBAs: the summer job is, in effect, an extended observation—by multiple people at the firm—of the candidate's task behaviors before a full-time offer is extended. After immersion in the job's requirements, the firm *and* candidate are in a better position to select. Procter & Gamble and Met-Life provide sales candidates, days before an interview, with a case study of fifteen to thirty pages. It describes a selling situation, and the assignment is to plan a day, select target customers, and develop a sales pitch. The required work helps to check for motivation and preparation skills. At the interview, the candidate must explain his or her plan and then role-play the situation with a sales manager or trainer. Technology is increasing these possibilities via game-like simulations, virtual video environments, and online media that allow more behavioral assessments by more people with less travel and time. The real constraint in many firms, however, is the lack of assessment skills by sales managers. This underscores a point discussed in chapter 10: the importance of links between sales and HR. Sales managers know (or should know) the key sales tasks. But HR managers typically know a lot more about the tools, techniques, and options for assessing behaviors relevant to those tasks.

Be clear about what you mean by relevant "experience," which is the most frequently used criterion by sales managers. In one survey, over 50 percent cited "selling experience within the industry" as their key selection criterion, and another 33 percent cited "selling experience in [an] other industry."[12] Driving this view is a belief that there's a trade-off between hiring for experience and the amount of time and money that you *don't* need to spend on training and development. But these are very different things, and experience at another company—within or outside the same industry—is not easily portable. In a sales context, "experience" is an inherently multidimensional attribute. It may refer to experience with any (or any combination) of the following elements:

- A customer group (e.g., a banker, a broker, or another financial-services manager hired by a software firm to call on financial-services prospects; or, in health-care businesses, different companies sell very different products, but many sell to hospitals)

- A technology (e.g., an engineer or field-service tech hired to sell a category of equipment)

- A company or division of the selling organization (e.g., a customer service rep moved to a sales position because internal cross-functional coordination is an important sales task and the rep "knows the people and how to get things done here")

- A geography or territory or culture (e.g., a member of a given nationality or ethnic group who knows, and has credibility within, the norms of the relevant customer's culture)

- Selling (e.g., an insurance agent or a retail associate with experience in another sales context)

The relevance of each type of experience varies with *your* sales tasks. In appraising talent, some sales managers "know it when they see it," and many don't. So consider what kind(s) of prior experience is truly relevant, and then require the people doing the selection to clarify what they mean when they see it.

Develop the Fundamentals: Training and Development

Training at many firms merits Hamlet's critique of Elsinore Incorporated's values statement: more honored in the breach than the observance. In a given year, over a third of firms do not train salespeople at all. Most companies budget their training according to last-in-first-out accounting principles: training budgets (like advertising) increase when sales are good, and get cut when times are tough. So it's hard for managers to determine cause and effect. Sales training also affects other functions in the firm. Product managers, for instance, are likely to take interest in how much sales training concerns information about their products; market managers are interested in how much training reps get in the demographics, psychographics, and purchase criteria of their segments. So "a little bit of everything" is often a default rule in sales training programs.

Selling is not a science reducible to timeless rules that can be specified ex-ante and conclusively verified ex-post. Many variables affect market performance and sales effectiveness. But effective sales training, like most worthwhile development, cannot be a single event. People need reinforcement, periodic upgrading and adaptation of skills to new circumstances, and the motivation that is a by-product of any good developmental process. Stated more bluntly: training for salespeople—as for other professionals, like pilots and doctors, who deal with a range of situations—should heed the "8 P's" used in the U.S. Air Force: "Proper Prior Planning and Preparation Prevents Piss-Poor Performance." And this has implications for what to do before, during, and after training initiatives.

Customize to Your Strategic Goals and Sales Initiatives. Many companies have competency lists, but the lists rarely incorporate particular sales tasks. Before a training initiative starts, always consider the behavioral goals and desired outcomes, which can vary significantly: selling against competition, introducing a new product, negotiation or closing skills, improving customer selection and call patterns, and so on. Sometimes an off-the-shelf training tool can address the desired outcome. But often customization is required, for several reasons.

New salespeople—experienced or inexperienced—have much to learn about the strategy and selling environment at *your* firm, *not* simply about the industry at large. They also need to learn about the company and how other functions affect, and are affected by, selling behaviors. They don't need to know how to do other jobs in the firm. But they do need to know what those jobs are and how those activities affect selling. In addition, as discussed below, buyers in many industries now conduct online research about products and price points *before* meeting with a salesperson. Buyers are less reliant on the salesperson for product information. Conversely, sales training must focus more precisely on key tasks, selling skills, and the rep's value added during the customer encounter.

Finally, sales training is about cultural values as well as skills. This is especially important when reps are now more likely to work from home, rather than a branch office with other reps. Customization allows salespeople to hear success stories, role-play exercises that reflect issues inherent in *your* ideal-customer profile (chapter 7), and learn via modeling behavior—a key component in adult learning. Good sales reps also represent their company's culture and values as well as products and services. This should be practiced and taught, not left for individuals to improvise.

Experiential Learning. How do you get to Carnegie Hall *and* to desired training outcomes? *Practice*: studies show what game designers know—active learning is more effective than lectures or passive learning. *Practice*: adults do best with experiential learning by doing. *Practice*: acquiring behavioral skills (versus concepts) requires repetition; people must try a new behavior multiple times (from three to twenty times, according to different studies) before it becomes practiced enough to be comfortable and effective.[13] This means that on-the-job learning is crucial. The problem is that in most busy sales forces, *on-the-job training* is a euphemism for no real training at all. It's a random-walk process.

During formal training programs, therefore, it's important to incorporate action-learning initiatives. People learn to handle unpredictable environments through relevant practice. A good analog is the "stop and shoot" video simulations used for years in police training. The basic format arms trainees with unloaded pistols and faces them toward a screen where vignettes are shown: the alleged perpetrator is running across a suburban lawn where children are playing, or using a hostage as a shield. The trainees must decide whether to shoot, balancing multiple factors in the moment: applicable law, observational skills, the safety of bystanders, and the consequences of action versus inaction. This approach contains many of the core elements of action learning for professionals. The exercises are experiential but simulated: case studies, role plays, and other exercises provide similar benefits. They allow for practice, and inevitable mistakes, in a safe environment. And trainees accelerate their experience of multiple situations and scripts they may encounter in the field, instead of in the training manual.

An example is Work-Out programs at GE and their use in sales training. Focused on topics that affect go-to-market tasks in a business unit, the programs involve participants in interviews internally and externally—building cross-functional as well as market knowledge. Company-specific case studies and other materials may be part of this process, and available research data is provided. Then, at training initiatives lasting from one to five days, managers and reps discuss, simulate, and analyze relevant actions and behaviors, while addressing actual sales opportunities or problems. In many sales Work-Outs, key customers also tell the participants about their experiences with GE products and sales approaches, and in recent years the emphasis has increasingly shifted to using Work-Out for real-time, collaborative problem-solving *with* customers. Experiential learning like this also takes advantage of another developmental fact: adults learn best when they can apply new information or a skill and see results.[14] As a result, most impactful adult education is task-driven and requires follow-up.

Follow-up. The greatest impact from training may have less to do with the content itself, but more to do with what happens *after* the formal training sessions: follow-up actions aimed at ensuring that people apply skills. In sales training, follow-up focuses on three dimensions: the specific sales tasks addressed at training, the selling or strategy concepts at the core of the training initiative, and sales careers.

A common way to follow up—typically as part of performance evaluations—is ride-alongs by the first-level manager. As discussed in chapter 10, managers' commitment to coaching and constructive performance reviews is key. *Win-loss analyses* can also reinforce training goals and improve sales effectiveness, but only if you link them to an ongoing process. Too often, win-loss analyses focus on losses and not on wins and rely primarily on the salesperson's view of "the facts," and the manager adopts the role of the prosecuting attorney in a courtroom drama. But wins are as important as losses: they provide information about your strengths, competitor weaknesses, buying behavior, and elements of the selling firm's business model or positioning pitch—all factors that can be used to measure and increase the odds of success. To complement the salesperson's perspective on a win or loss, customer visits are helpful.[15] Similarly, an after-action review (AAR) helps to focus on diagnosis *and* follow-up actions, not just apportioning credit or blame. An AAR moves systematically through the following questions: What was our intent? What happened? Why: what did we do well and what could we have done better? What can we do to improve?[16] Most importantly, effective win-loss analyses are not one-off events; they are part of an ongoing performance cycle approach and process, as outlined in figure 8-1.

Follow-up on training concepts, webinars, videos, and online self-study courses is becoming less expensive. Internal online discussion boards are useful in keeping the message fresh, disseminating best practices, and tapping field experience to adapt best practice to various situations. They also draw on a powerful motivator in many sales forces: peer feedback and peer pressure. Design of the training program can anticipate follow-up: a modular design rolled out sequentially in a series of short sessions acknowledges the cost of nonselling time inherent in training, while anticipating the

FIGURE 8-1

Win-loss analyses as part of an ongoing performance cycle approach and process

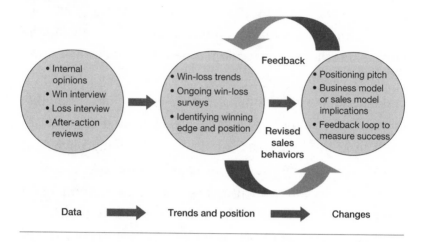

need and opportunities for practice and refresher training on concepts, skills, and peer feedback.

Finally, follow-up also refers to development over the course of a salesperson's career. Figure 8-2 outlines a common situation. The average salesperson's performance tends to flatten out over time, due to changes in product, technology, market demographics, and other factors besides effort. But the fully burdened cost typically increases. This raises issues for the rep and the firm: how to remain at the top of one's game over time, even as sales tasks change, and how to ensure that a specific type of expertise remains important to the selling firm. And whether they admit it or not, every sales rep in a competitive market faces the following challenge over time, and every sales organization has this choice: how can the salesperson continue to offer a better deal to the firm than a less-experienced person who may cost less, yet (simply by virtue of more recent education) may be *more*

FIGURE 8-2

What tends to happen in a sales organization over time: implications for careers and productivity

The challenge:

- How to remain at the top of one's game over time: nature of rep's contribution to the firm and its strategy?

- How to ensure that a specific type of expertise remains important to the firm?

- How to offer a better deal than reps who cost less, may be *more* technically up-to-date, and provide "80% of the job for 50% of the fully burdened cost"?

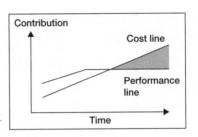

technically up-to-date and so able to provide 80 percent of current performance for less than 80 percent of the current fully burdened cost?

It's in the interests of *both* parties to keep performance aligned with contribution and cost. For the salesperson, the human implications are dramatized in plays and movies from Willy Loman in *Death of a Salesman* to Shelly Levene, the over-the-hill salesman in Mamet's *Glengarry Glen Ross*. For the firm, ignoring or passively acquiescing to the pattern where fully burdened cost outpaces individual performance contribution means incurring the costs and uncertainties associated with hiring and account reassignments. Also, 80 percent of performance is not 100 percent. Follow-up training is often a more cost-efficient and effective way of addressing the gap. Recall Terry Gou's attitude about people as headaches. It's often said that many companies maintain their equipment better than they develop their people. If so, you ultimately get what you don't maintain.

Sales Organization: Choose Your Strengths and Limitations

Hiring, development, and structure always interact. Skills affect organizational options. But because learning by doing is so important in developing sales skills, organization affects the skills that are developed. Sales organization is ultimately about the primary focus of your people at a point in time; it is about where and how to play in the field, and so linked to scope and advantage choices. As a result, there simply is no one best way to organize a sales force. Table 8-1 outlines the strengths and limitations inherent in common ways to structure a sales force: by geography or territory, by product or service line, by customer or account size, and by industry or vertical market segment. As Goethe said, "Where the light is brightest, the shadows are deepest." Each structure allows certain tasks to be accomplished more effectively and inhibits behaviors for others.

TABLE 8-1

Strengths and limitations of common sales force organizational structures

Strengths	Limitations
By geography or territory	
Often the most economically efficient structure: minimizes travel, office, and administrative costs and can maximize salesperson's face time with customers	Limits of salesperson's product knowledge: this structure can dilute rep's expertise across a broad or technically complex product line
"Clean" coverage if full-line selling within a territory: clear responsibilities and few turf battles; full-line selling and cross-selling or system sales opportunities	"Cherry-picking" and "flight to comfort zone" behavior by rep: impact on product mix and firm's trajectory of business development
More opportunity to develop knowledge of economic, cultural, competitive conditions in a territory	Attention to new products can suffer; applications development often fragmented

Strengths	Limitations
By geography or territory	
Market and CRM data often most accessible geographically and thus helpful in sales force and salesperson performance evaluations	Unsuited to buying organizations that span multiple territories: account coordination issues with large, multilocation customers
By product or service line	
Develops sales force product knowledge/expertise: important when firm has a broad or complex line, or early in the product/market life cycle	Low geographic efficiencies and typically incurs higher selling expenses: travel, training, administrative/support overhead
Helps to differentiate and position competing lines, and often easier to coordinate and align sales metrics with the selling firm's product groups	Can generate internal competition between separate product-oriented sales forces, with external customer confusion or pricing issues
Helps salespeople adapt to different technical or decision-making criteria for different products in the line (e.g., capital equipment vs. supply items)	Potential opportunity costs: • Cross-selling across the line to key accounts? • Adaptability to changes in technology?
Focus, attention, commitment of salespeople for a given product line or product group	Salespeople focus on product features over best customer solution among firm's options
By customer or account size	
Helps sales force develop customer-specific knowledge and account management capabilities	Resource duplication in the field, and often increased service/support expenses
Helps develop knowledge of total purchasing patterns in an account, and accommodates different buying processes/criteria within customer organizations	Assumes account size is an appropriate variable for capturing important differences in buying criteria or purchasing behaviors over time
Full-line selling within assigned accounts or customer groups: cross-selling or "systems" sales opportunities	Often conflicts with firm's product structure, and harder to measure sales effectiveness
Often acknowledges the 80-20 rule in many markets: most current sales volumes and market potential often concentrated in relatively few key accounts	Potential boundary problems: must manage customer migration over the life cycle; sales attention to smaller growing accounts suffers
By industry or vertical segment	
Accelerates sales force's ability to share learning across customers in a given industry or segment	Often the most expensive way to structure a sales force: SG&A and training expenses
Stimulates applications development that can be leveraged across customers in a vertical segment	Requires a critical mass of accounts within a segment to justify the costs
Develops expertise and credibility of salespeople about industry/vertical issues, trends, ecosystem	Danger that salespeople lose effectiveness and value as segment matures or declines

In academic and consulting studies, organization is often treated as a linear-programming exercise where the objective is to optimize deployment of salespeople. The optimum occurs when the incremental return from additional sales effort on all products and markets is equal, and the return equals the incremental cost of additional effort. Nice idea. But decisions about sales organization typically occur in conditions of change, uncertainty, and competition. Hence, sales managers usually and rightly focus at any one time on a few major threats or goals. In a technologically dynamic industry from the mid-1960s to the mid-1980s, IBM's sales force was organized and then reorganized into each of the structures in table 8-1 and soon demonstrated the strengths and limitations of each structure.[17] This wasn't silly. It was a response to market facts and changing sales tasks. As Thomas Learson, a senior executive at IBM during this time, commented, "In any given period in as fast-moving a business as this, we have a given set of problems to manage, a given set of opportunities to exploit."

Sales organization is about the best use of people "out there" in the marketplace, where value is ultimately created or destroyed. And in most markets, new technologies are affecting buying behavior and, therefore, sales organization and training.

Focus on Buying Behavior: Multichannel Management

Today's customers "channel surf" freely. In the United States, nearly two-thirds of purchases now involve some form of customer-initiated online research before the sale—less in categories like groceries or household products but even higher percentages in categories like automobiles and electronics. This shift in buying behavior has sales implications. Most buying moves through stages that, in turn, are reflected in the so-called sales funnel in place at selling organizations.[18] Figure 8-3 categorizes, grossly, these stages of buying behavior. The buyer moves from *shopping* (which includes becoming aware of the product set and gathering comparative information about features, price, and other factors) to *purchasing* (which includes the selection and buying decision as well as payment and order fulfillment terms) to *owning* (which, depending upon the purchase, includes any postsale usage, customer support, and maintenance needs).

Customers are indeed buying more online. In 2012, according to U.S. Department of Commerce data, online spending reached almost $200 billion. That may sound like a lot, but it's less than 5 percent of total retail spending, even in a recession, and less than half of what just one retailer, Wal-Mart, sells annually. A lot of people may "like" a Facebook

FIGURE 8-3

The customer has escaped

Driven by technology, choice, and information abundance, many customers are effectively unbundling and realigning supplier-driven tasks and arrangements throughout the buying cycle.

Shopping	→	Purchasing	→	Owning
• Awareness		• Select		• Usage issues
• Gather information		• Pay/Lease: financial terms		• Customer support
• Inspect/Compare		• Order fulfillment		• Customer maintenance

Examples:

• Automobiles, financial services, pharmaceuticals
• Retail supply chains
• B2B buyers in many industries

Source: Adapted from Paul F. Nunes and Frank V. Cespedes, "The Customer Has Escaped," *Harvard Business Review* (November 2003): 117–126.

entry and tweet on Twitter (retired Pope Benedict reportedly tweeted in nine languages). But 140 million people actually *buy* stuff at Wal-Mart *weekly*.

Don't believe the hype: the issue facing most sales organizations is *not* the specter of disintermediation, which has been periodically announced for decades. Back in the 1930s, when the social network called the telephone was being rolled out across the United States, the business press trumpeted the "death of the salesman" and the rise of what we now call networked buying cooperatives. Didn't happen. In the 1960s, when the national highway system was built, pundits proclaimed the demise of sales functions because people would simply drive for miles to get the best prices. Didn't happen. Then, in the twenty-first century, when the internet's "information superhighway" captured headlines and investor capital, sales disintermediation was again standard analysis. But it's simply not true that ecommerce is eliminating, or even downsizing, most sales forces. In fact, if you peek behind the server farms of online firms themselves, you will find big and traditional face-to-face sales organizations as the engine of revenue acquisition and firm value: at Groupon in 2012, over 45 percent of employees were in sales; at Google, it's over 50 percent; and at Facebook, the sales force's ability to translate "likes" into advertisers will make or break that company's valuation and fortunes going forward.

What is true is that buying is realigning sales tasks. An example is selling cars. Relatively few cars are actually bought online. But an estimated 90 percent of Americans research the purchase via Edmunds.com or TrueCar.com or other online sources before going to a dealer. According to AutoTrader Group, the average car shopper now spends more than 11 hours online researching cars and only 3.5 hours offline, including trips to dealerships.[19] As Ludwig Willisch, president of BMW North America, notes, "They visit dealerships less frequently when deciding which car to buy. So our salespeople have to be better at closing the sale on the spot—they usually have only one shot, and there's not really a warming-up period anymore."[20] Smartphones, online reviews, social media, blogs, apps that identify where a shopper is and send a text message about product, price, and outlets in the area—all these tools are increasing buying options. The net effect is "escaped customers" who can realign the activities outlined in figure 8-3 and not necessarily as the selling company's sales structure assumes. This change in buying affects relevant sales training, development, and the organization of go-to-market activities.

The technological options available to customers put more pressure on the reps' value added during the sales experience—how they make a difference. But the options also have a supply-side dimension, with training implications. The same technologies can improve lead generation and qualification (e.g., through search engine optimization, tailored online communities, and social media); determination of specifications, RFP preparation, and evaluations (e.g., through use of third-party websites, webinars, and online demos); and price negotiations and closing (e.g., online tracking systems and the smart use of big-data analytics). Salespeople must be trained in these capabilities. Equally important, sales and C-suite leaders should know how to use the capabilities to alter the business model, offload administrative tasks from salespeople, and thereby increase selling time.

In development, the need for cross-functional links (discussed in chapter 12) increases. Because customers can realign their buying activities, more groups in the selling organization now deal with customers through the buying cycle. At a minimum, these groups need a shared understanding of their firm's strategy, value proposition, sales tasks, and corresponding selling behaviors. The selling firm also needs to revisit and develop relevant performance metrics to deal with the next issue concerning organization.

The reality is that no matter how you organize sales, more firms today require a multichannel approach: online and face-to-face sales initiatives and both direct and indirect distribution channels. This is increasingly the norm. But perhaps because many managers are persuaded by over-hyped talk about disintermediation and a misunderstanding of how new technologies affect buying behavior, an effort to help salespeople deal with this added complexity is, in my experience, largely absent from sales training programs. Nor is such an effort supported by current sales performance metrics in many companies. For many firms, it's now less meaningful to track sales volume or market share, for example, than to track share of individual customer purchases in the category. Similarly, tracking the cost to serve different customer groups (discussed in chapter 10) becomes crucial in this environment.

Human Performance

Talk about hiring "the best" or knee-jerk reorganization decisions are too frequently the easy fix for more fundamental sales and strategy issues confronting firms. They're easy but, by themselves, typically not a fix. Even the best hiring, training, and organizing practices can't substitute for a flawed strategy, or frontline sales managers not committed to coaching and performance reviews, or a senior management team unwilling or unable to make changes in response to altered buying behavior. Companies must ultimately be worthy of real talent. And to benefit from talent, they must provide the right incentives and environment for people to flourish—the topics of the following chapters.

9

Control Systems

Sales Compensation and Incentives

Compensation is the most discussed aspect of sales. But most discussions are versions of compensation hydraulics that make Pavlovian assumptions: push this pay lever, and you'll get this kind of behavior. Answering the question "How should we pay the people responsible for dealing with customers?" implicates multiple aspects of your business model: goals, recruitment, training, the types of orders the firm gets, evaluations, and daily interactions between sales and others in and outside the firm. This chapter outlines a process for designing a sales compensation plan aligned with strategy. But it also discusses issues to address *before* you set specific numbers or debate different incentive plans:

- The roles and limits of compensation

- Links between compensation, motivation, and evaluation

- Conventional wisdom about sales compensation that merits constant reexamination

Roles and Limits of Compensation

By the twenty-first century, 85 percent of US companies used incentive plans, which, on average, accounted for about 40 percent of total sales compensation.[1] That's a lot of money and managerial effort. Yet, in a 2012 survey of seven hundred firms, a whopping 20 percent reported that their comp plans had "minimal or no impact on selling behavior," 12 percent said they "do not know," and only 8.9 percent said their pay policy "consistently drives precise selling behavior."[2] This finding is even more striking when you consider a common assumption about salespeople: "it's all about the money." But examine this assumption. Do we really believe that others are *not* motivated by money—unlike you? unlike me? Or that sales reps are somehow genetically distinctive in their responses to financial incentives and immune from other factors that affect behavior in organizations: priorities, processes, promotions, pride, professionalism, and so on?

Max Weber rightly ridiculed these assumptions a century ago. Weber noted that what needs explaining is not whether people like money—of course they do: "Light purse, heavy heart," as Ben Franklin said. As Weber put it, "The notion that our rationalistic and capitalistic age is characterized by a stronger economic interest than other periods is childish," Weber wrote, "[because] the impulse to acquisition, pursuit of gain, of money, of the greatest possible amount of money . . . exists and has existed among waiters, physicians, coachmen, artists, prostitutes, dishonest officials, soldiers, nobles, crusaders, gamblers, and beggars . . . It has been common to all sorts and conditions of men at all times and in all countries of the earth, wherever the objective possibility of it is or has been given."[3]

Money is powerful. Business history is full of firms that got what they paid for (e.g., reps who, responding to their volume-driven incentives, failed to execute a premium-priced strategy) and didn't get what they didn't pay for (individually focused incentives in a team selling approach). What's more, there's evidence that monetary incentives affect behavior *and* how people see aspects of reality. For example, a study of bank loan officers found that incentives can change the officers' perceptions of how a loan will perform. It wasn't simply that an origination bonus made the banker more likely to approve the loan; the bonus made him or her truly *believe* that the loan was lower risk and merited approval.[4] The researchers might have noted the wisdom in language: "credit" is from the Latin *creditus*, or "belief." Money talks.

But that talk is part of a wider dialogue among people, their peers, the organization, and the market. Appropriate compensation is a necessary but not sufficient cause of desired behaviors, especially in sales, where there are rejections, social influences from customers and colleagues, and other elements of the boundary role discussed in chapter 6. That's why recognition ceremonies, "100 percent Clubs," the trip to Hawaii, pink Cadillacs, and all the other panoply of sales meetings are so prevalent. Moreover, a sales force is a heterogeneous group of people, who respond differently to the same incentives. This heterogeneity was also demonstrated in the bank loan study: while the overall effect of the incentives was to change the loan officers' perceptions of risk, the effect varied by age (older officers were less responsive to incentives), by organizational unit (public-sector bankers were less responsive than private bankers), and by gender (women were more likely than men to make lenient lending decisions when origination bonuses applied. Tell the truth: not what you expected? Then stop the stereotypes!).

The purpose of any sales comp plan is to motivate the sales force to achieve the firm's goals. Hence, compensation is always part of motivation and ongoing management practices. These factors—money, motivation, management—affect each other and execution. They should be linked in a strategically effective pay plan. Money counts, but you can't substitute money for management.

Compensation, Evaluation, and Motivation

Motivation is core to management. Getting other people to do the right kind of work is at the heart of most managerial responsibilities. In sales, motivation involves multiple factors. Figure 9-1 depicts the factors as links in a chain in order to illustrate connections that might otherwise be ignored.[5]

One big factor affecting motivation is how you manage the choices outlined in chapter 8 concerning hiring, development, and organization. These choices affect not only the personal characteristics of the sales force, including their knowledge, skills, and attitude, but also the territory and account characteristics of the customers they deal with. In turn, market characteristics define the opportunities available to the sales rep and thus the level of potential earnings. In most businesses, some territories and accounts have a higher close rate, independent of the salesperson assigned to that territory or account. The relationship between market characteristics and sales possibilities lends itself well to territory-design models that are a useful input to quota setting and comp design.

FIGURE 9-1

Links between compensation, evaluation, and motivation

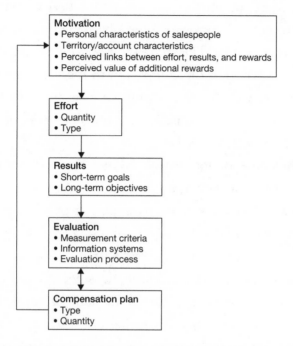

Source: Adapted from Frank V. Cespedes, *Concurrent Marketing* (Boston: Harvard Business School Press, 1995), 218–222.

The salesperson's perception of the connections between effort, results, and rewards is also a factor. Working harder may not mean better results because of product, pricing, or the competitive situation. Or more effort may generate more sales, but the firm's measurement or comp systems may not recognize or reward incremental results. Conversely, the perceived value of additional rewards affects motivation. The comp plan may indeed link effort, results, and rewards, but salespeople may see the required effort as disproportionately high relative to the additional rewards received. Many sales incentive systems, for example, pay for volume increases over the previous year's results. The intent is to motivate salespeople to develop new business, increase share of wallet, or cross-sell a new product. But the effort to do this is often seen as not worth it by reps with a base of mature but steady accounts. They are essentially managing current customers as annuities. The strategy-in-relation-to-sales issue is whether to redesign the comp plan to increase the value of additional rewards *or* to redeploy the sales force so that new business has its own focus. It's a management decision—not just a compensation decision.

An outcome of motivation is the amount and type of effort. Call frequency, the number of accounts in the pipeline, and orders booked are examples of effort quantity. In pharmaceuticals, call frequency on doctors correlated with sales results, so pharma reps had to make daily call quotas to make bonus. As managed-care firms became more prominent in purchasing, they reduced the number of relevant call points. In this situation, comp design needs to change, or you're paying for motion not results. Type of effort refers to factors like account development versus maintenance, effort on new versus current products, or an emphasis on selling products that generate volume and utilization versus products with higher margins but lower unit sales. Comp plans influence both the quantity and the type of sales effort.

Effort leads to results when goals are clear and aligned with evaluation criteria. What goals should guide efforts toward desired results? Important choices are discussed later in this chapter. Once established, results must be measured, raising issues about appropriate measurement criteria, the information available, and the performance evaluation process—topics discussed in the next chapter.

Finally, you must indeed consider the mechanics—both the type and the quantity—of the comp plan. Here, *type* refers to the relative emphasis on base salary or incentive pay, and how to adjust the mix when market conditions and sales tasks change. *Quantity* refers to the total compensation relative to target labor-pool norms, and how the firm allocates that total among selling activities.

There are always links (intended or unintended) between compensation, evaluation, and motivation. In turn, *how* you pay will affect the kind of person attracted to your sales force. Figure 9-1 provides this advice: start with the engine (the efforts and behaviors you want from salespeople), and *then* design the transmission (the specific pay plan aimed at encouraging those efforts).

Rethinking Conventional Wisdom about Compensation

When you view compensation in this manner, it leads you to reconsider conventional wisdom about sales compensation. Let's consider three common assertions that, in my experience, are often false.

"Comp Plans Must Be Simple"

The fear is that "complex" plans can cause salespeople to spend too much time calculating payoffs instead of selling and taking care of customers. Conventional wisdom is that "a good compensation plan is simple and predictable . . . A well-designed plan fits on a card small enough to be carried around in the salesperson's wallet."[6] Maybe not. Many sales situations involve complex bundles of activities: group sales efforts, product plus service offerings, multibusiness participation on solutions sales, and so on. Given the multichannel selling requirements discussed in chapter 8, this complexity is increasing. You can pretend the complexity isn't there, but it is.

Behind the simplicity assertion is an implicit view of salespeople: they may not be bright enough to understand a comp plan that's bigger than a business card. But this claim is contradicted (often by the same person making the assertion) by fears that a complex plan will drive gaming behavior by salespeople who maximize income with minimal effort. Will reps game the system, *any* system: complex or simple? Yes. But then the issue is crafting a win-win plan, not fear of taxing their brains. In a strategically effective plan, the company wins when the salesperson wins a bonus. Consider sales comp plans at firms like IBM, Oracle, and others that have strategies with complex sales tasks. The plans are many pages long, with multiple permutations and complex payout schemes. That complexity reflects selling realities. I have yet to meet the sales force that, in the aggregate, does not understand within a week the implications for (in the phrase used at IBM) "hitting big casino" and maximizing income. Available data across firms indicates *no difference* in the percentage of reps who meet and beat quota under more or less complex comp plans.[7] As one CEO says, "Salespeople become experts in their sales plan, regardless of its simplicity or complexity, and you can count on unintended consequences." Why? If a policy determines how you will eat, you will study it in detail. As for predictability: it's the market that ultimately determines predictability or volatility, not your comp plan.

The simplicity assumption reflects another issue: "what gets measured gets managed." People tend to produce the performance measured and often ignore other important tasks. In fact, many CEOs, when they advocate simple sales comp plans, are reflecting their experience with boards, executive compensation consultants, and Sarbanes-Oxley-Dodd-Frank regulations. Jeff Ubben, an activist investor, has served on many boards. He notes that, often overwhelmed by conflicting requirements and eager to keep the CEO's pay out of the papers, "boards become servants to formulas and solve for the dollar amount to be delivered, losing focus on desired outcomes and the design of incentives."[8] Too bad for the conceptually challenged board of directors, but that's no reason to inflict this oversimplification on your sales force.

"We Pay for Results, Not Process"

Here, the reasoning is that because sales tasks are contingent on specific customers and market conditions, the field rep will always know more about ground truth than anyone at headquarters. As managers, we should therefore ignore process (because we're not sure what the best process is) and simply reward results: pay (or don't pay) for actual outcomes, not the process in the sales sausage factory. But the process for administering compensation is always at least as important in effecting desirable behavior as the level of pay. For one thing, a pay process reflects strategic choices and management norms—explicit or implicit. At many companies, for example, salespeople receive big bonuses for results. But the process for providing the bonus is at odds with the firm's formal performance evaluation of that person. That is, the basis of the bonus (e.g., orders booked by an individual rep) often contradicts what the company, its espoused strategy, and sales managers *say* they want in performance-evaluation sessions (e.g., cross-referrals, joint presentations, or other aspects of team selling). The result is de-motivation or, worse, motivation toward the wrong type of sales effort.

Like other people, salespeople want both to maximize rewards *and* to know why they succeeded or failed in achieving a goal. In fact, they want to use that information to make more money next week, next quarter, next year. The process for discussing these questions—a process based on objective data or subjective conjectures—affects future behavior. Research shows that a perceived fair process increases acceptance of and compliance with decisions, even if people don't agree with the decision. When the process violates procedural fairness, it can undermine core purposes of compensation: to reward, retain, and motivate appropriate behavior.[9] We may "pay for results, not process," but if we ignore process in a sales environment, we often don't get what we've already paid for.

"Money Is the Only Motivator"

The assertion here is that, yes, we may talk nice, but at the end of the day, it is (as Fagin in the musical *Oliver* puts it) "money in the bank, that's what counts / money in the bank, in large amounts." But people are, alas, not just rote profit-maximizing agents. Behavioral economics shows this again and again in aspects of consumer behavior and risk perceptions. Do people suddenly become different people when they join a sales force? Anyone who has managed in a market with hierarchical cultural traditions knows the value that salespeople and others put on titles, relative rank, and other nonmonetary impacts on behavior. Recognition ceremonies reflect this human need.

In most organizations, it's common to display reps' sales numbers publicly—on a chart in the branch office or the spreadsheet sent to the sales force monthly or quarterly. Why? Because people are social creatures concerned with their standing and how they perform relative to others. Studies demonstrate what managers learn. After a firm informed its workers how they ranked on pay and performance, their average productivity increased by nearly 7 percent and the effect showed no signs of abating over time.[10] In other words, providing feedback about relative performance is not a Hawthorne effect. Or, as I've heard more than one salesperson say, "we work for money, but strive for recognition."

Developing a Sales Compensation Plan

Like it or not, there's more to human behavior than money. But the comp plan is always a determinant of behavior. Developing a strategically effective plan requires answering five questions: What are the important sales tasks? What must the salesperson do to succeed? What is the labor-pool frame of reference? What should the salary-incentive mix be? How should the incentive be designed?

What Are the Important Sales Tasks?

As with other factors involved in aligning strategy and sales, the starting point for comp design is identifying the core sales tasks that you want to emphasize, reward, and monitor. What tasks involved in selling drive our strategy and results? In selling to retail trade customers, for example, there is a range of tasks that can usually be divided into three categories:

1. *Volume-Influencing Activities:* selling new items; getting more shelf space for established items; selling or managing point-of-sale materials or in-store displays or co-op advertising; negotiating and managing trade promotions

2. *In-Store Service Activities:* shelf audits; handling damaged merchandise; ensuring product freshness; pricing adjustments or corrections; handling queries from store managers

3. *Supply-Chain Management Activities:* sales forecasting by account; establishing and managing delivery schedules; coordination with product, manufacturing, and logistics groups at the seller's company or wholesalers; ad hoc management of deliveries

A comp plan should set priorities among these tasks. In turn, your strategic choices determine the priorities. Companies that use service merchandisers in their go-to-market efforts have less need to focus on in-store service tasks in their sales comp plans; companies that manage retail shipments on an automated replenishment basis have less need to focus on supply-chain tasks in sales comp plans because these tasks are largely handled in areas external to the sales force, such as IT.

Similarly, in B2B enterprises, comp plans affect which portion of selling is attention to delivery, price negotiations, building distributor relationships, presale applications support, postsale service, cold calling, or selling more to current accounts. The relative importance of these tasks typically changes over the course of a product-market life cycle. Early in the cycle, customer education and applications development are often key sales tasks. But as the market develops and standards emerge, salespeople spend more time selling against functionally equivalent brands or developing third-party relationships. Comp plans should keep pace with these task changes, or strategy execution falters.

It's not the responsibility of customers to inform you when these changes occur. It's the seller's responsibility to track and adapt to external changes. One reason for disconnects between comp plans and salesperson behavior is that, in many firms, the people designing pay plans do so according to an obsolete vision of sales tasks. There is no substitute for ongoing field interaction, including actual sales calls. It's a necessary complement to aggregate data about markets and comparable pay levels.

What Must the Salesperson Do to Succeed?

If wining, dining, and attending trade shows or conferences are important, the plan's treatment of expenses should not discourage salespeople from developing the contacts and relationships. If, in a multichannel world, working with intermediaries is important, then the plan should provide incentives to work with influential resellers through cross-referrals, training, or joint sales calls. If it doesn't, then salespeople often sell *against* the firm's intermediaries or colleagues and both parties lose the sale, with consequent acrimony between the groups.

This approach may mean doubling commissions. Many managers resist this method of compensation and use moralistic language about "it's their job and they should do it."

But this is ultimately a math issue, not an issue of character development. Consider team selling, where sharing sales credit is always contentious. In many situations, a firm can give full credit to those involved and still not pay twice for the same sale. The keys are understanding the sales tasks and having information systems capable of tracking performance so that shared sales results can be taken into account when a firm is setting goals. Here's an example:[11] two reps last year sold $500,000 each to individual accounts and $500,000 to shared accounts. Their combined sales thus amounted to $1.5 million. Two approaches to sales credit are possible:

- Set targets and bonuses so that each rep receives $25,000 for $750,000 in sales, with shared-account sales credit split fifty-fifty. If each rep sells $500,000 individually and $500,000 to shared accounts, each makes the $750,000 target and gets a bonus. Payout cost to company at target is $50,000.

- Pay a $25,000 bonus for $1 million in sales with all shared-account volume double-counted and fully credited to both reps. Each rep must then rely on team effort for about 50 percent of target sales, but each also receives full credit for team sales. Payout cost to company at target is $50,000.

A rep in the first plan may reason that an incremental $250,000 in individual sales (developed by spending less time on the more complicated joint sales effort) is an easier way to reach the $750,000 target. That rep would then focus on individually assigned accounts, encourage his or her "colleague" to keep working hard on the team accounts, and hope to get some of the half-credit team sales with little or no effort.

Coordination and shared account penetration are likely to suffer. In the second plan, there is at least no incentive barrier to expending effort on the team sales, and the firm's payout is the same. The choice depends on the firm's strategy and the relative importance of team-selling tasks in that strategy.

Salespeople cannot control many elements that affect sales success (e.g., macroeconomic conditions, a customer's financial problems, competition). But the comp plan can encourage attention to these factors by rewarding accurate forecasting or market intelligence. For example, in most firms the annual operating plan is launched from a sales forecast. Yet in many comp plans, salespeople have an incentive to forecast low so they can earn more and look like star performers. But this is not a fact of life; it's not inevitable that tying bonuses to forecasts means "paying people to lie."[12] For years, IBM and others have used pay plans that motivate salespeople to forecast more accurately. Having forecast sales in their territory or account, the rep receives increasing compensation as he or she sells more. But the numbers are set so that while there is no cap on sales levels and commissions (message: continue selling as much as possible), the largest interim payout occurs where actual sales match the salesperson's forecast, and lower forecast sales receive lower payouts (message: don't cap your earnings for next year by lowballing your forecast).

As these examples illustrate, the comp plan should focus on factors that salespeople *can* control. If not, links between motivation, effort, results, and compensation are broken. Be clear and up-to-date about how, fundamentally, the salesperson makes a difference with customers. That difference is what the comp plan should reinforce and support.

What Is the Labor Pool Frame of Reference?

A firm with uncompetitive pay levels will eventually lose its best people and fuel what one sales manager calls "the finishing school syndrome": "At my previous company, we hired new people, trained them, gave them experience selling in this industry, and then, like me, they moved to better-paying jobs at competitors." Information about comparative pay levels in an industry is typically available through public sources as well as trade associations, recruiters, and outside hires.[13] Different sources often provide different numbers because each source defines and aggregates its categories differently. But that should spur thinking about the sales activities that are and aren't relevant for *your* strategy at *your* sales force.

Another issue is the salesperson's influence on the buying decision and the abilities required to exert that influence. When selling requires technical skills, firms must often recruit people who have opportunities in different industries and in areas besides sales. This affects pay levels independent of competitors' wage rates. What economists call *transaction-specific assets*—expertise and relationships built over time by the people selling a product—also affect compensation. The costs of replacing effective reps can be significant and—whether you like it or not—the comp plan must consider replacement costs. Ask, "Who owns the customer: the company or the salesperson?" Sometimes the rep does.

For example, a good private banker needs an array of skills: knowledge of multiple bank products and the ability to develop relationships, referrals, and support from others across the bank. And personalized service is the heart of the client value proposition, since any one bank's products are easily imitated by competitors. Thus, personal trust, a compatible personality, and other elements of good chemistry drive the relationship. This combination of skills does not grow on trees or in MBA programs, narrowing the relevant labor pool. It's highly dependent on accumulated transaction-specific expertise with the company and the client. Over time, many clients see themselves as doing business with the private banker, not the bank, and will transfer assets if that banker moves to another bank. As a result, in the 1990s and until the recession, private bankers' compensation increased at rates two to three times that of most other bank personnel. These pay decisions were about the value of the relevant assets and the salesperson's replacement costs.

What Should the Salary-Incentive Mix Be?

Most sales forces receive both salary and incentive pay. Several factors make a higher salary component attractive: when there is inherent difficulty or administrative complexity in measuring a salesperson's performance in a reasonable period; the need for salespeople to coordinate efforts; the complexity and length of the selling cycle; the importance of service activities; the amount of missionary selling involved; and the volatility of market demand.[14] These factors tend to make salary a bigger component of total comp. But a firm can have a highly leveraged plan (i.e., high commission or variable bonus) and still sell complex products in markets where service activities and long-term relationships are important—*if* other aspects of the sales system support the required tasks. Many manufacturers' rep firms do this very successfully on commission.

Decisions about the salary-incentive mix also affect sales culture and the level of influence on salespeople the firm seeks. This choice has been examined in studies about "outcome-based" versus "behavior-based" controls.[15] There is less managerial direction with outcome-based controls; the emphasis is on variable pay triggered by desired outcomes without much attention to how (within legal and ethical boundaries) the outcome is achieved. Salespeople in outcome-based pay plans bear bigger risks and have more autonomy to adapt to differences in the customer base. Managers in outcome-based plans are typically few and often expected to generate their own sales.

In highly leveraged outcome-based plans, reps are essentially entrepreneurs or franchisees. In contrast, behavior-based control means more managerial oversight, monitoring, and intervention about selling tactics. Because the majority of total comp is fixed salary, the variable component is often tied to what salespeople *do* (number of calls, expense management, and so on) as well as outcomes. When such supervision is both possible and determinative of outcomes ("we *know* the following steps increase the likelihood of sales success"), then there's less reason for customer-specific learning, adaptation, and variable pay.

Real estate and financial brokerages have long emphasized the outcome components. They also have high turnover rates, and salespeople often take "their" customers with them. You can argue that such firms' comp plans encourage turnover, easy entry, and a winnowing process for identifying sales talent. And/or you can argue these firms are not good sales managers and know it. Other industries emphasize the salary and behavior components. Overall, the US average (according to annual surveys by Dartnell Corporation) tends to oscillate around a fifty-fifty salary-incentive split. A common rule of thumb voiced by sales managers is that, for a given incentive to be material in the eyes of salespeople, it should be at least 15 percent of total comp and, to affect behavior, at least 30 percent. One sales vice president puts it this way: if less than 10 percent of total comp is at risk, that's barely noticeable by most reps; at 10 to 25 percent, you get their attention; at 25 to 50 percent, it affects their behavior and management can control a few key things; and at more than 50 percent, management control over field behavior diminishes significantly, while salespeople operate according to "make quota or quit" criteria. But there's no definitive study that validates these informal guidelines.

What *is* clear, however, are the forces affecting salary-incentive mix decisions. On the one hand, either straight salary or straight volume-based commission plans are easier to administer. So they are often the default options for firms that lack the systems or managerial skills required for more complex plans. On the other hand, new technologies that help monitor sales activities affect the cost-effective balance available to you. For example, CRM systems that provide an accurate window into sales funnels and calling patterns also allow for more behavior-based control.

How Should the Incentive Be Designed?

Although their variations are legion, the major types of incentive compensation are few. *Bonuses* are lump sums paid for attaining specific objectives. They can be based on quantitative or qualitative objectives or administered at the discretion of a sales manager. *Commissions* are typically a percentage of sales volume or margins. Some firms apply a standard rate to all sales, while others vary the rate by product, customer, or other metric to reflect profitability or competitive goals. Sometimes commissions are only paid for sales above quota, or different rates apply at levels above and below quota. *Sales contests* are lump-sum payments for performance relative to goals or to other salespeople in attaining a specific near-term objective.

In any incentive, the devil is in the details. Paying when orders are booked instead of when shipped, for example, can make big differences in cash flow, production scheduling, and focus of selling efforts. The company context is crucial. But there are general principles to follow in designing incentives that align strategy and sales. They concern the purposes, timing, and measures used.

Sales incentives have three allied purposes:

1. *Communicate Management's Goals and Direct Sales Efforts toward the Most Strategically Attractive Opportunities:* Incentive plans are always important company communications about what's really important and are read that way.

2. *Increase the Return on Investment (ROI) in the Firm's Sales Capacity:* Sales incentives should increase effort, and should direct that effort toward areas where both the firm and the rep prosper when sales are closed.

3. *Motivate:* The incentive should be structured so that total comp reflects individual performance, and given the spread of performance in most sales forces (see chapter 8), the spread in incentive pay should be meaningful to have impact.

Whenever possible, the time frame for an incentive should be short enough to make an impact but long enough to make each payment significant. The principle here is that the incentive structure should make visible the cause-and-effect relationships between effort, results, and rewards. Think about why many firms publicly "ring the bell" when certain sales goals are made. Generally, linking incentives to effort and results means trying to design incentives so they mirror the typical selling cycle and do *not* unwittingly discourage sales effort. For example, many firms base incentives on achieving minimum thresholds of sales with certain products: unless reps reach sales of X with product Y, they're not eligible for incentive payouts tied to sales of other products or activities. The firm wants to focus efforts on particularly profitable or strategic products. But the all-or-nothing incentive can backfire: if it becomes clear that reps won't make the threshold within the incentive period, they are likely to "save" orders for the next period or, worse, drop effort on the target products—behaviors arguably tied to the timing and structure of the incentive.

Finally, base your incentives on measures that reflect important objectives. Sales volume is the most common metric used for incentives. But often, other measures more accurately reflect strategic choices and the underlying go-to-market economics of a business model. For example:

- *Product Mix:* The mix is important when the firm sells different items often used as a system.

- *Pricing:* Linking incentives and pricing is especially important when negotiations are a key sales task and the rep has discretion over discounts or price-exception requests.

- *Bad Debt or Returned Goods:* In many businesses (e.g., medical devices, service merchandisers, cable TV), these are big chunks of total selling expenses and profitability.

- *Type of Sale:* Outright sale versus rental or subscription has a big impact on cash flow, the nature of the installed base, and after-market revenues.

- *Training:* Training is important when user training is both a core sales task and a source of revenues and profits for the selling firm (e.g., corporate software, many professional services).

Clearly, no one type of incentive is optimal for all companies, all business units, or even all sales locations within a business. The right form depends upon your strategy and analysis of relevant sales tasks. Again, start with the engine (the desired efforts and behaviors), and then paint the chassis.

Effective Sales Compensation Plans

Sales compensation cannot be approached in isolation, because it affects many other dimensions of the business. Let's look at the characteristics of strategically effective comp plans (figure 9-2).

Focus (versus a "Little Bit of Everything" Allocation of Efforts and Incentives)

Too many plans succumb to the everything-is-important fallacy. In one case study I teach, top management outlines

FIGURE 9-2

Effective sales compensation systems

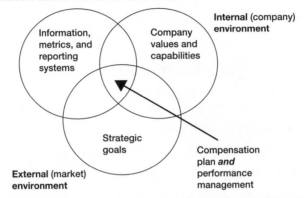

- Focus, build on current strategy, link to performance management
- Related to external and internal environments

the following objectives for its sales comp plan: obtain greater sales effort and control of selling behaviors; retain the best performers; develop cross-functional and team-selling capabilities; improve customer service; alter the sales mix among the firm's products; lower SG&A; minimize administrative "hassle"; generate more "accountability" in sales . . .[16] And the list goes on, stopping just short of solving world hunger, and this is not uncommon. But when everything is important, no one thing is truly important and efforts, rewards, and motivation suffer.[17] Strategy is choice.

Build on Current Strategy (versus a "Tweak-the-Previous-Year" Approach to Goal Setting)

Many comp plans align with the firm's previous year's results, not the market. The most common approach to setting quotas and goals is to tweak last year's targets. In other words, firms raise or lower quotas depending upon whether more or fewer reps made quota the previous year.[18] But selling is about today and tomorrow, not yesterday, and in the marketplace, not in-house comparables. Effective plans operationalize strategic choices by linking sales tasks, efforts, and the firm's IT and reporting systems.

Link to Performance Evaluation Processes (versus Confusing Pay with Performance Management)

Some firms try to substitute pay policies for management. But in the final analysis, an effective sales comp plan is what some call an *organizational hygiene factor*: necessary but insufficient by itself to motivate the behavior you want. A comp plan is part of, not a substitute for, ongoing performance management practices. You can't just manage by algorithm. People manage people.

No comp plan is likely to be effective, therefore, without attention to the topics in the next chapter: the role of sales managers in measuring effectiveness, giving performance feedback, and building field capabilities.

10

Sales Force Environment

Performance Reviews and Measuring Effectiveness

Performance reviews and the metrics used to evaluate performance are crucial alignment tools. They powerfully influence the sales environment in which strategy is or is not executed in the field. This chapter concerns the why and how of performance feedback and measuring sales effectiveness.

Performance Reviews

Performance reviews are among the most underutilized levers for influencing behavior in most organizations. HR executives repeatedly bemoan the managerial avoidance and cursory drive-by status of reviews in most firms. A typical result is that everyone is above average until budget constraints make cuts genuinely shocking to those let go. Here I want to focus on why performance conversations are necessary and yet hard to do, especially for many sales managers.

For the recipient, feedback has intrinsic and extrinsic value. Across fields, research shows that people become high performers by identifying specific areas where they need to improve and then practicing those skills with clear feedback on performance.[1] Numerous studies about how people learn and develop over time indicate the importance of on-the-job experience. One classic study found that work experience (job assignments, organizational relationships, and especially performance feedback) accounts for about 70 percent of the learning, versus about 15 percent each for formal training (e.g., exec-education courses) and life experience (hobbies, interests, family—the other things you do and love outside work).[2]

For the giver, feedback is key to getting people to practice the right things, stop bad habits, set priorities, and clarify accountabilities owned by the rep and not the manager or the firm. It's a key to effective leadership. Like the term *strategy*, *leadership* runs the risk of becoming a weasel word because it's used so promiscuously. But a tenet in virtually all definitions is that leaders manage group as well as individual performance. The higher you go in any organization, the more you depend on subordinates' performance. As the head of an IT firm says, "I'm betting my job on everyone who works for me."

Why, then, is conducting performance conversations so perennially hard to do, especially for many sales managers? There are systematic reasons. It's important to acknowledge them, or the next pep talk about "talent management" will do nothing after the applause dies down.

Conflict Avoidance and Wanting to Be Liked. Giving feedback can often mean confronting and managing conflict. Conversely, holding back can often mean cheating people out of a chance to learn and improve. But most sales managers approach performance reviews after years as salespeople, where their tasks involved avoiding conflicts with clients and eliding objections: "To win an argument is to lose a sale," as the old adage puts it. Indeed, research does indicate that salespeople generally have above-average affiliation needs, or, as Willy Loman told his sons, "The important thing is to be well-liked."[3]

Reluctance to Deliver "Bad News." A natural concern for hurting the recipient's self-esteem also inhibits effective reviews. Despite macho talk by management authors about separating the "eagles" from the "turkeys," there is an emotional paradox at the heart of good performance conversations. On the one hand, the giver of feedback must spend time and attention learning about subordinates' behaviors, temperaments, strengths, and weaknesses. On the other hand, in framing and delivering effective feedback, the giver must also stay detached from those inherently social interactions when he or she needs to make unpleasant but proper decisions. Many of us can't do this with our kids, and it's not much easier with workplace colleagues. But it's necessary.

Fear of Backlash, Resistance, or Disruption. Salespeople are famous for their independence. Many are "lone wolves" in biz-speak, or "counterdependent" (resistant to authority) in social-science lingo. Such people are not shy about challenging bad news about their performance. Sales managers know this, and many avoid it. Fears of selling disruption also inhibit reviews, especially when the choice is putting up with suboptimal performance or recruiting someone else and incurring the costs and risks of ramp-up time and transferring established client relationships while still needing to make territory quota. As a result, managers and customers (recall chapter 7) have a status-quo bias.

The Need to Keep Emotions in Check and in Balance. Most impactful conversations about performance (for reasons discussed shortly) are not about stars or clear nonperformers. They're with people in the middle of a bell curve, where incremental additions to productivity will, in the aggregate, make the biggest impact on overall group performance. But it's precisely in this area where emotional balance—for the giver and the receiver of feedback—is most fraught and necessary. Tone and body language in reviews count for as much as the numerical evaluation or overt message. Carl Bass, the CEO of Autodesk, describes the balance required of a manager in a performance conversation: "You're the one who's driving the bus, and if you're erratic while you're driving, everyone gets pretty nauseous." Especially in sales, it's important to project optimism about productive change even when pointing out flaws and weaknesses. Unless it's a firing discussion, you will still work with that person after the review. Hence, motivation is part of a performance conversation, and as the saying goes, motivation, like bathing, doesn't last that long, so that's why you should do it daily.[4]

Rationalization. How often do your managers say, "Yes, these conversations are important, but I'm too busy right now"? Delivering feedback effectively *does* take time. But invoking time constraints is ultimately a way of saying that performance reviews are not a priority, and that's a mistake.

Lack of Process. Finally, many sales managers lack a template for preparing and delivering feedback. In their gut, most managers understand that whatever makes a performance conversation hard to do is precisely why they need to do it. But without a process, all of the time and emotional energy invested in reviews can unintentionally de-motivate high performers, fail to motivate weaker performers, and send mixed signals to the entire sales force.

Giving Effective Performance Feedback

The aim of reviews is increased competence and commitment: to ensure that strategic goals and choices are understood *and* embodied in sales activities and the allocation of resources such as money, time and attention, call patterns, and reps' discretionary efforts. A prerequisite is identifying people who perform and people whose performance you invest in. It's common to say, "We invest in everyone." But it's not true. Few managers, especially in firms with flattening hierarchies and wider spans of control, truly invest equally in all of their direct reports. Most manage by exception. They deal with problems or opportunities as they arise and find ways of differentially allocating their time and attention. The issue is not whether managers do this; the issue is whether they do it effectively.

As discussed in chapter 7, a sales force is composed of people with different temperaments, capabilities, and learning styles. Some people improve when made aware of better approaches, others through modeling behavior when they watch stars perform the relevant tasks, and others learn best via specific assignments. To be effective, a manager must adapt feedback to the individual. Further, as discussed in chapter 8, the performance variance of individuals in sales tends to be greater than in other functions. The same is true about the impact of coaching *on* individuals. Matthew Dixon and Brent Adamson summarize the findings of research in this area: "When you improve coaching quality, the performance curve doesn't shift, it *tips*. The middle moves, but the feet don't."[5] In other words, overall performance improves but in a segmented manner. Coaching appears to have little impact on either weak or star performers. Why? The stars are already high performers, and, absent market or strategy changes requiring changes in sales tasks, coaching is mainly about marginal improvements or maintaining motivation. Weak performers who stay weak despite coaching do so in large part because they are simply a poor fit for that sales job. You hire your problems, and it's no coincidence that conducting reviews often makes new managers more rigorous and selective in hiring. The real impact of coaching is on the median group, where data indicates a performance boost of nearly 20 percent due to effective feedback.

It's with those people that sales managers ultimately get paid to manage and, therefore, where performance feedback needs to be concentrated, customized, and actionable. This has implications for what managers must do before, during, and after the review.

Before the Review

Sales managers must first make clear the standards, including the ethical standards, by which performance will be judged: what's important and how much you expect. This step may seem obvious, but it's often not done, and the reasons are various. Some new managers are unsure or uninformed about how sales goals align with strategy; other, more experienced managers may have lost touch with market or strategy changes. Additionally, over time, managerial turnover can generate mixed signals to reps about performance behaviors. A classic case study concerns a salesperson named Bob Marsh in a company disguised as Cabot Pharmaceuticals.[6] The case tracks Marsh's career from his hire through his dealings with various sales managers to his firing after twelve years and the aftermath of customer complaints. Discussion of this case always generates intense responses from executives, who never fail to diagnose (in *another firm*!) the impact of inconsistent performance reviews on Marsh's devolution from good hire to median performer who manages his accounts passively in the face of opaque standards. The best comment I've heard was from an executive who described Cabot's performance evaluation process as "a genius of inadequacy": conducted annually but, because of unclear standards, with negative impact on behavior and motivation.

Second, performance reviews are about what salespeople do for a living, their relationship to both sides of the boundary role discussed in chapter 6, and often their pay and job assignments. These important topics take time to discuss. Managers must make time on their and their reps' calendars to avoid "quickie" reviews that leave people feeling confused or unvalued. Managers must also take the time to pay attention to those reps' behaviors far in advance of a formal review date if they're going to be helpful and specific about the impact of selling behaviors. The need for ongoing attention and feedback underscores the importance of ongoing feedback via ride-alongs, debriefs, win-loss analyses, and other activities discussed in chapter 8.

Third, effective reviews also require judgments about the root causes of performance. For example, is poor performance the consequence of deficiencies in motivation or ability? Some reps may work hard, but lack certain capabilities: can training or coaching enhance their capabilities? Others may have relevant abilities but lack motivation: can different incentives or programs increase motivation? Others may seemingly lack both motivation and relevant ability: is this the right sales job for that person? Can their abilities be better utilized in a different role? Or is it time to replace this person? Finally, stars often have both high motivation and ability: what can be done to reward, retain, and learn from their behaviors? These are not easy judgments to make about human beings. But they're necessary and imply different action plans. Without them, it's difficult to be mutually productive during the review.

During the Review

Figure 10-1 outlines five steps for guiding a sales performance conversation.[7]

1. *Convey Your Positive Intent:* A performance review is about feedback aimed at augmenting the strengths of that person to increase his or her effectiveness.
   If you in fact don't really have this intent—if you believe that issues of motivation and/or ability overwhelm the potential contribution—then it's not a performance conversation and you can ignore the following steps, because the conversation is different: it's about moving that person out of that job.

FIGURE 10-1

Giving effective feedback: during the review

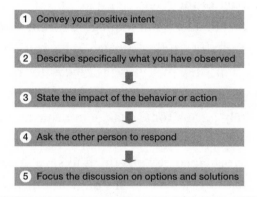

1. Convey your positive intent
2. Describe specifically what you have observed
3. State the impact of the behavior or action
4. Ask the other person to respond
5. Focus the discussion on options and solutions

2. *Describe Specifically What You Have Observed:* The more specific and descriptive your feedback about strengths and weaknesses, the more likely the other person will understand. Describe illustrative or critical incidents that indicate the impact on performance. Too much feedback in organizations is of the broad "do good and avoid evil" variety. That may sound harmless, but overly general feedback actually increases feelings of defensiveness, rather than openness to behavior change, because it involves such broad judgments. For example, saying, "Your pitch was terrible" is little more than a perception and invites counter-punching rather than open discussion. Saying, "It didn't include information on demographics, total life cycle costs, and payment terms" makes it easier to "hear" negative comments and take corrective action. But specificity requires that you take the time to observe and record throughout the year, not just the week or two before the review.

3. *State the Impact of the Behavior or Action:* Few people *want* to underachieve, but many are often unaware of the impact of their actions on outcomes. That's why we have managers. But managing means discussing cause-and-effect links between behaviors and outcomes. This step in reviews is crucial for both the rep *and* the manager. For the rep, improving performance ultimately means some change in behavior. So the manager should focus on specific behaviors, actions, and performance. It's one thing to say, "You didn't connect with the buyer." It's quite another to say, "You interrupted people throughout the meeting, and therefore, that buyer was less open to listening to your ideas." Also, few people change their core personality after a review. So focus on the impact of behaviors within a rep's control. In sales, feedback about personality rarely adds much value and can deter improvement. For the manager, a focus on behavior also helps to minimize a common cloning bias: is there really a problem with that rep's performance, or is the performance achieved using a style that the particular manager would not use to do the job? Always be clear about the difference.

4. *Ask the Other Person to Respond:* Effective reviews tend to be two-way transfers of information, not only directions from the manager. As discussed in chapter 9, most salespeople want to know about the impact of their behaviors on performance, if only to use that information to make more money. But the Rashomon effect is alive and well in sales. Two people can observe the same event or outcome yet interpret it differently.

Two-way dialogue is important, therefore, not just because it's polite, but also because it tests assumptions and reasoning about customers: "Does my view of your interactions with that account make sense?" "Here is the data I'm using to make this assessment: what am I missing—is it an issue of resources or something else?" "Here are the priorities inherent in the account plan and our strategy: do you understand, and do you agree? If not, why not?" Dialogue also opens other relevant purposes of a review: the possibility that the manager's behaviors, policies, or style may be part of the performance problem and opportunity.

5. *Focus the Discussion on Options and Solutions:* "So, now what?" Reviews are about today and tomorrow in the marketplace, not yesterday in the office or training seminar. A review is incomplete without a discussion of next steps in which both parties—rep and manager—take appropriate responsibility for possible change options. And responsibility for this closure rests with the manager. On what assets can you and the rep capitalize to increase effectiveness? Are there assignments that can increase learning, deliberate practice, or other elements relevant to those sales tasks? Can HR help? What timetable and benchmarks will we use to measure progress after the review?

After the Review

As with training, the greatest impact from performance conversations is what happens after the review. Too often, nothing happens: the review is an isolated annual event and therefore has little real impact beyond the size-of-bonus discussion. But behavioral change requires setting goals and then providing ongoing feedback about progress toward goals. Here's a non-sales example with relevance to sales performance. Lose It! is a weight-loss app and website that allows users to pick a desired weight and timeline with a daily calorie count. Lose It! then lets users track their eating and physical activity by holding up their phones to a food package's barcode or by tapping the screen at the start and finish of activities, including a walk, exercise, and even sex. The app provides ongoing feedback about daily progress toward the goal (the impact of dessert, for example, versus a walk or run) and a chat room for discussion with others. The result is an estimated ten million users whose average weight loss is twelve pounds, an amount doctors consider a major health benefit for most people.[8] Lose It! illustrates the basics of effective performance follow-up in many activities: feasible goals, regular and relevant feedback, and reinforcement from and relative to peers. In sales, effective follow-up typically requires making connections between the performance review and the following:

1. *Link to Account Planning:* In theory, a core vehicle for follow-up in most sales organizations is the account planning process. In practice, however, account plans in many organizations are WORN documents: Write Once, Read Never.[9] Follow-up means linking discussed behaviors to account management goals and activities. At HubSpot, for example, performance reviews indicated to Mark Roberge that customer retention rates varied by rep, not customer segment.

So Roberge linked follow-up to account plans and compensation: commissions were paid via metrics tied to account retention and peer performance quartiles. Churn decreased 60 percent in six months.

2. *Put Follow-up on the Schedule:* Technology is lowering the costs of doing this. For example, studies of programs designed to increase people's savings find that follow-up text messages, simply informing people of their savings rates versus their goals, are about 80 percent as effective as in-person meetings.[10] Other studies, in areas from health care and voting to energy usage and drinking habits, find that text-messaging reminders affect behavior and improve performance.[11] Managers can use this technology, in addition to meetings and ride-alongs, to provide regular feedback, while tapping an important motivational force in sales: peer pressure and comparisons. The key is making follow-up an iterative process from which individual reps and the firm derive value.

3. *Look for Patterns:* Regular follow-up also provides the opportunity to look for patterns and create a virtuous cycle of assessment and investment by potentially reallocating money, time, and people to align better with strategic imperatives. Carrier IQ sells to telecom providers of cell phones, tablets, and other mobile devices. Its products tell the wireless operator about signal strength, any problems with battery life or streaming data, and other issues that enable the operator to improve service and fix a problem faster. It's a complex technical sale with fifty-plus steps and traditionally a 24- to 30-month selling cycle. Jeff Althaus, vice

president of sales at Carrier IQ, detected the following pattern that emerged from reviews: it was taking 9 to 12 months to complete the trial or proof-of-concept portion of the selling task—a cash drain for a venture-capital-funded start-up. He also saw commonalities in the evaluations customers wanted in trials. So, Carrier IQ developed a platform with an online trial system that took customers through the process with the assistance of the firm's professional services and hosting operations group, *not* salespeople. The result has been to reduce the selling cycle to 12 or 14 months and make better use of limited sales resources.

Measuring Effectiveness

A performance review ultimately relies upon the metrics used to evaluate and reward performance. Most firms focus on sales volume. But aligning strategy and sales requires more granular measures of effectiveness, for a variety of reasons. First, revenues are often disconnected from economic profit and the cost of capital. Earnings per share (EPS) and sales growth are the two most common measures used by companies for communicating externally, especially with security analysts. But do those metrics actually measure shareholder value? Not necessarily. As Michael Mauboussin and others point out, EPS growth is good for firms that earn high returns on invested capital, neutral for a firm with returns equal to its cost of capital, and bad for firms with returns below their cost of capital. Sales growth, as discussed in chapter 4, has a similar, contingent connection to enterprise value.[12]

Second, it's important to distinguish between efficiency (doing things right) and effectiveness (doing the right things) in measuring sales activities. Depending upon the strategy, some sales forces require efficiency (usually, cost-efficiency) measures, while others require effectiveness metrics. But the most commonly used aggregate metric for evaluating a sales force is the sales expense-to-revenue ratio. This ratio can shed light on the relative cost efficiency of selling activities, but not (by itself) on their cost effectiveness, which is a more complex relationship between selling costs, revenues, sales margins, and customers acquired through one or another means of organizing the sales effort.[13]

Third, performance metrics should change as the market or strategy changes so that, in their reviews, managers are coaching and motivating the right things for today and tomorrow, not yesterday. When commercial airplanes went from piston to jet engines, the relevant unit of evaluation changed from cost per hour of flight to cost per passenger-mile, in turn changing the economic analysis of routes, competition, pricing and selling of airline services. But many airlines stuck to the cost-per-hour metric and declined.[14] Similarly, many executives resist abandoning existing sales metrics even as technology and other factors change the underlying performance drivers in the business.

Measuring sales effectiveness usually depends upon more than just sales revenue. Big-data analytics make more granular metrics accessible. But the average US company with more than a thousand employees already has *more* data in its CRM system than in the entire Library of Congress.[15] The role of data is not to make a manager sound analytical. In business, it's more important to be contextually right than it is to be school-smart. Its role is to help you make better decisions, and you won't separate signal from noise unless you know where to look. So, for purposes of aligning strategy and sales, the following sections describe places not to overlook in measuring selling activities and conducting performance conversations.

Price versus Cost to Serve

Back to basics: profit is the difference between the price a customer pays the seller and the seller's actual cost to serve that customer. The costs of serving customers can vary dramatically for the seller. Some customers require more sales calls, or geography makes them more or less expensive to serve; some buy in a few, large, production-efficient order quantities, while others may buy more in overall volume but with many just-in-time orders that affect setup time, delivery logistics, and other elements of cost to serve. Customers also differ in their product customization and postsale service requirements. Table 10-1 outlines factors that correlate with high- versus low-cost-to-serve customers.

These differences are important if you, or your investors, take seriously the notion of economic profit, because many capital costs are embedded in cost-to-serve differences. If the differences are ignored in the measurement of sales effectiveness, there are consequences for account management and competitive strategy. Why? If you can't measure your cost to serve, then you usually face several challenges. Your salespeople will be driven by competing pricing proposals. And when you chase volume, you can wind up damaging profits and your business system. You won't allocate available sales resources optimally. Finally—and perhaps most damaging—you are ultimately at the mercy of competitors

TABLE 10-1

Characteristics of high- and low-cost-to-serve customers

High-cost-to-serve customers	Low-cost-to-serve customers
Order custom products in small quantities with variable-order arrivals	Order standard products in big quantities with predictable patterns
Significant presales support in the form of marketing, production, technical, or sales resources	Little or no presales support: generally standard pricing and order terms
Significant postsales support in the form of installation, training, warranty, or field service resources	Little or no postsales support: self-service accounts or standard postsales terms and conditions
Require seller to hold inventory and/or will usually pay slowly: accounts-receivable and other working-capital requirements	Replenish as produced, and pay on time: cash-flow benefits

Source: Adapted from Robert S. Kaplan and Robin Cooper, Cost & Effect: Using Integrated Cost Systems to Drive Profitability and Performance (Boston: Harvard Business School Press, 1998).

who can measure their true costs and do these things more effectively.

An example is Fortis (disguised name), a seller of strapping equipment, tools, and consumables to manufacturing operations globally. Fortis was for years a market leader, selling a bundled solution of equipment and strapping with pre-sale applications support and postsale technical service. But Fortis lost share and profits as accounts increasingly unbundled the product-service package after their initial purchase. Meanwhile, Fortis's sales force continued to be evaluated, and compensated, according to sales volume. Fortis eventually conducted a study, charting the net price paid by each account (after discounts or price exceptions) versus the cost to serve that account (including sales expense, and pre- and postsale application and engineering costs attributed to that customer). The result is figure 10-2.

Pricing is a market test of strategic choices and sales efforts. In any business, we would expect some variability

FIGURE 10-2

Analysis of price paid and cost to serve by account

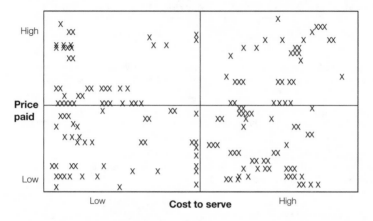

Source: Rowland T. Moriarty Jr., David May, and Gordon Swartz, "Fortis Industries, Inc. (A)," Case 9-511-079 (Harvard Business Publishing, 2010).

between price paid and cost to serve. But figure 10-2 is basically a random-walk result and, according to much research, not atypical.[16] Chart these variables—price paid and cost to serve by account—in your firm, and see what you find. If the result is like Fortis, notice the implications. Customers in the upper-right and lower-left quadrants are paying more or less, depending upon their cost to serve for the seller. But customers in the lower-right quadrant are negative economic-profit customers, and selling to them is not sustainable (even if, as at Fortis, they generate commissions for salespeople). Finally, customers in the upper-left quadrant are profitable but vulnerable because they are in effect subsidizing other customers in the portfolio. Sooner or later, a competitor, a supply-chain consultant, or their own finance people will alert those buyers to the reality and cost-savings opportunity.

What can a firm do in this situation? These differences are often only revealed and dealt with at the account level and via conversations with those account managers. Effective reviews can look at options ranging from pricing changes to reflect cost to serve, reducing or eliminating technical support, changing the locus of relevant support (as Carrier IQ did), different ordering and delivery options, and perhaps a channel strategy that offloads some parts of cost to serve to resellers whose economies of scope allow them to perform certain tasks more efficiently. Aligning strategy and sales also means sometimes "firing" customers that, despite all attempts by the seller, remain unprofitable accounts.

Cash Flows and Selling Cycle

Cash flow is always important for start-ups and LBOs. It's increasingly important for others in an environment where capital markets and banks are less liberal lenders after the financial crisis. Cash flows are closely correlated with the length of the selling cycle. Yet, salespeople can be dogged optimists in their call patterns, often assuming that "there must be a pony in there somewhere." Conversely, many customers in their official procurement processes are set up to evaluate, not necessarily to buy.

Consider the experience of Skyhook, which sells innovative software using Wi-Fi to determine a user's location.[17] Customers include manufacturers of phones, laptops, and other mobile devices. Skyhook had over sixty meetings with Nokia, yet no sale. At Nokia, there were groups for individual product lines, other groups responsible for core technology decisions, application services groups, a headquarters group for location services, *and* a recent $8 billion acquisition called Navteq, which provided location data. At other potential customers, such as Qualcomm, technical and engineering groups required elaborate field trials but had little incentive to adopt a new platform technology. Conversely, mainly because of the interest of then-CEO Steve Jobs in adding location capabilities to the iPhone while finding a credible counterparty to Google, it took just a few calls on Apple to reach an agreement.

It's not the responsibility of the customer to inform sellers that they are barking up the wrong tree. It's sales management's responsibility to make that judgment and react accordingly. Studies show how targeting sales efforts can affect profitability and cash flows, especially when the seller deals with customers across diverse sectors of the economy.[18] The selling cycle and level of customer access required also typically vary by the nature of the sales opportunity: new buy, rebuy, cross-sell, and so on. In practice, managing these differences is an account review issue and then a sales deployment decision.

Information about buying patterns and whether reps have access to the relevant decision makers is best gathered in performance reviews because this information is inherently account-specific. In turn, access is an important metric because it affects cash flows and the selling cycle. It should be an input into sales organization and where reps devote their efforts. For many B2B firms, it can mean shifting the selling emphasis from big accounts (high potential volume but also longer selling cycles) to small and medium-sized businesses where individual volume is less but access to decision makers is greater. For other companies, access can mean better concentration and leveraging of available sales resources. Selling into ethnic markets in the United States is an example. Nearly 40 percent of Asian Americans reside in the Los Angeles, San Francisco, New York, and Chicago areas: if you're a supplier of food or other products to this group, why invest direct selling resources nationally when four metro areas offer this kind of opportunity? Similarly, hospitalization rates for different types of diseases differ markedly by geography, with implications for the best use of selling resources at many medical-device and other health-care suppliers.

Duality of Sales Tasks

Markets are messy. Recall the distinction between transaction and relationship buyers and the implications (see chapter 6): managing customers is a choice but not simply a binary, yes-or-no decision; it requires understanding the differences and then directing selling behaviors and resources appropriately.

In many emerging markets, manufacturers that sell to retail channels must deal with both types of accounts. There are traditional indigenous retailers: an array of shops, kiosks, street vendors, and small proprietors who offer their neighborhood customers a bit of everything from groceries to electronics. And there are modern retail giants— multinationals like Carrefour, Tesco, or Wal-Mart and country-specific retail leaders like CR Vanguard in China, Grupo Pao de Acucar in Brazil, or Migros in Turkey. In this situation, a one-size-fits-all approach to measuring sales effectiveness makes little sense. Effective selling requires segmented performance reviews and metrics that deal with the differences.

Big chains in these markets typically command high slotting allowances and are more disciplined than mom-and-pop proprietors in tracking stock turns and discontinuing slower-moving items. They care a lot about merchandising, displays, automated-replenishment delivery processes, and reps' abilities to manage these tasks. The point-of-sale systems of these chains provide data for crafting sales promotions through a variety of media. Migros is a leader in using its loyalty card to target and align promotions across suppliers by store. By contrast, sales data from traditional stores in emerging markets are often either unavailable or unreliable. A key sales task is estimating an outlet's potential sales and inventory requirements by criteria such as store size, proximity to workplaces or schools, or other local characteristics. Smaller retailers in these countries often value free equipment or flashy outside signage that helps them stand out in a physically crowded market. Some sellers have found that paying a proprietor's electricity bills, or offering to paint the store annually, is more effective than traditional promotions. Performance reviews and metrics must focus reps on these different tasks, often within the same sales office.

Team Selling

For many firms, selling is not only an individual's task. It involves a team that must coordinate efforts across product lines (often made and sold by different divisions) to multilocation accounts that require an integrated approach. Global customers and key accounts are common examples. The selling cycle can be long, and sales depend on the selling firm's ability to marshal its resources effectively across a range of external buying influences and internal organizational boundaries. Coordination in these situations affects SG&A, pricing, the ability to retain and develop business, and sales force morale.

Some firms react to the more protracted and complicated nature of shared-account sales by relaxing or even ignoring measures. That's a mistake.[19] It's *because* these sales demand sustained attention and coordination that measures are important. Without them, the pull in most organizations is toward the shorter-term accounts. In turn, team-selling metrics affect compensation and performance reviews.

If multiple salespeople call on accounts and teamwork is important, then a bonus based on total account sales, margins, or profitability often makes more sense than individual incentives. And both qualitative and quantitative measures may figure in performance evaluations. At some investment banks and IT service providers that face this situation, evaluating individuals at bonus time includes input from account colleagues. Account executives and product specialists may evaluate each other on criteria such as the other's contribution in selling, service, or account management efforts. As one HR manager notes, simply knowing that these surveys are an input to measuring effectiveness and performance reviews often keeps salespeople sensitive to the coordination requirements of their jobs and keeps sales managers aware of potential problems and opportunities.

Selling through Distribution Channels

In supplier-reseller relationships, both have something the other wants and values; that's why exchange takes place. Both presumably want to maximize profitable sales of the supplier's products or services. On the other hand, channel relations involve each party in an implicit or explicit struggle to retain a larger share of the pie and control over the product or service. Also, the goals and operating procedures of

producer and reseller are often very different, leading to conflicts in implementing sales tasks. Because there are mutual
interests and inherent conflicts, the rhythm of these relationships is analogous to an ongoing tug-of-war with implications for measuring effectiveness.[20] If you sell through
third-party channels, answering the following questions can
help you craft the relevant metrics:

- What is the role of intermediaries in your strategy and
  sales efforts? Is it cost efficiency—the reseller does
  certain tasks more efficiently? Or do intermediaries
  supplement scarce resources in areas like warehousing
  or after-sale service? Clarifying the intermediaries' role
  makes a practical difference in areas ranging from the
  size of distributor discounts to the tasks performed by
  your salespeople with intermediaries.

- What level of quality control is required for those
  channel functions? Too often, sales managers speak of
  distribution as a homogeneous category. But distribution can refer to activities ranging from product customization for specific customers, demand generation,
  physical distribution, after-sale service, to absorption
  of credit risks and so on. Different channel functions
  will require different levels of quality control by your
  salespeople. Metrics, and channel terms and conditions, should recognize these differences.

- What options are available for shifting a function to
  a different point in the channel? A purpose of performance reviews and metrics is to analyze patterns and
  improve sales productivity. As products mature or as a
  technology establishes standards, for example, postsale

service, which initially required specially trained personnel by the supplier, can often be performed more efficiently and just as effectively by third-party service firms. As B2B customers gain more familiarity with a product category, they often develop in-house personnel capable of performing functions previously handled by the manufacturer or distributor.

The Necessity of Managers

Beyond these specifics, performance reviews and metrics also involve crucial intangibles for sales managers. These leaders must establish the foundational conditions: dialogue and ongoing communication. They must demonstrate that they care for their people and their people's true best interests and are therefore worthy of trust in assessing performance, conducting reviews, and applying relevant measures of effectiveness. Sales managers must also stand and deliver: make the decisions that are theirs to make. The best firms proactively involve at least two other functions in aiding sales managers' performance evaluation and feedback skills.

One function is human resources. HR managers can, as one group of researchers puts it, "create a line of sight between strategy, culture, and individual behavior" and, in so doing, have more business impact than any other set of HR activities measured.[21] To do this, however, HR managers must have a working knowledge of their firm's strategy and sales tasks. Conversely, sales managers must be able and willing to partner with HR in core people activities such as structuring performance reviews.

The other group is finance. Establishing relevant metrics takes data, analysis, and ongoing interpretation informed by field realities. Finance should be a forward-looking partner with sales, not only an after-the-fact scorekeeper. But this partnership may require a change in how sales thinks about finance and how finance thinks about itself. As others note, many CFOs focus internally, with too little time spent on understanding their firm's customers and sales activities.[22] A good counterexample is eBay, where a two-year program rotates finance hires across divisions to expand their professional networks across the company, and then includes sales and shipping activities as part of their finance responsibilities. Dinesh Lathi spent years in finance at eBay, where he says he learned to be "relentlessly customer-focused."[23]

The good news is that everything discussed in this chapter is *within* a manager's and company's circle of influence, not in the less controllable external environment. But exercising that influence requires managers who can translate strategic choices into locally relevant selling behaviors, work with others in their firm, and provide effective reviews. This raises issues at the fulcrum of strategy execution that are discussed in the final section of this book: the transition from salesperson to sales manager, making connections across the organization, and managing the cycle of strategy and sales performance.

Part Four

CLOSING

From too much business they didn't close.

**—A waiter at Ratner's Restaurant in New York City, explaining
why a competing restaurant had gone out of business (quoted in
Jeffrey Steingarten, *The Man Who Ate Everything*)**

Chapter 11
Company Environment:
Building Human and Organizational Capabilities

This chapter focuses on a key fulcrum and perennial sore point in many firms: developing sales managers who can translate strategic choices into performance behaviors and thus manage as well as sell. If you're a current or an aspiring sales leader, the chapter provides career advice and a way of assessing whom you select for sales management roles. And if you're in human resources, it can help you to forge better links with the management teams in sales.

Chapter 12
Making Connections

The final chapter examines the coordination between sales and other functions that's required for sales success. It provides some practical ways of improving team effectiveness in your organization. I also conclude with summary advice to sales leaders about improving sales productivity, and to strategists about how and why that improvement is fundamental to financial outcomes and overall enterprise value in a company.

11

Company Environment

Building Human and
Organizational Capabilities

"Culture eats strategy for breakfast" is an assertion made by many executives, because it points to realities in implementation. Consider the first situation in figure 11-1: a firm with a great strategy that it cannot implement well. If a tree falls in the forest and no one was there to hear it, was there a sound? That question has vexed great thinkers. But in business, which is a performance art, the answer is clear: there was no sound and the business is a failure—or, in street-smart parlance, nothing happens until you make a sale. By contrast, consider a firm with an average strategy—a coherent alignment of objective, scope, and advantage but not a strategy likely to be featured in *Harvard Business Review* or TED conferences—*and* an organization that can execute well. That's success.

But companies don't execute strategy; people do. Any culture is heavily determined by how managers shape the organizational environment via hiring, selection criteria, performance

FIGURE 11-1

Importance of implementation

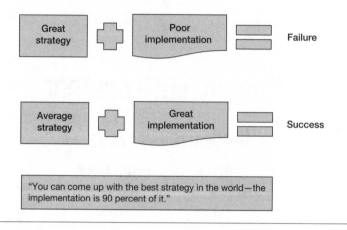

"You can come up with the best strategy in the world—the implementation is 90 percent of it."

expectations over time, and development. That's true in sales and other parts of a company. So this chapter looks at issues and options involved in selecting and developing sales managers who can translate strategic choices into relevant sales tasks and the performance behaviors discussed in part III. Then, because a coherent strategy requires aligning activities across the firm (as discussed in part II), chapter 12 looks at types of coordination important for effective selling and implementation: coordinating interactions between sales and marketing as well as finance, service, and other areas that affect product, pricing, and other elements of selling success.

Selecting Sales Managers

Frontline sales managers hire reps and influence their training; they organize and allocate sales efforts and incentives across market possibilities; they conduct (we hope!) performance reviews, and so reinforce good or bad behaviors. And when other functions or the C-suite need something from sales, it's sales management they contact. In most firms, sales managers *are* the means by which the core levers for aligning strategy and sales—people, control systems, and sales force environment—are utilized.

This crucial role gets mixed reviews. On the one hand, studies find that, in the short term, excellent reps with an average manager outsell average salespeople with an excellent manager. But over time, people working for an average manager tend to decline in performance.[1] Why? Many of the best reps eventually get promoted, retire, or otherwise leave, and the average manager is likely to replace them with average salespeople. As the saying goes in talent management, "First class hires first class, and second class hires third class." In addition, an excellent rep is excellent *within* his or her territory or accounts, while a manager has, for good or ill, more influence across multiple areas and customers.

On the other hand, decades of research indicate that—across functions, including sales—first-line management is the level from which come the most reports of incompetence, burnout, and excessive turnover.[2] Moving from doer to manager is difficult in any circumstances. You move from being selected—typically for outstanding performance in the doer role—to being the new person, at the low rung of the management hierarchy, who does not know the ropes. This transition even has a piquant social-science label: *heap reversal theory*.[3] As noted in chapter 10, moreover, sales managers must do this while learning about their people, judging diverse strengths and weaknesses, interacting with others in the organization, performing administrative tasks, *and* making the numbers.

Nearly every firm has examples of successful salespeople who are disasters as managers because they persist in their behaviors as reps rather than managers. You can't just excel at sales to be a good sales manager. Yet, that's precisely how most companies select new frontline managers.[4] For this reason, some consultants believe the answer to better sales and execution is to change these selection criteria: "This approach to hiring is the root cause of many organizations' high manager failure rates."[5] But choosing salespeople as sales managers is not silly or a willful disregard by operating executives of what is "obvious" to bright consultants. It reflects organizational and human realities in implementation.

One fundamental responsibility of sales managers is to provide opportunity by allocating clients or territory assignments and establishing quotas. This allocation affects what salespeople *do* daily in their jobs, their performance benchmarks, and their compensation—that is, how they are *evaluated* and how well they *eat*. Organizationally, this responsibility is best accomplished by people who already know the relevant selling activities. Humanly, it's even more difficult to develop the credibility required for candid performance reviews, necessary customer reallocations, compensation decisions, and other vital matters if the new manager has not demonstrated selling excellence. The novels of Joseph Conrad, the trial-by-fire memoirs of leaders across fields, conversations in hallways during sales meetings, and studies of managers all testify to the ubiquity of testing new people in these roles—as in other situations where some people must make tough decisions about others.[6] One new sales manager speaks for most in recounting a conversation he overheard between two reps who reported to him: "They had checked up on me [and] found I had only been a big producer, not a super producer. They couldn't be sure if my decisions were really backed by experience . . . They were actually questioning my qualifications."[7]

Selecting salespeople to be sales managers is not stupid. It's *how* the selection is made and what happens before and after the promotion that determines effectiveness. Managing the transition to becoming a manager is a joint responsibility of the individual and the organization.

Becoming a Manager

Sales manager is not just a bigger sales job. For one thing, it occurs at a pivotal point in a career. It represents both a reward for past performance and a bet on a person's potential talent contribution to the managerial hierarchy (and there's always a hierarchy, despite casual clothes, pizza, bicycles hanging from the ceiling, and the other now-standard accoutrements of millennial cool). This transition is not unique to sales. Many people across functions never adjust successfully to the change from individual doer to agenda-setter with administrative responsibilities. Years ago, John Miner devised a series of tests to measure "motivation to manage." A key part is a "sense of responsibility in carrying out the numerous routine duties associated with managerial work." Miner explained this component:

> The managerial job requires getting the work out and keeping on top of routine demands. The things that have to be done must actually be done. They range from constructing budget estimates to working on committees . . . to filling out employee rating forms and

salary-change recommendations. There are administrative requirements of this kind in all managerial work . . .
To meet these requirements a manager must at least be willing to face this type of routine.[8]

In other words, the test of a vocation is love of its drudgery. But consider again how, for years before becoming managers, most salespeople actively (and, often, correctly) resist internal "bureaucratic" activities in order to focus on external client requirements.

Also, the manager's role is to keep the sales funnel productive and make trade-offs for the business in doing so. A sales manager is an agent of firm strategy as well as coach, evaluator, and administrator. A common complaint from executives about sales managers is the latter's inability to embrace this role and "own the business," not only customer relationships. Keith Block ran Oracle's North American sales organization and sat on the firm's executive committee. He's adamant about sales managers dedicated to the firm's strategy: "I don't want sales managers. I want sales executives. I want people who don't think just about sales. [They] have one eye on a sales number [and] another eye on serving a market, making customers successful, and representing the company."[9] Helmut Wilke worked for Sun Microsystems and Microsoft. He emphasizes that "the best sales managers think like 'company guys' not like 'sales guys.' A good salesperson closes a deal, makes a commission, and moves on to the next deal. A good manager, on the other hand, sees the bigger picture and can judge the best way to use resources."[10] The litany goes on. So why so difficult?

Linda Hill studied transitions from salesperson to sales manager. Rich in human reality, Hill's study is about more than sales while providing practical advice about hiring or being a sales manager. She found that new managers had to *unlearn* attitudes and habits they developed when responsible only for their own performance. Conversely, they had to learn how to examine issues in more holistic ways; discover and use new measures of success; and—last but not least—draw on different sources of personal motivation and satisfaction. Becoming a manager means "evolving an entirely new professional identity" and involves three kinds of learning: learning new tasks, changing one's mind, and changing oneself. Hill points out that companies and business schools devote most attention to the task-learning aspect. But most new managers in her study were "*more* surprised and unnerved by the unexpected necessity of developing new attitudes, mind-sets and values (i.e., the personal learning involved in changing one's mind or oneself) consistent with their new positions." That is, they gradually came to realize that behaviors that were assets in selling roles (e.g., hands-on approach to client relationships) became liabilities in management roles where things get done through others—some of whom report to the manager (the reps) and others who do not (marketing, finance, and other functions). The managers who survived eventually learned the truths voiced by Block, Wilke, and others. Comp plans rewarded these managers "for making quota and customer satisfaction." But in performance reviews, new managers initially reported that their bosses devoted "disproportionate" time to issues other than quotas: what the managers were doing to implement company strategy, their future plans for their unit, people development, and how they were getting along with others in the organization.[11]

Like others, Hill found that sales managers largely learn from experience. But people don't always learn from experience, and it's no coincidence that on-the-job learning is called the "school of hard knocks."[12] Hence, a task facing companies is how best to capitalize on and accelerate on-the-job learning. The first step is to acknowledge, explicitly, the need and expectation to do this. Then, a company requires a shared language of development in sales (and other areas). That common language helps leaders to clarify performance expectations and it helps individuals to understand what's expected of them and so play a more proactive role in their own development; it helps the company to provide meaningful development support (versus after-the-fact evaluations); and it helps individuals to identify the required transitions and take responsibility for conceptual, behavioral, and personal change.

Developing Sales Managers

There are many models of career development. But once we get beyond the snack-crackle-pop level of "dress for success" or "be your personal best," most career models are psychological in emphasis. They focus on individual motives (e.g., achievement and affiliation) and/or quasi-spiritual dimensions of life. Like many people, I resent those who try to impose their political, religious, or lifestyle preferences on others in the workplace (even if they own or run the company), and I do not equate work with life: there are other places beyond the office where I and many others go for spiritual sustenance and fulfillment. Hence, I've found that the model that communicates and helps best with busy folks in organizations focuses on how people behaviorally solve the practical problems of developing and increasing their professional contributions over time—what they *do* to increase their ability to transition and grow as managers, and so handle responsibilities of greater scale and scope.

Often called a Four Stages model, it's based on research originally done by Gene Dalton and Paul Thompson.[13] Starting in the 1970s, they looked at knowledge worker productivity and asked, Why are some professionals highly valued past their technical prime while others aren't making the transition? They found no silver bullet or one set of traits that reliably predicted career success. Instead, they identified a more interesting pattern: high performers who *stayed* high performers moved through stages, delivering increased contribution to the organization as they progressed through each stage of their careers. To do this, the high performers had to assimilate behaviors that previously made them successful *and* pick up new skills and perspectives needed for performance at the next stage. Dalton and Thompson's model is best described by the core contributions at each stage:

1. Helping and learning

2. Contributing independently

3. Contributing through others

4. Shaping organizational direction

Among its virtues, the model maps nicely onto the individual-contributor-to-manager transition that characterizes many in sales, and it highlights the necessary coordination requirements as sales managers take on more responsibility and higher goals in a company.

Stage 1: Helping and Learning

Whenever someone joins an organization, he or she must learn the ropes and, equally important, demonstrate relevant competencies and a willingness to learn in *that* organization. She must learn which activities are truly critical and prioritized, no matter what the job description may say. He must learn how to get things done using both the formal channels outlined on the org chart and the informal channels that characterize "how we do things around here." Finally, she and he must do this while working under supervision that is both guidance and evaluation of his or her competence and potential. People at this stage learn and demonstrate the following behaviors, among other tasks:

- Willingly accept supervision of a more senior professional in the field, while exercising "directed" creativity and initiative (e.g., sell in the way that best fits your personality, while adhering to the firm's value proposition, scope choices, and call assignments)

- Often work on a portion of a larger project or activity, and demonstrate facility and ability to do the detailed or routine work on time, on task, and on target (e.g., make your portion of territory quota or do your part of a team account assignment, and file your call reports or CRM information in a timely, accurate, and informative manner)

- Perform well under time and budget pressures, and actively learn how "we" do things

Stage 1 could be called an apprenticeship, but as Dalton and Thompson pointed out, many people stay there for their careers. This is a model of professional development, not job titles. How many people reporting to you require hands-on supervision even after years in the same role? It doesn't matter whether those people are called reps or vice presidents; they are in stage 1. As the aphorism has it, "Some people have twenty years of experience, while others have one year of experience twenty times." Behaviorally, new hires must adjust to the role, and, again, it doesn't matter how long they may have worked successfully in other places. What matters is contribution *here*—in our market, customer, and organizational context—not there. As chapter 8 explained, much performance stems from firm-specific qualities and resources. Hence, a new hire's responsibility is to learn, actively and practically, what's required and feasible in the current organization while building trust with people whose resources affect his or her performance. At the same time, new hires must show the kinds of initiative that lead to the opportunity to do more—and more independent—work, or they can stay in stage 1 indefinitely.

One purpose of a shared language of development is to communicate joint responsibilities early and consistently. In stage 1, it's the individual's responsibility to accept supervision, demonstrate initiative, learn the organization, and perform the core tasks. It's the organization's responsibility to make these expectations clear at the outset.

Stage 2: Contributing Independently

Those who make the transition to stage 2 do so by developing a track record and reputation as someone who can work without detailed supervision and produce significant results. Often, that track record is based on depth in a certain area—whether it's a geographical market, vertical sector, type of product or application, or something else. It's often by focusing that, in sales as in other professional work, we show capacity to generate results and increase our visibility in the organization. In effect, a stage 2 individual is establishing and behaviorally fulfilling a professional identity. Stage 2 is, by far, the most populous stage in most firms, with 40 to 50 percent of employees there. People at this stage take on the following responsibilities, among others:

- Assume responsibility and accountability for definable projects from start to finish (e.g., build the business in a new market or account, work well with those who don't report to you but whom you need to do the assignment, and demonstrate personal ownership for results even when those outcomes are affected by other things besides your own efforts)

- Manage more of their time and job responsibilities on their own, because they demonstrate resourcefulness in solving problems or overcoming obstacles and so implicitly or explicitly renegotiate their supervisory relationship by identifying ways to improve performance

- Are known and knowing in their workplace: develop credibility with peers, in large part because of their reputation for accomplishment and reliability in their area of responsibility

Technical competence is the necessary condition and coin of the realm in stage 2. The stage 1 person is learning his or her craft. Stage 2 contributors are expected to know and perform at a level of proficiency consistent with widening responsibilities. The analyst must be able to analyze it, and the sales person must be able to sell it—profitably, consistently, appropriately. In any organization, moreover, expertise is bestowed as well as acquired. Success in stage 2 means not just being competent, but also being recognized as such. Reputation matters. It's how individuals attract opportunity and position themselves as candidates for more responsibility. For this reason, relationships with peers, supervisors, and others within the team and function become more important at this stage.

It's from the ranks of successful stage 2 performers that sales managers are typically chosen. So note the issues at this stage. Many salespeople are inclined to remain in stage 2: they are valued and often highly compensated. But their contribution is ultimately limited by what they can personally accomplish. In effect, their performance extends "as far as their arms can reach." To remain highly valued, they must also remain at the top of their game in terms of competence, as the technology, market, or customer's buying behavior, and therefore important sales tasks, change. If not, they cannot expect to continue to progress. A shared framework for development can help to establish relevant expectations and responsibilities: it's the individual's responsibility to recognize the benefits, risks, and requirements of remaining in stage 2, and it's the organization's responsibility to clarify those expectations and provide the relevant support—more technical or sales-skill support if he is going to stay there; increased management training or mentoring if she is going to be a candidate for sales manager.

Stage 3: Contributing through Others

So far in our pilgrim's progress, the focus has been on individual competence and performance. In this respect, our heroine, despite her ability to sell and contribute to the opera (perhaps even as a star), has sung an aria whose basic lyrics are "me-me-me-me." But the only way to perform beyond the limits of individual contribution is to leverage the contributions of others. That's precisely what good managers do. They support and influence others to adopt relevant courses of action, or align multiple efforts, without themselves needing to "be there"—to open the client door, get access to decision makers, close the sale. Their own experience and credibility as reps enable them to understand and communicate key sales tasks. Further, they now have enough self-confidence that they are not threatened by the success and delegated decisions of subordinates, while accepting responsibility for group performance in relation to wider enterprise goals. Here are some of the tasks and behaviors that stage 3 people accomplish and demonstrate:

- Broaden themselves in breadth and organizational knowledge; stage 3 people may not remain state-of-the-art in their technical or selling expertise, but compensate by learning how to make the right connections between technical specialties (in a word, act as integrators)

- Develop a wider business perspective, and help others understand the bigger-picture context, needs, interdependencies with other groups, strategic choices, and requirements

- Increase the performance of others as a manager,
  mentor, idea/best-practice leader, *and* represent their
  unit to others on important issues

Effective stage 3 professionals in all functions, but especially sales, must soon learn and demonstrate their abilities in two crucial sets of activities. To broaden perspective, they must understand the interdependencies that condition their unit's performance. In turn, they proactively develop networks beyond their own function so that they can access the resources and cooperation of other units that are required for their group's effectiveness. It's at this stage, for instance, that sales and marketing coordination is typically a vital part of a sales manager's de facto responsibilities.

Second, as Linda Hill's study documents, a key shift in moving from stage 2 to 3 is the nature of personal development. Stage 2 individuals had to learn to develop and take care of themselves. But stage 3 managers must learn to take care of others and assume responsibility for collective behaviors. They spend much time developing their subordinates, not because the managers are natural coaches or nice people. They do this because it's a business necessity: the only way to keep increasing performance at this stage is to find and develop more people to whom the manager can offload responsibilities. That, in turn, enables managers to move on to additional opportunities and increase their contribution and impact. In other words, you do it because it's good for *you*, and them, and the company.

But note the tension here: you invest in me, and I become a valued subordinate and then I move on, leaving you to fill the gap by finding others. Faced with this dynamic, many managers become talent hoarders, not talent developers, because they don't want to lose good people. However, many of the best salespeople in any organization are ambitious and, blocked, will leave for more responsibility, status, or money. This is a big problem in many firms and contributes to unwanted turnover. Again, a shared development language can help by spelling out the joint responsibilities and expectations to the reps early in their career and doing the same for managers throughout their performance reviews by higher-ups in the firm. A good manager over time tends to be a "leader feeder," attracting high-potential talent *because* of a reputation for developing people rather than hindering their progression into new roles.

Stage 4: Shaping Organizational Direction

Going from stage 2 to 3 is about moving beyond the performance limitations of individual contribution. Most sales managers—*if* they are managers—should be at stage 3, and they can have successful careers without moving beyond this stage. But contribution at stage 3 is also limited by whom managers know and can influence directly in performing current activities. In effect, stage 3 managers are optimizing the cards they have been dealt. Stage 4 is about helping to reshape the deck and the continued relevance of the cards by finding ways to influence those that you don't know and may never interact with on a direct or personal basis. Hence, stage 4 is described as "shaping organizational direction." What does it take to influence the direction of an organization? At a minimum, it requires comfort with power and influence and with the needs and perspectives of powerful, influential people in the organization beyond your function. And that requires an informed point of view about the changing needs of the wider organization. People at this stage are responsible for the following tasks, among others:

- Represent the function to key external groups—across the firm and external to the firm—on important strategic issues

- Improve organizational performance and capability through changes in work systems, processes, practices, or direction

- Make the tough decisions and exercise power for the wider benefit of the organization

Successful stage 3 professionals are students of their functional area and its environs. Strong stage 4 people are students of their industry and its changing customer and competitive environment. In sales, stage 4 managers have a fact-based point of view about objectives, scope, advantage, and how the organization is or isn't dealing optimally with each component. Further, they don't just diagnose problems but also have feasible options for *doing* things about them. As one senior sales executive put it, "I'm not the smartest person in this company. But I have a clear perspective on the relationship between our assets and opportunities, and how to close the gap. My job is to ensure that our firm is utterly realistic about any difference between where we are and where we want to go in the external market, and the required changes to get there."

In any organization, the use of power is an important element of change. Stage 4 individuals know how to get organizational power beyond their scope of responsibilities—not only by means of formal authority, but usually and more importantly by making connections and clarifying the cross-functional rules of engagement (discussed in the next chapter).

They also know how to exercise power and balance long- versus short-term objectives in doing so. They understand that power is a depreciating asset that must be used sparingly but decisively when enterprise benefits are at stake. They also understand that part of power is being a role model in how to build the relevant constituencies, make informed arguments for the benefit of the enterprise, and develop a reputation as a straight shooter and not only an adept bargainer for your group's needs. Stage 4 individuals also broaden their role in development. They take an active interest in succession planning, especially their own successors. Why? Because it's from these ranks that firms find future C-suite executives.

A Shared Language of Development: Implications

Table 11-1 outlines the progression inherent in the four stages. The model highlights the differing roles, role adjustments, organizational relationships, and contributions

TABLE 11-1

Stage growth, in brief

	Stage 1	Stage 2	Stage 3	Stage 4
Role	Helper and learner	Independent contributor	Contribute through others	Shape organizational direction
Organizational relationship	Apprentice	Colleague and specialist	Manager and team leader	Sponsor and strategist
Role adjustments	Dependence	Independence	Assuming responsibility for others	Exercising power
Performance contribution	On-time and on-task support to others	Technical expertise	Relationships and best-practices leader	Development and change management

that enable high performers to stay high performers as they move from being individual contributors to effective managers.

In their research, Dalton and Thompson looked at what factors highly correlate with stage development. The usual suspects were noticeably absent. Whether individuals continue to grow and contribute over time seems to have little to do with what school they attended, their area of specialization, their length of service, or the type of academic degree. Dalton and Thompson found little connection, for instance, between an MBA and continued high performance over time. (Thesis supervisor to researchers: "Reexamine that data with *more* variables!") Rather, because adult learning is primarily experiential, the key factors are how people are managed in the early stages, their assignments, and the opportunities they are (or are not) given to develop. Qualities such as intelligence, curiosity, contacts, ambition, and interpersonal skills undoubtedly help. But the organizational factors are the primary drivers enabling some people to move through the transitions. This finding has actionable implications for developing sales managers.

Implications for Training and Development

The first task of training is to build relevant competence. Chapter 8 explained the guiding principles of training for salespeople: customize training to your firm's goals and sales tasks, use action-learning initiatives that provide repeated opportunities for practice, and follow up on both training and performance outcomes. For reps considered potential managers, the next task is to think stage-ahead, preparing the individual for the next stage of responsibility.

While training for reps focuses on what *we* do in *our* firm to execute *our* strategy, stage-ahead means more outside-in development for those with managerial ambitions. A stage-ahead approach can help to address a recurrent issue in many sales organizations, which spend lots of money and time on management training but often with little to show for it. One reason is that they lavish this time and money on the wrong people, depressing the potential ROI. It's current and future managers, not great reps who will stay reps, who especially need to be exposed to fresh facts and new ideas (from within and outside your organization). It's managers who are in a position to refine and leverage new concepts and tools that improve sales effectiveness and help to set a continuous improvement standard in your organization.

Implications for Job Design and Staffing

Every job, including selling and sales management jobs, has implicit required behaviors. But too often, the pivotal behaviors remain implicit. Indeed, in most firms, the rules of success have all the transparency of oatmeal. The experience of most people is that after being hired, the organization is basically saying to them, "*You* figure out what those broad statements in the job description actually mean for behaviors in your job." Some new hires do, and many don't. A shared language of performance encourages these behaviors to become explicit. It also allows reps and managers to acknowledge and deal with human realities: individuals make transitions at different rates. As the role evolves, managers and reps can renew and revise their agreement about expectations and assignments because, with a shared language, both understand what each needs to do differently to sustain and build performance at the next stage.

In turn, a shared language of development has implications for staffing assignments. Take, for example, the increasingly common requirement for team selling to multilocation or global accounts. One issue, as chapter 9 discussed, is compensation incentives. Another, as noted in chapter 10, is the metrics used to measure effectiveness in these situations. But often the most important factor driving effectiveness is *who* staffs the account team. Most companies adopt this rule: big account = big sales (or sales potential) = most successful rep in each region working with the most successful reps in the other regions. But those reps are often great stage 2 individual contributors with less-than-adequate tolerance or skills for team tasks. The result? Big account = individual misaligned efforts = time spent constantly relearning and reexplaining what "colleagues" in each region did (or, worse, squabbling over sales credit), *not* time and effort spent on external account management. It's those making the transition to stage 3 who are best in team selling situations. They are the people to whom the internal networking comes most naturally and for whom the broader organizational knowledge is most beneficial for future growth as a manager. A shared framework of development helps managers to make these staffing assignments, and it helps the people tapped for such assignments to understand the required behaviors and implications for career progression.

Implications for Performance Reviews

Chapter 10 discussed the role of performance feedback in the sales force environment. The Four Stages model, if it's a shared language, helps in the activities required before, during, and after a performance review. Before the review, it enables more focused observation and planning by the sales manager.

During the review, it aids the candid conversations required. For example, a manager might begin a discussion with a stage 1 individual by noting, "You've done a good job settling into the role and orienting yourself to our firm. But your challenge now is to transition to more independent roles over the next year. I have other new hires that require my hands-on attention. That means less specific task direction or intervention is available for you when problems arise. So I'm counting on you to handle more on your own, and involve me only when you think it's necessary. And I'll be evaluating that at our next review." The rep, if also familiar with the developmental arc, might respond, "I understand and welcome that. But it will help if you could sponsor me for training in certain areas over the next few months, and help me to clarify those judgments and decisions about customers where you should continue to be involved and those where I now have more say-so. Can we talk about that?"

Both manager and rep are now working on similar *behaviors*, not just slogans like "be more strategic" or "ask for forgiveness, not permission" or (the worst one!) "demonstrate leadership qualities." The shared language aids tremendously in the performance conversations after a review. Manager: "I like your progress in taking more responsibility and involving me at the right points. But one issue: you need to pay more attention to building required relationships within your territory. Because I'm not as involved, I'm no longer the one providing that air cover. Talk to X and Y about what they do to get more prompt responses from Service or the product managers here." Of course, all depends upon actual performance, and the conversation might go another way. Manager: "I wish I could see more progress in the transition we discussed. But you're still counting on me too much, while I'm expecting you to understand the goals and figure out the best tactics. You have potential, but I need a stage 2 for this job." In either case, both manager and rep now have a common reference point. They're more able to have a behaviorally based performance discussion because the facts of strength and need are on the table. Such a discussion also helps individuals take more proactive responsibility for their development.

Implications for Career Discussions

Inherent in any shared model of career development is a willingness to discuss careers. Employees want to do this. Dalton and Thompson surveyed two hundred thousand employees in over one hundred organizations: the respondents indicated a stronger desire for improvement in how their firms help employees manage careers than in any other area; twenty years later, the Gallup organization found the same thing. At any point in time, the nonfiction best-seller list includes a career how-to guide (Amazon.com lists over forty-nine thousand entries under "career development"), and careers are at the heart of gender equality and other important issues in society.[14] Careers are what we do for eight-plus hours a day and involve some basic needs: money, recognition, and potential geographical, educational, and social directions for our life and family. But careers are rarely discussed between people and their managers, especially in sales. Why?

Many managers want to avoid raising expectations. A firm is, after all, a hierarchy that's wider at the bottom than the top, so many managers believe that discussing careers can get people's hopes up and many will be disappointed. But ambitious people who are not promoted will be disappointed whether or not you discuss career requirements with them. Without that discussion, they will fill in the blanks as they see things (probably overestimating the performance leverage of their individual contributions) and feel mugged by reality if the promotion doesn't happen, and you will only have a tougher career discussion down the road. Other managers avoid the discussion because they want to *keep* good performers in their unit. As this happens in a firm, many managers fear that if they accept someone from another unit, they're getting someone else's reject. Finally, many managers simply lack a framework for discussing careers in any meaningful way, falling back on the platitude that "if you do good work, it will happen when it happens." Will it? Should it?

The lack of these discussions inhibits development in sales forces, and over time, the wider organization is held hostage to talent limitations in the field. A shared development model creates the space for the necessary career discussions. It also shines a light on key aspects of building capabilities. For the individual, the surest way to get stalled in a career is to have a manager who wants to hang on to you and thus keep you at stage 1 or 2. This model of development lets managers know that they do not "own" the talent that reports to them; that's an enterprise asset and they're just renting it for some time. For the organization, the model helps to raise the level of maturity and clarity in performance discussions, align expectations, and build the required links between wider HR capabilities and selling outcomes.

Coordinating Expectations and Behaviors

This approach to building and sustaining human and organizational capabilities does *not* imply that all or most people in a firm or function should be in stage 4. All organizations, as chapter 8 argued, need a portfolio of talent with people working effectively in different roles and therefore different stages. But it does imply that all organizations, and especially sales, need a communicable view about what it takes to maintain high performance in various roles and as market conditions inevitably change. And that's a joint responsibility. As Dalton and Thompson emphasized, "In a very fundamental sense, career development [and] maintenance of one's competence is an individual responsibility. No organization and no manager can do that job for the individual . . . But managers have a responsibility to design organizations so that they can remain capable of developing in the future."[15]

Developing sales managers ultimately means developing people who can move through the pathway outlined on figure 11-2 and thus increase their contribution across time and space for the firm.

FIGURE 11-2

Focus shift by stage

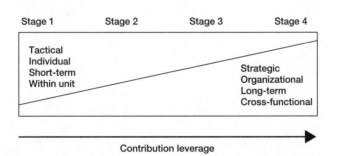

Conversely, aligning strategy and sales means having people who understand the tasks inherent in that progression of development. It also means communicating core requirements for increased contribution and promotion. Note that as the person moves from individual contributor, to manager, and to shaper of direction, the coordination requirements increase. Both selling and sales management tasks are increasingly reliant on coordinating a network of connections within the function and then across functions. Making those connections is the focus of the final chapter, because it's necessary for managing the cycle of strategy and sales performance in any business.

12

Making Connections

Senior executives often preach teamwork at strategy retreats and management meetings. But few firms focus on team effectiveness where it counts most: the cross-functional interactions involved in customer acquisition and retention. There are practical ways to improve the coordination required for strategy implementation. Those practices can improve the company as well as increase selling success.

Why Coordination Is So Important

Consider the order cycle in many businesses, especially B2B businesses that account for so much economic activity in industrialized countries. For the seller, an order touches multiple functions as it moves from a customer's request for specifications or quote to a purchase order and through any postsale service activities such as warranty or field engineering (figure 12-1).[1]

Sales is involved in nearly all the activities, if only because it's the sales rep who typically fields the customer's questions

FIGURE 12-1

Typical order cycle

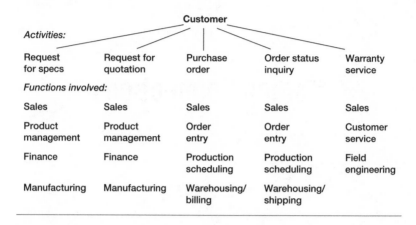

Activities:				
Request for specs	Request for quotation	Purchase order	Order status inquiry	Warranty service

Functions involved:

Sales	Sales	Sales	Sales	Sales
Product management	Product management	Order entry	Order entry	Customer service
Finance	Finance	Production scheduling	Production scheduling	Field engineering
Manufacturing	Manufacturing	Warehousing/ billing	Warehousing/ shipping	

or complaints and who then interacts with other functions to respond to the customer. In these interactions, people report to their functional bosses, and driven by its own operating procedures and metrics, each function is likely to have different priorities. Because that customer's order counts toward bonus comp for the sales rep, that customer is the most important thing and any customization is warranted. But it's one among many orders vying for the attention of operations or shipping, and customization has margin implications for product managers and finance. This is one reason why "customer focus" is a perennial slogan but not a behavioral reality in many firms.

Cross-functional coordination—and its evil twin, misalignment—is pervasive in selling efforts, although often hidden. At one point, IBM had a subsidiary, SRA, which sold self-study training programs that taught IT staffs how to use IBM systems. By many measures, SRA's courses were the best in the industry. But SRA was outsold eight-to-one by another, non-IBM training firm. SRA's sales and marketing activities were targeted exclusively at training managers, yet research indicated that over 80 percent of the time, the training manager had bought SRA courses because of specific requests from systems programmers in their firms. Even more: when an SRA sales rep left and a territory became vacant, there was no change in SRA sales. It turned out that in virtually all significant sales of SRA products, the IBM service engineers, who worked closely with programmers at customers, had recommended SRA courses as the only ones providing the depth needed for quick recovery in the event of a system failure or details concerning optional applications. But sales and service rarely communicated. As one executive said, "Our sales force isn't driving sales; they're really driven, haphazardly, by a hidden sales force."[2]

It's hard to solve this problem with reorganizations. Sales and service, for example, are different jobs requiring different types of expertise in most firms. As seen in chapter 8, any structure will encourage certain types of interactions and inhibit others. Monetary incentives affect behavior but, as discussed in chapter 9, compensation is a necessary but not sufficient cause of desired behavior in an organization. It's unlikely that you will pay every function the same way and unwise to assume that stock options or a profit-sharing goal can erase these differences. Further, the problem is getting bigger. Management structures in US firms, for instance, have changed significantly in the past few decades. The C-suite—the executives reporting directly to the CEO—has doubled since the 1980s, driven by an increase in functional managers responsible for specific activities (e.g., IT, product, legal) rather than general managers responsible for integrated business-unit activities across functions.[3] Why? The business world is more complex, required knowledge increases, and more specialists are needed to stay up-to-date with that functional knowledge. Hence, as I argued in a previous book, "to dismantle or diffuse this necessary expertise in the name of undifferentiated notions of teamwork is to short-circuit the continuing organizational learning required in the new market environment and to unwittingly encourage lowest-common-denominator approaches to the marketplace."[4]

What's needed are coordinating activities that are supported by structures and incentives but that go beyond those tools and create (a) a shared understanding of strategy and each group's contribution to that strategy's value-delivery requirements; (b) clarity about the cross-functional rules of engagement inherent in your strategy and selling tasks; and (c) the ability, and discipline, to manage the iterative process that I call the strategy → sales performance cycle.

This chapter looks at each issue in turn. First, let's look at sales and marketing—two functions that are interdependent but different in their concerns and procedures. Then, we'll examine how to establish rules of engagement between sales and other functions that affect selling success. Finally, I'll conclude by looking at the strategy → sales performance cycle and provide summary advice to strategists and sales leaders about aligning strategy and sales.

Sales and Marketing Coordination

Studies indicate that less than 40 percent of firms believe their sales and marketing units are aligned with what their customers want; that most marketing collateral is considered useless by salespeople and customers; and that, despite investments in CRM and now big data, simple lead generation from marketing to sales remains a constant source of complaints in both functions. Not surprisingly, the issue is frequently highlighted in articles and tops the agenda in a recent survey of B2B executives.[5]

Few managers are *against* teamwork. But coordination costs money, takes time, and prolongs decision making. Hence, it's important to isolate activities where coordination is important and the issues affecting groups that must coordinate. Figure 12-2 outlines activities associated with marketing and sales. On organization charts, these activities are often grouped into labels like *product management* or *distribution*. But as in figure 12-2, they can be viewed as a continuum where, as in a relay race, the achievement of each unit's tasks depends upon the plans and actions of other units.

FIGURE 12-2

A continuum of activities

Task Is Primary Responsibility of
Marketing . . . . Sales
Market research
   Competitive analysis
      Product development
         Product positioning
            Advertising/communications
            Lead generation
            Promotions
               Pricing
                  Account selection
                  Personal selling
                     Channel management
                       Account management
                          Pre- or post-sale service

For example, market research should be informed by selling activities at target accounts; pricing plans must be implemented by sales channels; and profit margins are affected by activities during the selling cycle. This continuum means that marketing planning without sales input, or sales actions without marketing plans, will be incomplete or contradictory and waste some significant portion of your firm's time, money, and morale.

Alone Together: Interdependencies and Differences

Although coordinating marketing and sales is vital, in most firms some differentiation of these activities occurs, so that specialized expertise—and accountability—for a subset of these tasks can be developed and maintained. And that's why coordinating marketing and sales is so important and difficult: inherent in these tasks are interdependencies that must be managed, yet each unit also faces different ongoing needs in executing its portion of the continuum of activities that affect customers.

Figure 12-3 provides a way of visualizing the interdependencies. Marketing needs certain kinds of input from sales, including sales forecasts, customer feedback about product performance, and ongoing market information about buying behavior and competitor activities. Sales needs from marketing an actionable translation of strategy into plans applicable to accounts, relevant leads, documentation about the product or service offering, and pricing. But with division of labor comes differences. Each group differs in its orientation to the market, time horizons, performance criteria and metrics, and required information priorities (table 12-1).

FIGURE 12-3

Typical interdependencies between marketing and sales

From marketing to sales → . . .

- Overall market strategies and plans
- Program/product information and training
- Market research data and analysis
- Pricing and promotion analyses, guidelines, programs
- Contracts, proposals, presentation support
- Customization support and resources
- ....

   ← From sales to marketing . . .

   - Sales forecasts and results
   - Relevant information re: buying behavior, competition
   - Customer access and feedback re: current/new products
   - Execution of product, pricing, promotion programs
   - Ongoing activities re: account management
   - Customer service information re: needs and opportunities
   - ....

TABLE 12-1

Marketing dialects

Marketing	Sales
Organization and orientation	
• Across geographies, with specific product or market responsibilities	• Within territories, with specific account responsibilities
Time horizon drivers	
• R&D/product introduction cycles	• Selling cycles at various customer locations
• Internal budgeting process	• External buying processes
• Career paths that emphasize frequent rotation among product assignments	• Career paths that emphasize account continuity in a sales assignment
Performance criteria and information priorities	
• Profit-and-loss and/or ROA criteria	• Sales volume
• Product/market/segment information	• Account information
• "Lumpers": aggregate for product development, costing, pricing activities	• "Splitters": disaggregate for selling and specific account management activities

In most firms, marketing managers operate across geographies and accounts but with specific product or market responsibilities. Their time horizons tend to be driven by internal R&D, and product introduction, planning or budgeting cycles. Because they manage markets, not accounts, marketing managers often have an incentive to amortize R&D costs and stretch a product's applicability *across* customer groups. By contrast, sales managers and reps tend to operate within geographical or account assignments. Their time horizons are driven by selling cycles at specific accounts, which are indifferent to the seller's budgeting or planning cycles. Because they manage customers, not markets, sales managers and reps have an incentive to customize product or service applications *within* a segment or an account. Career paths and metrics— how people are measured and get ahead in the organization— also differ. Marketing career paths often emphasize frequent rotation among products, brands, or markets, but with P&L or return-on-assets criteria as key metrics. In sales, career paths place more emphasis on account continuity, because relationships aid getting access to the appropriate decision makers, but usually with sales volume as the key metric.

These differences are not bureaucratic procedures. They reflect expertise requirements. But problems arise because of conflicting priorities or different "dialects": what each unit in its daily routine considers core versus discretionary in allocating its limited attention, resources, and efforts. Over time, these differences become "how we do things here" in separate silos. And if this is true for marketing and sales— areas directly concerned with customers—systematic differences also affect interactions between sales and the other functions whose efforts impact customer acquisition and retention.

Any attempt to manage this determinant of effective selling must understand its roots and requirements. The issue is *not* to eradicate the differences or abstractly insist that "everybody is responsible for customer satisfaction." In any firm, what in theory is "everybody's business" tends in practice to be *nobody's* business, because of the lack of accountability. Rather, the issue is how to link effectively the knowledge, capabilities, and operational buy-in that are located in different areas across the firm.

Rules of Engagement

In business, you are what you eat and can digest: external responsiveness requires internal coordination, placing sales squarely in the crossfire of the differing mind-sets and metrics in each function in an organization. Think of the differences as toll gates: with each, your organization must slow down and pay, either in time, money, or decreased customer satisfaction. In any firm where these interactions are especially time-consuming or difficult, most sales reps will take routes that avoid the tolls and focus on what they *can* sell with minimal internal interactions. This approach may maximize the individual rep's return on effort. But it's usually a surefire way to inhibit scaling a business in accord with strategy. Louis Gerstner, reflecting on his experience at IBM in the 1990s, put it well: "I came to see, in my time at IBM, that culture isn't just one aspect of the game—it is the game. In the end, an organization is nothing more than the collective capacity of its people to create value."[6]

How, practically, can a firm improve these interactions—is there the equivalent of an "Easy Pass" that allows traffic to flow through organizational toll gates more efficiently? A first step is identifying those with whom you are dependent to get your job done and jointly clarifying the rules of engagement that should apply between these groups. Many managers find it helpful to outline these dependencies and rules. Figure 12-4 asks you to identify the key activities involved with another relevant organizational unit. For sales and marketing, for example, this could involve any or all of the tasks on figure 12-3, depending upon the objectives, scope, and advantage inherent in your firm's strategy. Then, construct a balance sheet to clarify what you must *get* from the other group to perform your activities effectively, and what your group must *give* to the other for that group to provide it most efficiently.

Reciprocity is at the heart of these interactions. In his studies of persuasion and influence, Robert Cialdini emphasizes that the rule of reciprocation—what Cialdini calls "the old give and take"—drives influence. He cites much evidence suggesting that virtually every human society subscribes to

FIGURE 12-4

Clarifying the rules of engagement

Key activities: _____   Groups: _____

What key interactions between your group and the other group affect your group's performance? What must your group *give* to the other group to *get* what you need?	
Give	Get

the rule, "and within each society it seems pervasive also; it permeates exchanges of every kind . . . and the cluster of interdependencies that bind individuals together into highly efficient units."[7] Especially in sales, it's usually better to overestimate rather than underestimate interdependencies and the reciprocities that follow. It's no coincidence that many sales reps leave a gift for the receptionist or other gatekeeper who handles the customer's schedule or, at their own firm, for the service rep who expedites their order up the queue. What happens individually should also happen organizationally. Leaders who rely solely on structure, compensation, or general goodwill and fail to clarify these give-and-get rules are handicapping their ability to align strategy and sales.

Here's an example from a company that I'll call Neptune. Its business is managing outsourced water supplies of municipalities in the United States and other countries. In this situation, contracts often span ten years or more and require an up-front allocation of capital by Neptune, and the investment cycle involves an initial cash trough that only generates a return for Neptune over the life of the contract. Neptune must provide a competitive bid for the contract with as full knowledge as possible of the risks involved. The selling cycle is long (usually eighteen to twenty-four months or more) and involves a complicated set of elected officials and other decision makers at the customer; it requires much due diligence, and sales (Neptune calls it "business development") is responsible—with other functions—for clarifying the risks, negotiating terms, and managing the process over time with an often changing set of buyers and influencers. Each proposed contract is ultimately reviewed by a cross-functional group at Neptune. Like a credit committee at a commercial bank, that group includes the finance group, the legal group (it's a regulated business), and the technical services group that, if Neptune gets the contract, must manage the business for years.

Over the years, this process generated a motley mix of business for Neptune. Much of the business was good for the customer (the outsourcing arrangement freed up capital and resources for other municipal activities like education, firefighters, and pension obligations) and for Neptune (the firm could typically manage the water supply more efficiently because its expertise was wider than that of any individual municipality). But many initially promising contracts also turned out to be money-losers. Unexpected risks appeared. Decision making suffered. Each function became skeptical about the assertions of others, and especially of sales/business development, whose bonus compensation was tied to contract acquisition. Execution was more expensive while also generating customer acrimony, because after-sale issues had to be managed in the context of fixed-price contracts. (This situation should sound familiar to those in other sectors where fixed-price contracts are common, or in outsourcing or software licensing businesses.) Finally, leaders at Neptune decided to clarify the rules of engagement between sales and the other relevant functions. The output (see table 12-2 for excerpts) seems simple, but is worth examining because, as always, the rules uncover behaviors that make or break the collective capacity to add value.

Why is sales requiring from finance the "critical few measures required for thumbs-up or thumbs-down" from the review committee? Think about the sales group's situation and experience: after eighteen to twenty-four months of cultivating relationships and providing multiple RFPs, sales was often told by finance that the proposed contract was rejected

TABLE 12-2

Rules of engagement: example from "Neptune, Inc."

Finance: gives to business development	Finance: gets from business development
Timely financial modeling with the "critical-few" measures required for thumbs-up or thumbs-down, not a laundry list of risks and returns. Clarify the targets: communicate ROA requirements and consider specific commercial factors.	Early involvement of finance and clear communication of needs early in the sales process and not just when the bid is at the end-of-process stage. Provide us with key value drivers and relevant data: e.g., customer counts, rates, etc.

Legal: gives to business development	Legal: gets from business development
Provide solutions-oriented legal advice with options and alternatives; seek to balance the company's commercial interests and legal mandates with customer relationships when dealing with prospects.	Seek legal input early in the cycle, giving a complete project description with all known risks and concerns. Identify "must-haves" vs. "nice-to-have" and explicitly list legal questions/ issues in account plans.

Technical services: gives to BD	Technical services: get from BD
Early technical assistance as needed to assess the opportunity, including risks, risk-mitigating options, and pricing/bid implications. Technical support should recognize the vagaries of customer purchasing processes and requests.	Thorough screening of opportunities, in accord with corporate criteria, before engaging tech services so that we can trust that BD has vetted the project and determined it is one we want to "win" and not just "explore."

because it failed to account for item X. "Tell me the key measures upfront," sales is saying, "and *not* after I've devoted almost two years of my life to this deal." Conversely, why is finance requiring from sales "early involvement . . . and not just when the bid is in the end-of-process stage" of review and approval? Think about the inevitable game-playing in any firm where the rules of engagement are not clarified. Many sales managers waited until the last moment before submitting the bid proposal, in effect saying, "Here's a $50 million or $100 million contract, and we must respond by tomorrow. Don't you want that business?" Finance's rule says, "Stop holding us hostage to last-minute ultimatums: if you want us to give timely financial modeling, then we need to get involved early and clearly."

Similarly, sales wants "solutions-oriented legal advice," meaning, "We don't want to break any laws, but your job in Legal is to be more than Doctor No: help us find other options that let us do business while maintaining regulatory compliance." Legal says, "To do that, get us involved with a project description that includes all risks. Don't treat us—colleagues with legal and fiduciary responsibilities to the firm—as a target for a sales pitch. Let's work together with full recognition of what's really involved with this prospect." With sales and technical services, you hear sales wanting service assessments early in the selling cycle because, in this situation, it's better to bail earlier rather than later: the rep can devote energy to other prospects. Conversely, you hear technical services requiring sales to do the customer profiling discussed in chapter 7 *before* sales brings in limited service resources.

These rules increase understanding between interdependent groups about how to interact to support growth and other strategic objectives. They help people understand how to channel behaviors to support each other *and* to hold each other accountable. In this respect, cross-functional rules of engagement are, in my experience, more actionable and real than the many abstract values statements that now adorn company websites and office ornaments.

Once a firm has clarified the relevant rules, it can *then* use *structure* and *compensation* to support those behaviors. After Gerstner arrived at IBM, he decided—against much advice—not to break up the firm. Instead, he based strategy on providing integrated product/service packages customized to vertical sectors. At the time, IBM was a wilderness of silos without rules of engagement for working across functions, sales units, and product groups. Step 1 was clarifying the required behavioral rules among these groups, given the strategy. Step 2 was then restructuring the business around specific industry groups and formally pairing product specialists with global industry teams in give-and-get relationships. Step 3 was to redo bonus compensation to give more weight to corporate results than to business-unit performance. Business history suggests that you can't do it the other way: starting with compensation or structure and then behavior. Gerstner is right: it's culture—human performance and behaviors—that drives operating and financial performance in any firm. Customers rarely see or care about the rules of engagement at their suppliers. But these behaviors ultimately elicit customer praise or complaints and help or hinder the translation of strategy into the right sales efforts and results.

Managing the Strategy → Sales Performance Cycle

In any organization, alignment is both an outcome and an ongoing process.[8] As an outcome, it refers to the fit of organizational activities in response to a set of external realities and objectives. But no firm can stay productively aligned for too long. Every strategy has a sell-by date, because every business operates in a changing market environment. As a process, therefore, alignment refers to a replicable series of activities, not just a single decision or action. Figure 12-5 outlines a process for managing the strategy → sales performance cycle.

The first step is strategy. As chapter 4 discussed, it's a coherent strategy that provides direction and, as chapter 5

FIGURE 12-5

The strategy → sales performance cycle

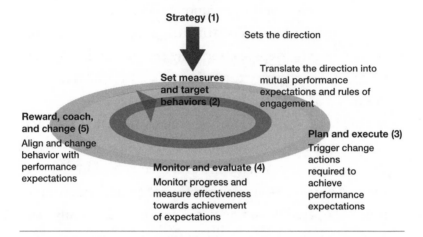

Strategy (1)

Sets the direction

Set measures and target behaviors (2)

Translate the direction into mutual performance expectations and rules of engagement

Reward, coach, and change (5)

Align and change behavior with performance expectations

Plan and execute (3)

Trigger change actions required to achieve performance expectations

Monitor and evaluate (4)

Monitor progress and measure effectiveness towards achievement of expectations

emphasized, that strategy must be communicated, simply and consistently, to peers and others deep into the relevant organizational units. Second, as chapter 6 indicated, the strategy must be translated into actionable sales tasks and performance expectations. Here is where the rules of engagement relevant to performance should be discussed, negotiated, and clarified.

Third, plans for executing tasks must be in place. Plans are more than checklists. They are actions to affect behavior and achieve performance expectations. As the U.S. Army After-Action-Review manual puts it, "There is no lesson learned until a behavior is changed." In sales, action plans involve the customer selection, hiring, training, and organizational choices examined in chapters 7 and 8.

Fourth, you must measure effectiveness in relation to performance expectations. Without those metrics, any sales organization is more likely to commit the sunk-cost fallacy, throwing good money after bad. As chapter 10 discussed, the relevant measures usually depend upon more than just sales revenue. They often should encompass price versus the cost to serve different customers, cash flow and selling-cycle dimensions of the strategy, and potential team-selling and/or channel-selling requirements.

But the process of aligning strategy and sales ultimately requires *managing* the cycle—the fifth and last step of the cycle. Metrics must be embodied in how field managers conduct performance reviews and, as chapter 9 outlined, how they and their people are rewarded for relevant behaviors and outcomes. Effective performance reviews and coaching and training initiatives are simultaneously the output of the strategy → sales cycle (how can you reward and coach effectively unless you know what you are rewarding and training for?) and the foundational conditions. It's human performance that ultimately drives the cycle and, as chapter 11 argued, that requires managers capable of stage 3 and 4 behaviors.

The process must be iterative, as the circular form of figure 12-5 indicates. Because the external market changes, most firms have two requirements that, while not mutually exclusive, do pull sales efforts in different directions. One requirement concerns what's necessary to maintain the skills, attention, and motivation needed to compete for current sources of revenue and profit. The other concerns the skills and capabilities that must be developed to compete in new markets or in response to changing buyer behavior. Sales managers often refer sardonically to these dual requirements as the "monkey theory of management"—that is, in making its way through a competitive jungle, the smart monkey never lets go of one branch (an established means of generating sales) until its other hand is securely fastened to the next branch. The problem is that this view of change is a prescription for inertia rather than adaptation and innovation. In fact, if you look at videos of monkeys swinging through a jungle, they often *do* let go of one branch before grabbing the next. But the smart monkey can calibrate the required leap.

More formally, these dual requirements are called a problem in *requisite variety*. When the complexity or variety in the environment exceeds the capabilities of the people who must manage it, then inertia or mistakes are usually the result. As studies indicate, a better match between people and a complex environment can occur in one of two ways: either the system becomes less complex or the human more complex.[9] During the past few decades, most advice to business has emphasized the latter: somehow making people more complex via leadership rather than management, overarching purpose rather than clarified strategic choices, and selecting stars rather than the ongoing management of the bell curve of capabilities that most organizations are. The approach developed throughout this book emphasizes the other and (in my view) more actionable alternative: linking discrete capabilities in a process that makes finite individuals capable of more in the aggregate than they are individually. As a great organizational scholar, James March, once noted, "Leadership involves plumbing as well as poetry."[10] That has implications for strategists and sales leaders.

Summary Advice to Sales Leaders

In the executive programs at Harvard, the participants are typically impatient. They face short-term pressures and want handy summations, even if—as with aligning strategy and sales—many interacting variables are relevant. But even if the advice is reductive, I've found that summary guidelines can add much value. I offer some here in the hope they are useful to readers who may be confronting these issues in real time.

Consider sales productivity—a recurring topic between sales leaders, strategists, and others in the C-suite. Reporting that the sales pipeline grew by so many dollars should *not* qualify as an adequate answer if the firm is serious about profitable growth. How did the pipeline grow? Did we add lower- or higher-profit and lifetime-value customers? Are we bringing in shorter- or longer-selling-cycle prospects? What are the implications of selling efforts for other functions and the center of gravity in our business strategy?

Figure 12-6 outlines a way of thinking about sales productivity and brings together themes in this book relevant to sales leaders. The productivity of a sales model is a function of *capacity* (how much the sales force can do in terms of call capacity and their capacity—or capability—to reach various customer groups), the *close rate* (what percentage of prospects the sales force sells), and *profit per sale* (what they sell

FIGURE 12-6

Analyzing sales productivity

Sales productivity = (a) capacity × (b) close rate × (c) profit per sale

a. Increase sales capacity by
- Longer hours, more calls, better lead generation
- More focus on high-impact selling tasks and activities

b. Increase close rate by
- Better customer opportunity and deal selection criteria
- Better account and/or channel partner management

c. Increase profit per sale by
- Better pricing, product mix, and/or sales per customer
- Lower selling costs and improved internal process efficiencies

and at what prices). What levers are available to sales leaders to improve each component?

To improve sales capacity, people can work harder: make more calls and/or do a better job at lead generation in the pipeline.[11] Among other things, that's the lesson of chapter 7: BPI sold more with fewer reps because the ideal-customer process improved lead generation and allowed more-productive sales calls. You also improve sales capacity by working smarter, which is the lesson of chapter 6—focus on the high-impact sales tasks inherent in the business strategy—and chapter 10: then translate that focus into relevant metrics for performance reviews.

To increase close rates and accelerate selling cycles, get better at identifying and selecting potential deals along the spectrum of opportunities that confront every firm. Which are solution customers where significant resources are required, and which are transaction customers where the issue is to take costs out of the sales approach? How can we embody these differences in the account management and channel-partner elements of our sales model? The major message from the research presented in chapters 8, 9, and 10 is that, in sales, *how* you allocate available resources is often more important than *how much* resource investment you make.

To improve profit per sale, constantly work on other elements that affect profitability: pricing, product mix, and sales per customer. Continuous improvement is always relevant and earns firms the "right" to worry about strategy. You also improve profit per sale by lowering selling costs. One message of part II is that articulating strategic choices and the implications for customer selection allows sales leaders to lower selling costs *without* harming selling, because then they know where and where not to cut, increasing resources for the key tasks. The message of part IV is that an ongoing understanding of the links between internal activities and external customer acquisition and retention requires making the relevant connections and rules of engagement between sales and others across the organization.

Bottom line: all orders are not equal. Which customers are core to our strategy, spend more with us over time, and cost less to maintain, and which customers cost us in time and money without a commensurate return strategically or financially? Every strategy has an implied sales productivity equation. For some firms, capacity, close rates, and profit per sale involve many presale applications and postsale service or support activities. Think about the selling situations for enterprise software or many professional services. For other firms, this equation can "collapse" into a single sales call. Think about Eureka Forbes, discussed in chapter 6, and the tasks involved in door-to-door sales of vacuum cleaners. But for both types of sales, this framework can help a sales leader track best practices in the business and then improve hiring, training, and performance management.

Summary Advice to Strategists

First, it's difficult for people to implement what they don't understand. One lesson of chapter 4 is not to confuse strategy with purpose, vision, or values, and chapter 5 shows that it's the responsibility of those crafting strategy in a firm to insist on the distinctions. Then, you must communicate that strategy and what it means for important choices in objective, scope, and advantage. Most firms' training programs rarely include much about the business strategy—either because the firm is not clear about its strategy or because leaders are wary that this information will get to competitors. If the issue is the former, then clarify strategy: it's an indispensable step in managing the strategy → sales performance cycle. And if the issue is the latter, then as explained in part I, you have bigger problems than competitors "knowing" your strategy, because you are inviting a dialogue that can never happen.

Second, the goal of strategy is profitable growth, meaning economic value above the firm's cost of capital. As figure 12-7 indicates, there are basically four ways to create value for shareholders: (1) invest in projects that earn more than their cost of capital; (2) increase profits from existing capital investments; (3) reduce the assets devoted to activities that earn less than their cost of capital; and (4) reduce the cost of capital itself. In my experience, most CEOs, CFOs, and others involved in strategy formulation typically know this. But far fewer understand and operationalize the core customer and sales factors that materially affect each value creation lever. Placing figure 12-6 next to figure 12-7 can help to highlight the links:

- Projects and initiatives in most firms are driven by revenue-seeking activities with customers. Hence, the customer selection criteria used in sales directly impact the first enterprise value-creation lever: *which* projects the firm invests in.

- To increase profits from existing investments, all elements of sales productivity are relevant, but especially the interactions between sales and other functions that accrete costs, time, and asset utilization patterns in the firm.

FIGURE 12-7

Linking customer value and profitable growth

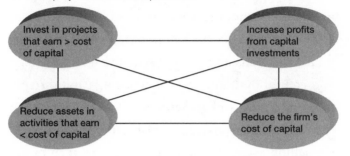

The goal is to maximize the financial value of customer relationships: the sum total of revenues from exchanges with each customer, minus the directly attributable costs—now and in the future. In turn, there are four ways a company can increase enterprise value.

- The third value-creation route—smartly reducing the assets devoted to activities that earn less than their cost of capital—requires good links with evolving customer realities and an understanding of the performance management issues outlined in part II of this book. Without that understanding of how hiring, development, organization, incentives, and performance metrics affect field behavior, asset redeployment in any firm becomes either an academic exercise that does not affect the behavior of those utilizing unproductive assets. Or, as chapter 2 suggested, asset redeployment becomes an unwitting impediment to the use of assets that in fact remain essential to profitable selling activities.

- It may seem that sales has little impact on the fourth value-creation lever, which is the firm's cost of capital. Isn't that a function of the debt-to-equity ratio (call the investment bankers for advice, since they've shown how smart they are in managing their leverage!) and the many weighted-cost-of-capital calculations in finance textbooks? At one point, for example, Stern Stewart identified more than 160 possible adjustments to measuring cost of capital, and sales rarely appears in business-school lectures about this topic.[12] But consider the basics (in fact, *always* consider the basics): financing needs are in large part driven by the cash and capital on hand and the working capital required for conducting and growing the business. Most often the single biggest driver of cash-out and cash-in is the selling cycle. Accounts payables are accumu-lated during selling, and accounts receivables are largely determined by what's sold, how fast, and at what price. That's why increasing close rates and accelerating selling cycles is a strategic issue and not only a sales task.

Interactions with customers affect all elements of enter-prise value creation, and in many firms, the sales force is effectively the sum of those interactions. Strategy, growth, or attempts to increase the stock price without attention to this fact are at best limited and, at worst, going down the wrong path.

Finally, if the bottom line to field sales leaders is that all orders are not equal, then a key takeaway message to strate-gists is voiced by a character in a John le Carré novel: "A desk is a dangerous place from which to watch the world." Strategy is about confronting market facts, because that's where value is created or destroyed. In turn, strategists, and not only salespeople, need continuing contact with customers to avoid a priestly but otherworldly role in the organization. Evidence suggests that, in many firms, the balance is out of whack. In surveys, nearly 80 percent of C-suite executives believed their products were highly differentiated, but only 8 percent of customers agreed; meanwhile, in high-performing businesses, it's reported that senior managers spend at least a third of their time with customers.[13] As I once heard Sam Walton remind his executives, "There ain't many customers at headquarters."

Because of sales' central role with customers, changes in sales requirements always have wider organizational implications. Today, those changes are at the heart of many challenges and opportunities confronting firms around the world: how to harness big-data technologies; how to respond to online channels that alter buying processes; how to deal with shorter life cycles yet more complex selling tasks; how to develop talent that can respond flexibly but coherently; how to encourage cross-functional efforts without destroying the necessary expertise and accountability. Linking strategy and sales is a basic building block required to meet these challenges. I hope this book helps managers in that effort.

Notes

Preface

1. The survey, conducted by Booz&Company, involved more than eighteen hundred executives from companies of various sizes and from various industries around the globe. It involved twenty-one questions on the topics of strategy development, decision making, priority setting, capabilities, growth, and cost cutting. See Booz&Company, "Executives Say They're Pulled in Too Many Directions and That Their Company's Capabilities Don't Support Their Strategy," Booz&Company web page, January 18, 2011, www.booz.com/global/home/press/article/49007867.

2. Data about the money spent on sales forces comes from Andris A. Zoltners, Prabhakant Sinha, and Sally E. Lorimer, "Are You Paying Enough Attention to Your Sales Force?" HBR Blog Network, April 12, 2013, http://blogs.hbr.org/2013/04/are-you-paying-enough-attention-to/. See also their article, "Building a Winning Sales Force in B2B Markets: A Managerial Perspective," in *Handbook of Business-to-Business Marketing*, ed. Gary L. Lilien and Rajdeep Grewal (Cheltenham, UK; Northampton, MA: Edward Elgar, 2012), 521. Data about the amount of money firms spend on media advertising comes from Barclay's Capital, "U.S. Advertising Revenue, by Medium," *Business Insider*, October 27, 2009, www.businessinsider.com/us-advertising-spending-by-medium-2009-10. The amount of money spent on online advertising is from Suzanne Vranica, "Digital Marketing Takes Center Stage," *Wall Street Journal*, September 23, 2013, B2.

3. Zoltners, Sinha, and Lorimer, "Building a Winning Sales Force in B2B Markets," 521.

4. Ankur Agrawal, Olivia Nottebohm, and Andy West, "Five Ways CFOs Can Make Cost Cuts Stick," *McKinsey Quarterly* (May 2010).

5. See Suzanne Fogel, David Hoffmeister, Richard Rocco, and Daniel P. Strunk, "Teaching Sales," *Harvard Business Review* (July–August 2012).

Chapter 1

1. Jim Koch, "How One Entrepreneur Learned to Sell (in a Barroom)," *Harvard Business Review* (July–August 2012): 103.

2. Jeffrey Pfeffer and Robert I. Sutton, *The Knowing-Doing Gap: How Smart Companies Turn Knowledge into Action* (Boston: Harvard Business School Press, 1999), 1–2.

3. Chris Zook and James Allen, "The Great Repeatable Business Model," *Harvard Business Review* (November 2011).

4. For studies about failure to implement, dating back now at least thirty years, see Walter Kiechel, "Corporate Strategists Under Fire," *Fortune*, December 27, 1982, 38; Ram Charan and Geoffrey Colvin, "Why CEOs Fail," *Fortune*, June 1999, 69–78; Robert S. Kaplan and David P. Norton, *The Strategy-Focused Organization: How Balanced Scorecard Companies Thrive in the New Business Environment* (Boston: Harvard Business School Press, 2001); and Mark Morgan, Raymond E. Levitt, and William Malek, *Executing Your Strategy: How to Break It Down and Get It Done* (Boston: Harvard Business School Press, 2007).

5. This data comes from a study by Marakon Associates, in collaboration with the Economist Intelligence Unit, of 197 companies worldwide with sales exceeding $500 million. See Michael C. Mankins and Richard Steele, "Turning Great Strategy into Great Performance," *Harvard Business Review* (July–August 2005).

6. Cynthia A. Montgomery, "How Strategists Lead," *McKinsey Quarterly* (July 2012).

7. The responses from sales executives are available in Andris A. Zoltners, Prabhakant Sinha, and Sally E. Lorimer, "Building a Winning Sales Force in B2B Markets: A Managerial Perspective," in *Handbook of Business-to-Business Marketing*, ed. Gary L. Lilien and Rajdeep Grewal (Cheltenham, UK; Northampton, MA: Edward Elgar, 2012), 525, table 28.1.

8. Michael C. Mankins and Richard Steele, "Stop Making Plans; Start Making Decisions," *Harvard Business Review* (January 2006).

9. For the survey methodology and results, see Booz&Company, "Coherence Profiler," accessed December 12, 2013, www.booz.com/coherence-profiler.

10. Jim Holden, *Power Base Selling: Secrets of an Ivy League Street Fighter* (New York: Wiley, 1992), 2–3.

11. Frank V. Cespedes, *Concurrent Marketing: Integrating Product, Sales, and Service* (Boston: Harvard Business School Press, 1995),

79–82. I borrowed the term from two great theorists of organizations: Barbara Levitt and James G. March, "Organizational Learning," *Annual Review of Sociology* 14 (1988): 319–340.

12. Martin Walker, "America's Edge," *Wilson Quarterly* (summer 2012): 38.

13. Mankins and Steele, "Turning Great Strategy into Great Performance."

Chapter 2

1. Clayton M. Christensen, *The Innovator's Dilemma: When New Technologies Cause Great Firms to Fail* (Boston: Harvard Business School Press, 1997).

2. The sin of pride does prompt me to inform the reader that we eventually did fix the problems at PPCo and the private-equity owners sold the business for a good multiple.

3. John Maynard Keynes, *Economic Possibilities for Our Grandchildren* (1931) and republished in John Maynard Keynes, *Essays in Persuasion* (New York: Classic House Books, 2009), 198.

4. David Dorsey, *The Force* (New York: Ballantine Books, 1994), xiii.

5. Ibid., xv.

Chapter 3

1. *The American Heritage College Dictionary*, 4th ed., s.v. "framework."

2. Emanuel Derman, *Models. Behaving. Badly.: Why Confusing Illusion with Reality Can Lead to Disaster, on Wall Street and in Life* (New York: Free Press, 2011), 195.

3. Emanuel Derman, *My Life as a Quant: Reflections on Physics and Finance* (New York: John Wiley, 2004), 266.

4. Ibid., 198.

5. Atul Gawande, *The Checklist Manifesto* (New York: Metropolitan Books, 2009), makes a wise, witty, and humane case for the humble checklist.

Chapter 4

1. These studies are detailed in two books by Chris Zook and James Allen, *Profit from the Core* (Boston: Harvard Business Press,

2010), and *Repeatability: Build Enduring Businesses for a World of Constant Change* (Boston: Harvard Business Review Press, 2012).

2. Chris Bradley, Angus Dawson, and Sven Smit, "The Strategic Yardstick You Can't Afford to Ignore," *McKinsey Quarterly* (October 2013). If anything, this study *understates* the skewed distribution of outcomes, because it omits "outliers"—that is, companies with economic profit greater than $10 billion during this period, like Apple, Exxon Mobil, Gazprom, and Microsoft.

3. James Atlas, *Saul Bellow: A Biography* (New York: Random House, 2000), xiv.

4. See the results of a survey conducted by the Association for Financial Professionals (AFP) and the excellent discussion in Michael T. Jacobs and Anil Shivdasani, "Do You Know Your Cost of Capital?" *Harvard Business Review* (July–August 2012): 43–51.

5. Michael Lewis, *The Big Short: Inside the Doomsday Machine* (New York: W.W. Norton, 2010). By the way, one participant-observer at the time was Emanuel Derman, who wrote years before the crash that "mortgage valuation models involve a witch's brew of assumptions . . . none of them well-tested [so] mortgage valuation is ugly . . . Still, mortgages were what I had signed on to deal with [at the investment bank]" (*My Life as a Quant: Reflections on Physics and Finance* [New York: John Wiley, 2004], 193–194): a smart, wise, *and* intellectually honest man.

6. Steven Kerr, "On the Folly of Rewarding A, While Hoping for B," *Academy of Management Journal* 18 (1975): 769–783.

7. Michael Porter was swimming against the prevailing tide when he pointed out these factors in "Strategy and the Internet," *Harvard Business Review* (March 2001). But as the old saw has it, when the tide goes out, you can see who's been swimming naked. Porter was correct.

8. See Sarah Needleman and Angus Loten, "When Freemium Fails," *Wall Street Journal*, August 22, 2012, B8.

9. See Zook and Allen, *Repeatability*, 10, for the final definition of "strategy" cited here and, more generally, Joann S. Lublin and Dana Mattioli, "Strategic Plans Lose Favor," *Wall Street Journal* (January 25, 2010), B7.

10. Fritz Machlup, "Structure and Structural Change: Weaselwords and Jargon," in *Essays on Economic Semantics*, ed. Merton Miller (Englewood Cliffs, NJ: Prentice-Hall, 1963), 73–75.

11. Ibid., 73.

12. Jim Collins and Jerry I. Poras, *Built to Last* (New York: HarperBusiness, 1995); and Jim Collins, *Good to Great* (New York: HarperBusiness, 2001).

13. Kenneth R. Andrews, *The Concept of Corporate Strategy* (Homewood, IL: Richard D. Irwin, 1971; rev. ed., 1980), 12.

14. These statements are taken from James C. Collins and Jerry I. Poras, "Core Purpose Is a Company's Reason for Being," in "Building Your Company's Vision," *Harvard Business Review* (September–October 1996), 69, and they are still widely cited by many others in discussions of vision and purpose and strategy.

15. Barney Jopson, "Visionary Talk at P&G Fades as It Seeks Growth," *Financial Times*, February 1, 2013, 17.

16. For the Apple values, see Tim Cook, "Apple Inc. Q1 2009 Earnings Conference Call Final Transcript," Thomson StreetEvents, January 21, 2009. For Merck, Nordstrom, and Disney, see Collins and Poras, "Core Purpose," 68. For Nike, see Zook and Allen, *Repeatability*, 106.

17. See, for example, the pertinent discussion of corporate planning processes in Michael Birshan and Jayanti Kar, "Becoming More Strategic," *McKinsey Quarterly* (July 2012).

18. "Appalachian Trail, at 75, Is a Portal to the Natural World," *Boston Globe*, August 14, 2012, editorial.

19. Alan Greenspan, interview in *Bloomberg Businessweek*, August 13–26, 2012, 65.

Chapter 5

1. Quoted in Jerry Useem, "America's Most Admired Companies," *Fortune*, February 18, 2003.

2. Robert S. Kaplan and David P. Norton, "Having Trouble with Your Strategy? Then Map It," *Harvard Business Review* (September–October 2000): 167.

3. Here, I am stating in condensed terms the time-honored advice about strategy from Peter Drucker's notion of integrated "management by objectives" and "concentration of effort" in *Managing for Results* (New York: Harper & Row, 1964) originally titled "Business Strategies," by the way, but as Drucker later recounted, "Strategy, we were told again and again, belongs to military or perhaps to political campaigns but not to business"; to the notion of the 7S model of organizational effectiveness in Robert H. Waterman, Thomas J. Peters, and Julien R. Phillips, "Structure Is Not Organization," *Business Horizons*

(June 1980): 14–26; to Mike Porter's emphasis on "fit" in "What Is Strategy?" *Harvard Business Review* (November–December 1996); to John Wells's excellent discussion of "system causal logic" in *Strategic IQ: Creating Smarter Corporations* (San Francisco: Jossey-Bass, 2012).

4. Chris Zook and James Allen, *Repeatability: Build Enduring Businesses for a World of Constant Change* (Boston: Harvard Business Review Press, 2012), 83. Similar research findings are cited in work by Donald Sull and Kathleen M. Eisenhardt, "Strategy as Simple Rules," *Harvard Business Review* (January 2001); and "Simple Rules for a Complex World," *Harvard Business Review* (September 2012).

5. For providing employees with strategic and bottom-line information, see Gary L. Neilson, Karla L. Martin, and Elizabeth Powers, "The Secrets to Successful Strategy Execution," *Harvard Business Review* (June 2008). For communicating strategic identity, see Mark Morgan, Raymond E. Levitt, and William Malek, *Executing Your Strategy* (Boston: Harvard Business School Press, 2007), 33. For strategy maps, see Kaplan and Norton, "Having Trouble with Your Strategy?"

6. Kenneth R. Andrews, *The Concept of Corporate Strategy* (Homewood, IL: Richard D. Irwin, 1971; rev. ed., 1980), 23–24.

7. Steven Spear and H. Kent Bowen, "Decoding the DNA of the Toyota Production System," *Harvard Business Review* (September–October 1999).

8. Andrews, *Concept of Corporate Strategy*, 37.

9. For representative examples of this point of view, complete with the straw-man assertions that "approaches to strategy . . . assume a relatively stable and predictable world" or start from the assumption "that stability in business is the norm," see Martin Reeves and Mike Deimler, "Adaptability: The New Competitive Advantage," *Harvard Business Review* (July–August 2011); and Rita G. McGrath, "Transient Advantage," *Harvard Business Review* (June 2013).

10. See Alfred P. Sloan, "Change and Progress," final chapter, and "Transformation of the Automobile Market" ch. 9, in *My Years With General Motors* (Garden City, NY: Doubleday, 1963): if you substitute "social media," "apps," "the digital revolution," or other phrases, you will find Sloan's description of changes in the auto market from 1924 to 1926 (three years!) to be one of many historical examples of what some now call "internet time" or a "flat" world and believe is somehow specific to twenty-first-century information technologies and global markets.

11. David J. Collis and Michael G. Rukstad, "Can You Say What Your Strategy Is?" *Harvard Business Review* (April 2008): 82–90.

12. Fred Smith, quoted in George Labovitz and Victor Rosansky, *The Power of Alignment* (New York: John Wiley, 1997), 40.

13. Zook and Allen, *Repeatability*, 186, based on a study of forty companies during the period 1980–2010.

14. Ibid., 163. The survey was conducted by Bain and Company and the Economist Intelligence Unit.

15. Ibid., 94.

16. Betsy Morris, "What Makes Apple Golden," *Fortune*, March 17, 2008, 72.

Chapter 6

1. Walter A. Friedman, *Birth of a Salesman: The Transformation of Selling in America* (Cambridge, Ma.: Harvard University Press, 2004), 6–7.

2. Ibid., 85. For a pertinent critique of currently popular neuroscience techniques and the fad for pseudoscientific neuromarketing advice, see Sally Satel and Scott O. Lillienfeld, *Brainwashed: The Seductive Appeal of Mindless Neuroscience* (New York: Basic Books, 2013). As the technology stands today, brain scanning has major limitations, and despite gee-whiz headlines, there's little evidence these techniques work any better than old standbys like surveys and focus groups (and the touted techniques often work far worse). But there's one born every minute!

3. Kevin Bradford and Barton A. Weitz, "Salesperson Effectiveness: A Behavioral Perspective," in *Handbook of Business-to-Business Marketing*, ed. Gary L. Lilien and Rajdeep Grewal (Northampton, MA: Edward Elgar, 2012), 418.

4. *American Heritage College Dictionary*, 4th Edition (Boston: Houghton Mifflin, 2002), p. 1355.

5. Stephen Leacock, "The Perfect Salesman" in *The Garden of Folly* (New York: Dodd, Mead, 1924).

6. "10 Greatest Salespeople of All Time," *Inc.* magazine, accessed January 7, 2014, www.inc.com/ss/10-greatest-salespeople-of-all-time#1.

7. See Friedman, *Birth of a Salesman*, ch. 5, "The Pyramid Plan: John H. Patterson and the Pursuit of Efficiency," for an excellent discussion of NCR during Patterson's time and Patterson's place in sales history.

8. James B. Stewart, "The Matchmaker: Erica Feidner Knows the Piano You Want," *The New Yorker*, August 20 and 27, 2001, quoted in ibid.

9. Philip Delves Broughton, *The Art of the Sale* (New York: Penguin Press, 2012). His quoted comments are from Philip Delves Broughton, "The Most Important Predictor of Sales Success," *HBR Blog Network*, June 27, 2012, http://blogs.hbr.org/2012/06/the-most-important-predictor-o/.By the way, this conclusion about people and selling has ancillary support in the conclusions of knowledgeable brain researchers. As Stephen Kosslyn, formerly director of Stanford's Center for Advanced Study in the Behavioral Sciences, notes, "It is tempting to think of the brain as a muscle, that as it gets stronger at one thing it is also stronger at everything, but it isn't. The shocking truth is that the opportunities to generalize are very limited. If you practice some cognitive task, you are basically practicing that thing. If something else is very similar in its underlying structure, there may be some transferability, but rarely 100%." See "Brain Sells: Commercializing Neuroscience," *The Economist*, August 10, 2013, 56–57.

10. Some years ago, this important point was made in articles by Ben Shapiro and Steve Doyle. See Stephen X. Doyle and Benson P. Shapiro, "What Counts Most in Motivating Your Sales Force?" *Harvard Business Review* (May–June 1980): 133–140; and Benson P. Shapiro and Stephen X. Doyle, "Make the Sales Task Clear," *Harvard Business Review* (November–December 1983): 74–76.

11. Figure 6-1 and the discussion in this section is adapted from Frank V. Cespedes, "Aspects of Sales Management: An Introduction," Case 9-589-061 (Boston: Harvard Business School, 2006). The academic literature on boundary roles is extensive. For an excellent overview and application to sales, see Jagdip Singh, Detelina Marinova, and Steven P. Brown, "Boundary Work and Customer Connectivity in B2B Front Lines," in *Handbook of Business-to-Business Marketing*, ed. Gary L. Lilien and Rajdeep Grewal (Northampton, MA: Edward Elgar, 2012), 433–455.

12. Jim Koch et al., "The View from the Field: Six Leaders Offer Their Perspectives on Sales Success," *Harvard Business Review* (July–August 2012): 104.

13. Ibid., 105.

14. Michael Chu and Joel Segre, "A Note on Direct Selling in Developing Economies," Case 9-310-068 (Boston: Harvard Business School, 2010).

15. See Friedman, *Birth of a Salesman*, ch. 1, "Hawkers and Walkers," for a history of peddling in nineteenth-century America.

16. See Koch, "The View from the Field," 109; and Das Narayandas and Kerry Herman, "Eureka Forbes Ltd.: Managing the Selling Effort (A)," Case 9-506-003 (Boston: Harvard Business School, 2005; rev. 2009).

17. I am grateful to Row Moriarty, chairman of Charles River Associates, for this distinction. Figure 6-3 is adapted from his discussion of buying behavior in the book based on his doctoral work at Harvard. See Rowland T. Moriarty, *Industrial Buying Behavior: Concepts, Issues and Applications* (Lexington, MA: Lexington Books, 1983), 123. For a complementary discussion, see also Thomas V. Bonoma and Benson P. Shapiro, *Segmenting the Industrial Market* (Lexington, MA: Lexington Books, 1983).

18. This example is based on information in Kamran Kashani and Inna Francis, "Xiameter: The Past and Future of a 'Disruptive Innovation,'" Case 433 (Lausanne, Switzerland: IMD International, 2011).

Chapter 7

1. P. D. Reynolds and R. Curtin, "Panel Study of Entrepreneurial Dynamics II: Data Overview," *Social Science Research Network eLibrary*, November 2, 2007, http://papers.ssrn.com/sol3/papers.cfm?abstract_id=1023086.

2. In the Capital IQ database, which provides data on public and private companies, investment firms, and capital transactions, there are 43,785 companies founded in the year 2000, of which 5.8 percent reached $10 million in sales and 1.6 percent reached $50 million by 2010. For the 36,689 companies in the class of 2003, 5.1 percent reached $10 million and about 1 percent reached $50 million; and for the 32,086 companies founded in 2006, the comparable figures are currently 3.7 percent and about 1 percent, respectively. In other words, this is a fairly constant secular trend, not a one-off aberration for a given year.

3. Quoted in Nicole Perlroth, "Growth Without Revenue Loses Allure," *International Herald Tribune*, January 15, 2013, 14.

4. The seminal work on adaptive selling and scripts is Barton A. Weitz, "Effectiveness in Sales Interactions: A Contingency Framework," *Journal of Marketing* 45 (1981): 85–103; and Thomas W. Leigh

and Arno J. Rethans, "A Script-Theoretic Analysis of Industrial Purchasing Behavior," *Journal of Marketing* 48 (1984): 22–32.

5. Michael Polanyi, *The Tacit Dimension* (Garden City, NY: Doubleday, 1966).

6. Donald A. Schon, *The Reflective Practitioner: How Professionals Think in Action* (New York: Basic Books, 1983).

7. For a superb discussion of *metis* in varied circumstances and the disasters perpetrated by disregard for local circumstances, see James C. Scott, *Seeing Like a State: How Certain Schemes to Improve the Human Condition Have Failed* (New Haven, CT: Yale University Press, 1998), especially ch. 9, "Thin Simplification and Practical Knowledge: Metis."

8. Quoted in Dick Cavett, "Comedy Pain and Comedy Pleasure," *Opinionator*, a blog of *New York Times*, August 3, 2012, http://opinionator.blogs.nytimes.com/2012/08/03/comedy-pain-and-comedy-pleasure/?_r=0.

9. Some of the material in the section about understanding customers is adapted from Frank V. Cespedes, Thomas Eisenmann, and Steven G. Blank, "Customer Discovery and Validation for Entrepreneurs," Case 812-097 (Boston: Harvard Business School, 2012).

10. Nate Boaz, John Murnane, and Kevin Nuffer, "The Basics of Business-to-Business Sales Success," *McKinsey Quarterly* (May 2010).

11. A classic statement and demonstration of the difference between attitude and behavior is M. Fishbein and I. Azjen, "Attitudinal Variables and Behavior: Three Empirical Studies and a Theoretical Reanalysis," monograph (Seattle: University of Washington, 1970). A good review of the relevant literature since then is Aric Rindfleisch and Kersi D. Antia, "Survey Research in B2B Marketing: Current Challenges and Emerging Opportunities," in *Handbook of Business-to-Business Marketing*, ed. Gary L. Lilien and Rajdeep Grewal (Northampton, MA: Edward Elgar, 2012), 699–714.

12. Theodore Levitt, "Marketing Myopia," *Harvard Business Review* (July–August 2004; originally published in 1960).

13. See Clayton M. Christensen, Scott Cook, and Taddy Hall, "Marketing Malpractice: The Cause and the Cure," *Harvard Business Review* 83 (December 2005); Clayton M. Christensen, Scott D. Anthony, Gerald N. Berstell, and Denise Nitterhouse, "Finding the Right Job for Your Product," *MIT Sloan Management Review* 48 (spring 2007); or for a good summary of this research, see Clayton

M. Christensen, "Integrating Around the Job to be Done," Case 9-611-004 (Boston: Harvard Business School, 2010).

14. For guidelines and a process for conducting customer visits and understanding usage situations, see Frank V. Cespedes, "Customer Visits for Entrepreneurs," Case 812-098 (Boston: Harvard Business School, 2011).

15. Neil Rackham, *SPIN Selling* (New York: McGraw-Hill, 1988), 99–111. Memo to management: when in doubt about whether all the talk about selling tactics is simply anecdotal, revisit Rackham's book which (in my view) remains the best and most discriminating research-based discussion of what does and doesn't work on different types of sales calls.

16. For the core academic research and concepts, see Daniel Kahneman and Amos Tversky, eds., *Choices, Values, and Frames* (Cambridge, England: Cambridge University Press, 2000). For a witty and accessible review of this research, see Daniel Kahneman, *Thinking, Fast and Slow* (New York: Farrar, Straus and Giroux, 2011), 278–309.

17. John T. Gourville, "Eager Sellers and Stony Buyers," *Harvard Business Review* (June 2006). Other research supports the general direction of this analysis but at a slightly lower magnitude than Gourville suggests: see Promothesh Chatterjee, Caglar Irmak, and Randall L. Rose, "The Endowment Effect as Self-Enhancement in Response to Threat," *Journal of Consumer Research* 80 (October 2013), where experiments indicate that, on average, people value current goods 2.2 times more than they value new products.

18. For an example of these contrasting sales approaches, see Ashlee Vance, "The Two Horsemen of the Enterprise Software Apocalypse," *Bloomberg BusinessWeek*, June 14, 2012, 52–58.

19. See Geoffrey A. Moore, *Crossing the Chasm: Marketing and Selling High-Tech Products to Mainstream Customers* (New York: HarperCollins, 1991; revised 2002); and Geoffrey A. Moore, *Inside the Tornado: Strategies for Developing, Leveraging, and Surviving Hypergrowth* (New York: HarperCollins, 1995; revised 2004).

20. The best research about lead users is the work of Erich von Hippel: *The Sources of Innovation* (New York: Oxford University Press, 1988); *Breakthrough Products with Lead User Research: Methods for Uncovering the Ideas and Prototypes of Leading Edge Users* (Cambridge, MA: MIT Press, 1998); and *Democratizing Innovation* (Cambridge, MA: MIT Press, 2005).

21. See Amar Bhide, *The Venturesome Economy: How Innovation Sustains Prosperity in a More Connected World* (Princeton, NJ: Princeton University Press, 2008).

22. This example is also discussed in Frank V. Cespedes, James P. Dougherty, and Ben S. Skinner III, "How to Identify the Best Customers for Your Business," *Sloan Management Review* 54 (winter 2013): 53–59.

Chapter 8

1. Quoted in John Markoff, "Skilled Work, Without the Worker," *New York Times*, August 19, 2012, D1.

2. See Mark A. Huselid, Richard W. Beatty, and Brian E. Becker, *The Workforce Scorecard: Managing Human Capital to Execute Strategy* (Boston: Harvard Business School Press, 2005).

3. Thomas Baumgartner, Homayoun Hatami, and Jon Vander Ark, *Sales Growth* (New York: John Wiley & Sons, 2012), 166–167.

4. For a review of studies about manufacturing productivity, see Chad Syverson, "What Determines Productivity?" *Journal of Economic Literature* 49 (2011): 326–365.

5. The studies (among others) supporting these assertions about productivity differences in knowledge work are, respectively, John E. Hunter, Frank L. Schmidt, and Michael K. Judiesch, "Individual Differences in Output Variability as a Function of Job Complexity," *Journal of Applied Psychology* 75, no. 1 (1990): 28–42; Robert Kelley and Janet Caplan, "How Bell Labs Create Star Performers," *Harvard Business Review* (July–August 1993): 128–39; Francis Narin and Anthony Breitzman, "Inventive Productivity," *Research Policy* 24 (1995): 507–519; and Derek Price de Sola, *Little Science, Big Science . . . and Beyond* (New York: Columbia University Press, 1963; rev. ed. 1986). The technical term for this distribution is a *Lotka curve*, a hyperbolic curve that skews sharply left toward a relatively small number of individuals accounting for a majority of output and then a long tail to the right. For a general overview and additional data about this distribution in the arts and the sciences, see Charles Murray, *Human Accomplishment* (New York: HarperCollins, 2003), ch. 6, 87–106.

6. Jim Dickie and Barry Trailer, "Sales Performance Optimization: 2012 Sales Rep Hiring/Compensation Analysis" (Boulder, CO: CSO Insights, 2012).

7. Boris Groysberg, *Chasing Stars: The Myth of Talent and the Portability of Performance* (Princeton, NJ: Princeton University Press, 2010).

8. All quoted comments in this section are from Mark Roberge, "The Science of Building a Scalable Sales Team," *HBR Blog Network*, July 12, 2012, http://blogs.hbr.org/2012/07/the-science-of-building-a-scal/.

9. Dickie and Trailer, "Sales Performance Optimization," 10.

10. The difference between outcome impact and performance variability in jobs has a long history in HR studies. An excellent discussion, to which I am especially indebted, is Huselid, Beatty, and Becker *The Workforce Scorecard*. See also Eric Lesser, Denis Brousseau, and Tim Ringo, "Focal Jobs: Viewing Talent Through a Different Lens," Executive Brief, IBM Institute for Business Value, 2009, www.935.ibm. com/services/us/gbs/bus/html/understanding-focal-jobs.html.

11. A seminal study about results from interviewing versus other job success predictors is John E. Hunter and R. F. Hunter, "Validity and Utility of Alternative Predictors of Job Performance," *Psychological Bulletin* 96 (1984): 72–98. But there are now many studies indicating the poor validity of interviews in hiring decisions. For a review of the research (and a study indicating that interviews can *hurt* in selection decisions), see Jason Dana, Robyn Dawes, and Nathaniel Peterson, "Belief in the Unstructured Interview: The Persistence of an Illusion," *Judgment and Decision Making* 8, no. 5 (September 2013): 512–520. For a discussion of interviewing versus other predictive techniques in sales hiring, see Andris A. Zoltners, Prabhakant Sinha, and Greggor A. Zoltners, *The Complete Guide to Accelerating Sales Force Performance* (New York: AMACOM, 2001), ch. 6.

12. Dickie and Trailer, "Sales Performance Optimization," 8.

13. For the research supporting the assertions in this paragraph about practice and adult learning, see Donald A. Schon, *Educating the Reflective Practitioner* (San Francisco: Jossey-Bass, 1987); John Whitmore, *Coaching for Performance: Growing People, Performance, and Purpose* (Boston: Nicholas Brealey, 2002); and "Unlocking the DNA of the Adaptable Workforce," Global Human Capital Study 2008 (Somers, NY: IBM, 2008). For the importance of practice in sales training in particular, see Neil Rackham's wise and still-pertinent discussion in *SPIN Selling* (New York: McGraw-Hill, 1988), ch. 8.

14. See Harold D. Stolovitch and Erica J. Keeps, *Telling Ain't Training* (Alexandria, VA: ASTD Press, 2002).

15. For details about how to plan and conduct customer visits, see Edward F. McQuarrie, *Customer Visits: Building a Better Market Focus* (Newbury Park, CA: Sage Publications, 1993); and Frank V. Cespedes, "Customer Visits for Entrepreneurs," Harvard Business School Case 812-098 (Boston: Harvard Business School, 2011).

16. A useful discussion of the origins and conduct of an AAR is in Gordon R. Sullivan and Michael V. Harper, "Growing the Learning Organization,"ch. 11 in *Hope Is Not a Method* (New York: Random House, 1996).

17. See Frank V. Cespedes, "Agendas, Incubators, and Marketing Organization," *California Management Review* 33 (1990): 27–53, for details about IBM's sales organizations and strategies during this period and the comments by Learson.

18. Figure 8-3 and the basic argument here about the impact of online technologies on sales channel tasks are adapted from Paul F. Nunes and Frank V. Cespedes, "The Customer Has Escaped," *Harvard Business Review* (November 2003): 117–126. Please note: this article was written over ten years ago, when most business-press commentary was predicting—indeed, assuming—disintermediation and the demise of sales forces. They were wrong, and we were right.

19. Christina Rogers, "Say Goodbye to the Car Salesman," (sic!) *The Wall Street Journal* (November 21, 2013): B1-B2.

20. Quoted in Baumgartner, Hatami, and Vander Ark, *Sales Growth*, 189.

Chapter 9

1. Andris A. Zoltners, Prabhakant Sinha, and Greggor A. Zoltners, *The Complete Guide to Accelerating Sales Force Performance* (New York: AMACOM, 2001), 269.

2. Jim Dickie and Barry Trailer, "2012 Sales Compensation and Performance Management: Key Trends Analysis" (Boulder, CO: CSO Insights, 2012), 10.

3. Max Weber, *The Protestant Ethic and the Spirit of Capitalism*, translated by T. Parsons from the 1920 German edition of the 1905 original (New York: Scribners, 1958), 17.

4. The study referenced here was done by Shawn Cole of Harvard Business School, and Martin Kanz and Leora Klapper of The World Bank. It involved a series of experiments with over fourteen thousand lending decisions under different incentive schemes: volume incentives

that reward origination; "low-powered" incentives that reward origination conditional on loan performance; and "high-powered" incentives that reward performance and penalize default. In other words, Cole and colleagues were testing incentives whose emphasis is on volume versus profitability versus customer retention. See "Incentivizing Calculated Risk-Taking: Evidence from an Experiment with Commercial Bank Loan Officers," working paper (Boston: Harvard Business School, July 2012).

5. Figure 9-1 and the discussion in this section is adapted from Frank V. Cespedes, *Concurrent Marketing* (Boston: Harvard Business School Press, 1995), 218–222.

6. Zoltners, Sinha, and Zoltners, *Accelerating Sales Force Performance*, 320 and 324.

7. Dickie and Trailer, "2012 Sales Compensation," 23.

8. Jeff Ubben, "How to Revive Animal Spirits in CEOs," *Wall Street Journal*, November 30, 2012, A15.

9. See Joel Brockner, "Making Sense of Procedural Fairness," *Academy of Management Review* 27 (2002): 58–76; and W. Chan Kim and Renee Mauborgne, "Fair Process: Managing in the Knowledge Economy," *Harvard Business Review* (January 2003): 127–137.

10. Jordi Blanes I Vidal and Mareike Nossol, "Tournaments without Prizes: Evidence from Personnel Records," *Management Science* 58 (2012): 94–113.

11. For more detail on this example and the mechanics of shared-credit compensation systems, see Frank V. Cespedes, Stephen X. Doyle, and Robert J. Freedman, "Teamwork for Today's Selling," *Harvard Business Review* (March–April 1989): 26–35.

12. Michael C. Jensen, "Paying People to Lie: The Truth About the Budgeting Process," *European Financial Management* 9 (2003): 379–406. I agree with Jensen's description of most current de facto practice: coupling bonuses and forecasts usually means self-serving "negotiations" aimed at reducing performance targets (i.e., "paying people to lie"). But I disagree with his conclusion that this practice is inevitable and that, therefore, incentive payments should never be tied to achievement of budget targets. Many sales organizations (if not CEOs and board comp committees) effectively link bonuses with rep's forecasts through the means outlined in this chapter. For an example of how this works mathematically and in practice (at IBM), see Zoltners, Sinha, and Zoltners, *Accelerating Sales Force Performance*, 313–315.

13. For a guide to sources about pay data, see Robert G. Eccles, Boris Groysberg, and Ann Cullen, "A Note on Compensation Research," Case 9-408-114 (Boston: Harvard Business School Publishing, 2008; revised 2011).

14. A *missionary salesperson* attempts to build goodwill and/or educate the potential user or customer about the product and may never book an order personally; instead, purchase orders are booked through the firm's wholesalers or other stocking points. Examples include salespeople for many pharmaceutical firms, soft-drink companies, or distilleries: the missionary calls on doctors, restaurants, or pubs, respectively, but the customer buys from a pharmacy, bottler, or distributor, not from the salesperson. For an overview of the academic literature about salary-incentive splits, see Anne T. Coughlan and Kissan Joseph, "Sales Force Compensation: Research Insights and Research Potential," in *Handbook of Business-to-Business Marketing*, ed. Gary L. Lilien and Rajdeep Grewal (Northampton, MA: Edward Elgar, 2012), 476–482.

15. For reviews of these studies, see Coughlan and Joseph, "Sales Force Compensation." For a discussion of the sales management implications, see Erin Anderson and Vincent Onyemah, "How Right Should the Customer Be?" *Harvard Business Review* (July–August 2006): 119–127.

16. Benson P. Shapiro and Frank V. Cespedes, "Olympia Machine Company, Inc.," Case 9-708-490 (Boston: Harvard Business School, 2008).

17. A more general point about compensation and incentives is made by Michael Jensen, "Value Maximization, Stakeholder Theory, and the Corporate Objective Function," *Journal of Applied Corporate Finance* 14 (2001): 9–10: "It is logically impossible to maximize in more than one dimension at the same time . . . When there are many masters, all end up being shortchanged." You needn't view business as a linear-programming exercise with just one objective function—we expect senior executives to walk and chew gum at the same time, and we should replace them when they can't—to agree with the basic logic and practical truth of this point of view. For a value-maximization argument that follows this logic while relaxing the only one-dimension assumption, see Baruch Lev, *Winning Investors Over* (Boston: Harvard Business Review Press, 2012), 193–216.

18. This assertion about most goal-setting practice is supported, among other places, by the data in Dickie and Trailer, "2012 Sales Compensation," 6.

Chapter 10

1. See K. Anders Ericsson, "The Influence of Experience and Deliberate Practice on the Development of Superior Expert Performance," in *The Cambridge Handbook of Expertise and Expert Performance*, ed. K. Anders Ericsson, Neil Charness, Paul J. Feltovich, and Robert R. Hoffman (Cambridge and New York: Cambridge University Press, 2006), 683–703; and K. Anders Ericsson, Ralf Th. Krampe, and Clemens Tesch-Romer, "The Role of Deliberate Practice in Acquisition of Expert Performance," *Psychological Review* 100, no. 3 (July 1993): 363–406. For an engaging review of the research about deliberate practice and performance feedback, see Geoffrey Colvin, *Talent Is Overrated* (New York: Portfolio Books, 2008).

2. Morgan McCall, Michael Lombardo, and A. Morrison, *The Lessons of Experience* (Lexington, MA: Lexington Books, 1988). See also John Whitmore, *Coaching for Performance: Growing People, Performance and Purpose*, 3rd ed. (London: Nicholas Brealey, 2002), where, according to research at IBM, about 65 percent of development is attributed to experiential learning rather than formal education.

3. The core studies on the need for affiliation are E. G. Flamholtz and Y. Randle, *The Inner Game of Management: How to Make the Transition to a Managerial Role* (New York: AMACOM, 1987); and D. C. McClelland and D. H. Burnham, "Power Is the Great Motivator," *Harvard Business Review* (March–April 1976): 100–110, whose politically incorrect conclusion still bears repeating: they found that better managers have a higher need for power than affiliation. In fact, managers with high affiliation needs made many ad hominem and ad hoc exceptions, overlooking bad behaviors in attempts to stay on good terms with everyone, and they left "employees feeling weak, irresponsible, and without a sense of . . . where they stand in relation to the manager or even of what they ought to be doing."

4. This street-smart assumption about sales motivation, by the way, has support in research about the so-called hedonic treadmill that characterizes much human behavior. When people acquire a new item, they initially feel more satisfied, but then rapidly revert to their baseline of well-being. For a summary of the research, see Daniel Kahneman, *Thinking, Fast and Slow* (New York: Farrar, Straus and Giroux, 2011), 377–385.

5. For a summary of this research about the differential impact of coaching on sales performance, see Matthew Dixon and Brent Adamson, *The Challenger Sale* (New York: Portfolio, 2011), 151–153.

6. Frank V. Cespedes and John T. Gourville, "Cabot Pharmaceuticals, Inc.," Case 9-510-030 (Boston: Harvard Business School, 2010).

7. In addition to personal experience, for my advice in this section about conducting reviews, I am indebted to John J. Gabarro and Linda A. Hill, "Managing Performance," Case 9-496-022 (Boston: Harvard Business School, 1995); and to Catherine Braun, a former business colleague and an experienced executive coach.

8. David H. Freedman, "The Perfected Self," *The Atlantic*, June 2012, 42–52.

9. For this wonderful phrase that unfortunately describes accurately the status of account plans in many sales organizations, see Jim Dickie and Barry Trailer, "CRM 2.0: Strategic Account Planning Optimization," *CSO Insights* (2012): 2.

10. Felipe Kast, Stephan Meier, and Dina Pomeranz, "Under-Savers Anonymous: Evidence on Self-Help Groups and Peer Pressure as a Savings Commitment Device," working paper, Harvard Business School, Boston, September 2012.

11. See Ruth Rettie, Ursula Grandcolas, and Bethan Deakins, "Text Message Advertising: Response Rates and Branding Effects," *Journal of Targeting, Measurement and Analysis for Marketing* 13 (2005): 304–312; Allison Dale and Aaron Strauss, "Don't Forget to Vote: Text Message Reminders as a Mobilization Tool," *American Journal of Political Science* 53 (2009): 787–804; T. M. Da Costa et. al., "The Impact of Short Message Service Text Messages Sent as Appointment Reminders to Patients' Cell Phones at Outpatient Clinics in Sao Paulo, Brazil," *International Journal of Medical Informatics* 79 (2010): 65; Maria Gleerup et. al., "The Effect of Feedback by Text Message and Email on Household Electricity Consumption: Experimental Evidence," *Energy Journal* 31 (2010): 111–130; Brian Suffoletto et. al., "Text-Message-Based Drinking Assessments and Brief Interventions for Young Adults Discharged from the Emergency Department," *Alcoholism: Clinical and Experimental Research* (2012).

12. Michael J. Mauboussin, "The True Measures of Success," *Harvard Business Review* (October 2012): 46–56; and, more generally, his smart, wise and engaging discussion about metrics and the difference between skill and luck in business and other fields, *The SucceSS Equation* (Boston: Harvard Business Review Press, 2012).

13. For a more detailed discussion of expense-to-revenue ratios and their application as measures of sales and distribution productivity, see E. Raymond Corey, Frank V. Cespedes, and V. Kasturi Rangan, *Going to Market: Distribution Systems for Industrial Products* (Boston: Harvard Business School Press, 1989), 60–83.

14. Rob Docters, John G. Hanson, Cecilia Nguyen, and Michael Barzelay, *Contextual Pricing* (New York: McGraw-Hill, 2012), 57.

15. "Big Data: The Next Frontier for Innovation, Competition, and Productivity," McKinsey Global Institute Report, May 2011.

16. For studies of cost to serve, see Benson P. Shapiro, V. Kasturi Rangan, Rowland T. Moriarty, and Elliot B. Ross, "Manage Customers for Profits (Not Just Sales)," *Harvard Business Review* (September–October 1987): 56–68; Robert S. Kaplan and Robin Cooper, *Cost & Effect: Using Integrated Cost Systems to Drive Profitability and Performance* (Boston: Harvard Business School Press, 1998), ch. 10; Valarie A. Zeithaml, Roland T. Rust, and Katherine N. Lemon, "The Customer Pyramid: Creating and Serving Profitable Customers," *California Management Review* 43, no. 4 (summer 2001): 118–142; Anupam Agarwal, Eric Harmon, and Michael Viertler, "Cutting Sales Costs, Not Revenues," *McKinsey Quarterly* (2009): 77–85; and Jonathan L. S. Byrnes, *Islands of Profits in a Sea of Red Ink* (New York: Penguin Books, 2010).

17. Shikhar Ghosh and Thomas R. Eisenmann, "Skyhook Wireless," Case 9-809-119 (Boston: Harvard Business School, 2009).

18. For research about the links between customer selection and profitability, see Douglas Bowman and Das Narayandas, "Linking Customer Management Efforts to Customer Profitability in Business Markets," *Journal of Marketing Research* 41 (November 2004): 433–447; and Vijay Kumar, *Managing Customers for Profit: Strategies to Increase Profits and Build Loyalty* (Philadelphia: Wharton School Publishing, 2008). For research and a model for constructing a customer portfolio that reduces the volatility of cash flows, see Crina O. Tarsi, Ruth N. Bolton, Michael D. Hutt, and Beth A. Walker, "Balancing Risk and Return in a Customer Portfolio," *Journal of Marketing* 75 (May 2011): 1–17.

19. For the relevant stream of research about team selling, see Frank V. Cespedes, Stephen X. Doyle, and Robert J. Freedman, "Teamwork for Today's Selling," *Harvard Business Review* (March–April 1989): 26–37; Frank V. Cespedes, "Sales Coordination: An Exploratory Study," *Journal of Personal Selling and Sales Management* 12

(summer 1992): 13–29; Richard A. Guzzo and Marcus W. Dickson, "Teams in Organizations: Recent Research on Performance and Effectiveness," *Annual Review of Psychology* 47, no. 1 (1996): 307–338; Michael Ahearne et al., "The Role of Consensus in Sales Team Performance," *Journal of Marketing Research* 47 (June 2010): 458–469.

20. For more on the nature of channel relations, see Frank V. Cespedes, "Channel Management," Case 9-590-045 (Boston: Harvard Business School, 2006).

21. Dave Ulrich, Jon Younger, Wayne Brockbank, and Mike Ulrich, *HR From the Outside In: Six Competencies for the Future of Human Resources* (New York: McGraw-Hill, 2012), 114–129. Their research focused on eighteen HR competencies, clustered into three factors, and found that the cluster associated with aligning strategy, culture practices, and behavior had a greater business impact than the others measured.

22. See, for example, Robert A. Howell, "CFOs: Not Just for Finance Anymore," in the Wall Street Journal CFO Report, *Wall Street Journal*, February 27, 2012, R4.

23. Emily Chasan, "Where Startups Shop for Finance Pros," *Wall Street Journal*, October 22, 2013, B7.

Chapter 11

1. See the research cited in Andris A. Zoltners, Praghakant Sinha, and Sally E. Lorimer, *Building a Winning Sales Management Team* (Evanston, IL: ZS Associates), 2–7.

2. Core studies include J. A. Bayton and R. L. Chapman, "Making Managers of Scientists and Engineers," *Research Management* (November 1973): 33–36; D. E. Dougherty, *From Technical Professional to Corporate Manager: A Guide to Career Transition* (New York: John Wiley, 1984); M. London, *Developing Managers: A Guide to Motivating and Preparing People for Successful Managerial Careers* (San Francisco: Jossey-Bass, 1985); J. W. Lorsch and P. F. Mathias, "When Professionals Have to Manage," *Harvard Business Review* (July–August 1987): 78–83. For the frontline sales manager, in particular, core studies remain the discussions and data in Frederick E. Webster Jr., "Selling vs Managing" in ch. 2 of *Field Sales Management* (New York: John Wiley, 1983); and J. Falvey, "The Making of a Manager," *Sales and Marketing Management* (March 1989): 42–83.

3. M. K. Badawy, *Developing Managerial Skill in Engineers and Scientists: Succeeding as a Technical Manager* (New York: Van Nostrand Reinhold, 1982), 71.

4. For data supporting these assertions, see the four decades of research by Caliper provided in Herb Greenberg, Harold Weinstein, and Patrick Sweeney, "Why the Best Salespeople Often Don't Become Great Managers," in *How to Hire & Develop Your Next Top Performer* (New York: McGraw-Hill, 2001), 175–187.

5. The specific quote is from Matthew Dixon and Brent Adamson, *The Challenger Sale* (New York: Portfolio Books, 2011), 143. But this point of view is widely held, and you'll find it on many blogs.

6. See, for example, the review discussion by Jennifer A. Chapman and Jessica A. Kennedy, "Psychological Perspectives on Leadership," ch. 6 in *Handbook of Leadership Theory and Practice*, ed. Nitin Nohria and Rakesh Khurana (Boston: Harvard Business School Publishing, 2010).

7. Quoted in Linda A. Hill, *Becoming a Manager*, 2nd ed. (Boston: Harvard Business School Publishing, 2003), 93.

8. John B. Miner, *The Human Constraint* (Washington, DC: Bureau of National Affairs, 1974), 7.

9. Noel Capon and Gary S. Tubridy, *Sales Eats First* (Bronxville, NY: Wessex, 2011), 17.

10. Zoltners, Sinha, and Lorimer, *Building a Winning Sales Management Team*, 36.

11. Hill, *Becoming a Manager*, passim.

12. For an excellent discussion of studies about the role of experience in management development, informed by years of acquaintance with academic theory and actual practice, see Morgan McCall Jr., "The Experience Conundrum," ch. 23 in in *Handbook of Leadership Theory and Practice*, ed. Nitin Nohria and Rakesh Khurana (Boston: Harvard Business School Publishing, 2010).

13. For the research, the use of the model across cultural contexts, and examples of applications over four decades, see Gene Dalton, Paul Thompson, and Paul Price, "The Four Stages of Professional Careers," *Organizational Dynamics* 6 (1977); Paul Thompson and Gene Dalton, "Are R&D Organizations Obsolete?" *Harvard Business Review* (November–December 1976): 105–116; Gene Dalton and Paul Thompson, *Novations: Strategies for Career Management* (Glenview, IL: Scott, Foresman, 1986); and Jon Younger and Kurt Sandholtz, "Helping Professionals Build Successful Careers," *Research-Technology Management* (November–December 1997): 23–28. I am grateful to Jon

Younger of the RBL Group for initially introducing me to this research, explaining its relevance to issues in sales development, and demonstrating its usefulness and impact in a variety of company contexts over the years. In the section of this chapter about the Four Stages model, I have drawn on many conversations, joint work, and communications with Jon, a superb doer and developer of talent in multiple organizations.

14. Dalton and Thompson, *Novations*, 238–239. For the Gallup survey results, see Marcus Buckingham and Curt Coffman, *First, Break All the Rules* (New York: Simon & Schuster, 1999). For a recent and controversial discussion of career development and gender issues, see Sheryl Sandberg, *Lean In: Women, Work, and the Will to Lead* (New York: Knopf, 2013).

15. Thompson and Dalton, "Are R&D Organizations Obsolete?" 112–113.

Chapter 12

1. Figure 12-1 is adapted from Frank V. Cespedes, *Concurrent Marketing: Integrating Product, Sales, and Service* (Harvard Business School Press, 1995), p. 249.

2. I am grateful to Gerald Berstell for the details about the SRA example.

3. See Julie Wulf, "The Flattened Firm: Not as Advertised," *California Management Review* 55, no. 1 (2012): 5–23. For a discussion of the study's sample and methods, see Raghuram G. Rajan and Julie Wulf, "The Flattening Firm: Evidence from Panel Data on the Changing Nature of Corporate Hierarchies," *Review of Economics and Statistics* 88, no. 4 (2006); and Maria Guadalupe, Hongyi Li, and Julie Wulf, "Who Lives in the C-Suite? Organizational Structure and the Division of Labor in Top Management," working paper, Harvard Business School, Boston, March 2013.

4. Cespedes, *Concurrent Marketing: Integrating Product, Sales, and Service*, 271.

5. For the studies supporting the assertions in this paragraph, see the following: Miller Heiman, *Miller Heiman Sales Best Practices Study* (2008): only 37 percent of respondents agreed that their marketing and sales organizations are aligned with what their customers want and need; American Marketing Association, *Proceedings of the Customer Message Management Forums* (2002 and 2003): "80 to 90% of marketing collateral is considered useless by sales"; IT Buyer Survey, International

Data Group (2008): "58% of a vendor's marketing content is not relevant to potential buyers and reduces the vendor's chances of closing a sale by 45%"; "2012 Lead Management Optimization Study: Key Trends Analysis," *CSO Insights*, 2012: "Only 55% of the firms surveyed have a lead follow up rate of 75% or more"; Fred Wiersema, *The B2B Agenda: Current State of B2B Marketing and a Look Ahead* (State College: Penn State University, Institute for the Study of Business Markets, 2012), 31: "The biggest challenges for B2B Marketing . . . First, there is the need to build stronger interfaces between marketing and other functions, particularly sales."

6. Louis V. Gerstner Jr., *Who Says Elephants Can't Dance? Leading a Great Enterprise Through Dramatic Change* (New York: HarperBusiness, 2003), 182.

7. Robert B. Cialdini, *Influence: The Psychology of Persuasion*, rev. ed. (New York: HarperBusiness, 2007), 18.

8. George Labovitz and Victor Rosansky, *The Power of Alignment* (New York: John Wiley, 1997), 5.

9. Karl E. Weick, "Organizational Culture as a Source of High Reliability," *California Management Review* 29, no. 4 (1987): 112.

10. Quoted in M. Augier, "James March on Education, Leadership, and Don Quixote: Introduction and Interview," *Academy of Management Learning and Education* 3 (2004): 173.

11. Despite much easy-fix advice to salespeople, working harder *is* important in sales. Think of it this way: 1 more good sales call daily = 5 per week = 20 per month = approximately 240 additional calls per year. Evidence suggests that the incremental effort will usually pay off and, conversely, that employees tend to overestimate their work hours by 5 to 10 percent in relation to the work hours they report in time diaries. See John P. Robinson, Steven Martin, Ignace Glorieux, and Joeri Minnen, "The Overestimated Workweek Revisited," *Monthly Labor Review* (June 2011): 43–53. The effect also applies in many other professional categories besides sales, and the relationship is especially strong for young professionals: see Dora Gicheva, "Working Long Hours and Early Career Outcomes in the High-End Labor Market," *Journal of Labor Economics* 31, no. 4 (October 2013): 785–824.

12. For Stern Stewart adjustments, see Al Ehrbar, *EVA: The Real Key to Creating Wealth* (New York: John Wiley, 1998).

13. The surveys were undertaken by Bain and Company and reported in Chris Zook and James Allen, *Repeatability: Build Enduring Businesses for a World of Constant Change* (Boston: Harvard Business Review Press, 2012), 43 and 90.

Index

Page numbers followed by *f* refer to figures and page numbers followed by *t* refer to tables.

Acknowledgments

"If you take an idea from one person, that's plagiarism. But if you take from many people, that's research." I've had the help of many people in developing, testing, and refining the ideas in this book.

My first debt is to Lynda Applegate, chair of the Entrepreneurial Management unit at Harvard Business School when I wrote this book. Lynda suggested that I start the executive program on Aligning Strategy and Sales and championed that cross-functional initiative through the university labyrinth. She is one of the best managers and colleagues I know, in or out of academia. I also want to thank the HBS faculty who have taught in that program—David Collis, Walter Friedman, John Gourville, Linda Hill, Robert Simon, and John Wells—and people from industry who generously agreed to be guest speakers in the program, especially Paul Nunes of Accenture and Mark Roberge of HubSpot.

In addition to the reviewers at Harvard Business Review Press, the following people read all or parts of the manuscript and provided very helpful comments about form and content: Catherine Braun, Cass Gilmore, Larry Timm, Jon Younger, and especially Ben Shapiro (with whom, and from whom, I have learned so much over the years). Their advice was golden; the remaining errors and digressions are mine. Similarly, Jim Dougherty and Ben Skinner were coconspirators with me on the concepts and company example discussed in chapter 7.

I'm grateful to professors Thomas Eisenmann, Boris Groysberg, Das Narayandas, and Jan Rivkin of Harvard for conversations and teaching discussions about customer discovery, human resources, sales management, and strategy, respectively. Jim Aisner and professors Teresa Amabile and Anita Elberse offered excellent advice about "the making of books, of which there is no end." Outside the university, I have learned a great deal about strategy and leadership from Marty Becker, Lou D'Ambrosio, and Marc Simon (three excellent CEOs), and about strategy and sales from Alston Gardner.

So Young Kang was superb in helping with the multiple revisions of the manuscript. At the Press, my sincere thanks go to Tim Sullivan, Erin Brown, Julie Devoll, Kevin Evers, Jennifer Waring, and Patricia Boyd. I also thank Meg Chute, Eric Mankin, Janice Miller, and others at HBP Corporate Learning for the chance to discuss aspects of this topic with thousands of managers globally via webinars.

I thank my wife, Bonnie Costello, for her advice, and my daughters Elizabeth and Helen, now great young women who are writing their own narratives. In memoriam: my gratitude to my father, Edward Cespedes, and my uncle, Vincent Dorio, for their love, wit, and motivation.

I have now spent a good part of my career at Harvard Business School, which has long been a fertile place for linking theory and practice. I hope this book continues that tradition. My sincere thanks go to the hundreds of managers who attended the Strategy and Sales program at Harvard and in doing so kicked the tires and improved the ideas, examples, and relevance of this book. I also appreciate the invaluable help of Jacqueline Baugher, Sandra Mastorakos, and Maria Regan in launching that program.

Finally, I have a personal and intellectual debt to the many organizations where, as a consultant or board member, I was *paid* to observe, counsel, and tinker with strategy and sales issues in a variety of market, company, and cultural contexts. Having run a business, I want to acknowledge the immense luxury of learning with other people's money.

About the Author

Frank V. Cespedes is the MBA Class of 1973 Senior Lecturer of Business Administration at Harvard Business School. He has run a business, served on boards for start-ups and corporations, and consulted to many companies around the world. He is the author of five books as well as articles in *Harvard Business Review*, the *Wall Street Journal*, *California Management Review*, *Organization Science*, and other publications.